William Wickes

A Treatise on the Accentuation of the three so-called Poetical Books on the Old Testament

William Wickes

A Treatise on the Accentuation of the three so-called Poetical Books on the Old Testament

ISBN/EAN: 9783337293956

Printed in Europe, USA, Canada, Australia, Japan

Cover: Foto ©Lupo / pixelio.de

More available books at **www.hansebooks.com**

טעמי אמ"ת

A

TREATISE ON THE ACCENTUATION

OF THE THREE SO-CALLED

POETICAL BOOKS OF THE OLD TESTAMENT,

PSALMS, PROVERBS, AND JOB.

WITH AN APPENDIX CONTAINING THE TREATISE,
ASSIGNED TO R. JEHUDA BEN-BIL‘AM, ON THE SAME SUBJECT,
IN THE ORIGINAL ARABIC.

BY

WILLIAM WICKES, D.D.

Oxford

AT THE CLARENDON PRESS

1881

[*All rights reserved.*]

PREFACE.

In preparing the following treatise I have had to depend almost entirely on my own investigations. The Christian accentuologists of the 17th and 18th centuries, to whom we owe the discovery of the leading principles that underlie the Hebrew accentuation, were not successful (as, I presume, all who have consulted their Works will allow) in dealing with the peculiar system of the three so-called Poetical Books. I have gained therefore but little help from them. In the present century, only two scholars, Ewald and Baer, have ventured on an independent examination of the subject. Ewald's speculations[1] I have not been able to accept. Baer's treatises[2]—which shew very careful preparation, and are valuable, as containing (like Heidenheim's משפטי הטעמים for the twenty-one Books) the traditional views handed down by Rabbinical authorities—I did not find reach far enough for my purpose.

I may draw attention to one respect in which the present Work differs from any of those which have preceded it. It is founded, in a great measure, on an extensive examination of MSS. I soon saw that even our best texts need correction, as far as the accents are concerned; and that, without a correct text, I could not hope to establish any rules on a satisfactory basis. I therefore visited the leading Libraries of Europe, and collated, as far as seemed necessary, most of the known MSS. The main results are given in the course of the following pages. I venture to hope that this part of my Work will be particularly acceptable to scholars.

---

[1] Lehrbuch der Heb. Sprache, p. 227 ff.
[2] הורה אמה (Rödelheim, 1852), and Das Accentuationssystem der Psalmen, des Buches Iob und der Sprüche, überlieferungsgemäss seinen Gesetzen nach dargestellt, in an Appendix to Delitzsch's Commentary on the Psalms (Leipzig, 1860).

I have given, as an Appendix, the treatise assigned to Ben-Bil'am, in the original Arabic. This treatise is so far interesting as it contains the first known attempt to furnish a systematic account of the accentuation of the three Books, and as it remained, through the Middle Ages, the chief authority on the subject. The reader must, however, be prepared to find the rules given quite elementary.

In conclusion, I have to acknowledge my obligations to Dr. Baer, as a personal friend. The assistance he has willingly rendered me, whenever his extensive Masoretic and Rabbinical learning could be of service to me, has been very valuable. I am also indebted to Dr. A. Neubauer for much kind interest and advice.

W. WICKES.

11, Woodstock Road, Oxford,
    August, 1881.

MSS. CONSULTED FOR THE PRESENT WORK.

I. BIBLE MSS.

B. M.   MSS. in the British Museum. For the sake of brevity, I have given my own numbers to these MSS.[1] 1 stands for Add. 21161[2]; 2 for Add. 15250; 3 for King's 1, 271 E; 4, 5, 6, 7, 8, 9, and 10 for Harl. 1528, 5498, 5506, 5711, 5715, 5775, and 7622 respectively; and 11, 12, 13, 14, 15, 16, 17, and 18 for Add. 9398, 9399, 9402, 9406, 15251, 15252, 15451, and 18830.

Ber.   MSS. in the Royal Library, Berlin. The numbers given are those of the printed catalogue.

Cam.   MSS. in the University Library, Cambridge. See printed catalogue.

Cop.   MSS. in the Royal Library, Copenhagen. See printed catalogue.

De R.   De Rossi's MSS., now in the Royal Library, Parma. See De Rossi's printed catalogue.

Erf.   The well-known Erfurt MSS. 1–4, described by Lagarde in his Symmicta, p. 133 ff. (These MSS. are now in the Royal Library, Berlin.)[3]

Fr.   A MS. at Frankfurt on the Main, written A.D. 1294 by the grandson of the punctator Simson (now in the possession of Herr S. M. Goldschmidt).

Ghet.   Three MSS. in the Ghetto, Rome—No. 1 in the *Scuola del Tempio*, Nos. 2 and 3 in the Castilian Synagogue.

---

[1] It is a disgrace to our great national Library that there is no printed catalogue of the Hebrew MSS. Nor are steps being taken, as far as I can ascertain, to have one made. One has to hunt now, with loss of time and patience, through poorly prepared written catalogues—in one of which Heb. MSS. are mixed up with Sanskrit, Persian, &c. (and no Index)—to find what one wants.

[2] A very interesting and original MS. I have been able to identify it, as the one described by Kennicott, Cod. 201. (It was formerly at Nürnberg, whither I went some years ago to examine it, but to my great disappointment it had disappeared; nor could any one tell me what had become of it.) Kennicott is quite right in his estimate of it: *Codex antiquissimis præstantissimisque accensendus*. I believe that this and Erf. 3 are two of the oldest (perhaps the two oldest) MSS. we have, containing the three Books.

[3] Erf. 5, often quoted by Michaelis in the notes to his ed. of the Heb. Bible, is now in the Library of the Graf von Schönborn, at Pommersfelden, near Bamberg. I walked over in 1877 to see it, but was not able to gain admission to the Library.

Hm. MSS. in the Town Library, Hamburg. The numbers are those of the printed catalogue.
K. Where I had no printed catalogue to refer to, as in the case of the smaller Libraries, I have given the numbers according to Kennicott's list.
Ox. MSS. in the Bodleian Library, Oxford. See printed catalogue.
Par. MSS. in the National Library, Paris. See printed catalogue.
Pet. Refers to the MS. B. 19^a (A. D. 1009) in the Imperial Library at St. Petersburg. One or two other MSS. of this Library have been quoted by the numbers in the catalogue.
Vat. MSS. in the Vatican, according to Assemani's and Card. Mai's catalogues.
Vi. MSS. in the Imperial Library, Vienna, according to printed catalogue.

II. MSS. ON THE ACCENTS OF THE THREE BOOKS.

1. The Arab. and Heb. MSS., which contain, in whole or part, the treatise assigned to Ben-Bil'am on the accentuation of these Books. On these MSS. see p. 102 ff.

2. A MS. recently acquired by the British Museum (Or. 2375), containing a fragment of the Work הדאיה אלקאר (הורית הקורא). It was from this Work that the compendium was prepared, of which the above treatise, No. 1, is part. For a further description of this MS., see p. 103.

3. That part of חבור הקונים—written by Simson the punctator (circa 1230)—which refers to our subject. Simson does little else than copy the above treatise. Of this Work—sometimes called Simsoni, from its author—there are three copies known, one in the Br. Mus. (Or. 1016), one in the University Library, Leipzig (Or. 102^a), and one in De Rossi's Library, Parma (389). Having examined them all I am able to say that they agree almost *verbatim et literatim*[4].

4. Two treatises on the accents of the three Books—the second quite fragmentary—in the Royal Library, Berlin (Heb. Cat. 118, p. 123 ff.). The writers had evidently No. 1 before them, but handle it much more freely than Simson. They not only curtail it much, but add views of their own. What little is to be gleaned from them I

---

[4] Any one who is curious to know something more of this work may consult Hupfeld, *Commentatio de antiquioribus apud Judæos accentuum scriptoribus*, Partic. II, p. 11 ff. (Halle, 1846).

have quoted in the course of the present Work. I find, however, that I have made a slight mistake in saying here and there in the notes that the first of these treatises is assigned to Samuel the grammarian. It may indeed, with great probability, be attributed to him, for it is a necessary supplement to the part on the *prose* accentuation, which is distinctly assigned to him. Still there is no statement in the MS. to that effect[5].

III. MS. ON THE MASORA.

Erf. Mas. A MS. formerly at Erfurt (now in the Royal Library, Berlin), which contains the *Mas. parva*, with additions not found in the printed text. It is briefly described by Lagarde, Symmicta, p. 142.

THE PRINCIPAL PRINTED TEXTS
QUOTED IN THE PRESENT WORK.

Sonc. First ed. of the entire Heb. Bible, printed at Soncino, 1488.
Bomb. 1. 1st Rabbinical Bible, printed by Bomberg, Venice, 1518.
Bomb. 2. 2nd Rabbinical Bible, printed by Bomberg, Venice, 1525.
Jabl. Heb. Bible edited by D. E. Jablonski, Berlin, 1699.
Opit. Heb. Bible edited by H. Opitius, Kiel, 1709.
Mich. Heb. Bible edited by J. H. Michaelis, Halle, 1720. This ed. is valuable to the student because of the various accentual readings, taken from the Erfurt MSS.

The three last-named edd. are all much more correct, as far as the accents are concerned, than our common edd. Modern editors (excepting of course Heidenheim and Baer) have one and all gone on perpetuating the errors of the Van der Hooght text, without taking the trouble of enquiring whether more correct texts were not available.

Norzi. מנחת שי. A text of the Heb. Bible (Mantua, 1744), with critical notes (according to Jewish ideas). Norzi did not, however, understand much about the accents.

---

[5] The date of this Samuel, who is no doubt the same as the well-known punctator, I am able to fix from an epigraph, which I found in Kenn. Cod. 95 (in the Library of St. John's College, Cambridge), a copy of which I sent to Dr. Steinschneider, who published it in the Heb. Bibliographic, No. 109. This epigraph states that the Cod. in question was pointed by him in the year 1260.

Heid. Heidenheim's ed. of the Psalms (Rödelheim, 1825).

Baer. Edd. of the Psalms (Leipzig, 1880), Proverbs (1880), and Job (1875). In these edd. Baer aims at giving the correct Masoretic text, and at establishing the same by means of critical notes. I strongly recommend my readers to procure them for themselves. The price is very trifling.

Ben-Bil. My references are to Polak's ed. (Amsterdam, 1858) of Ben-Bil'am's treatise on the accents of the three Books, entitled שער טעמי ג׳ ספרים אמ״ת חברו ר׳ יהודה בן בלעם ספרדי. This is a mere reprint of the original ed. by Mercerus[6], from the Paris MS. (Paris, 1556). Polak's task has been poorly performed. The text is full of mistakes, most of which might have been corrected by a collation of the Ox. MS. A copy of this MS. was, to my knowledge, offered to him; but he did not care to accept the offer!

Wasmuth. *Institutio methodica accentuationis Hebrææ* (Rostock, 1664).

Ouscel. *Introductio in accentuationem Hebræorum metricam* (Leyden, 1714).

Spitzner. *Institutiones ad Analyticam sacram textus Hebraici V. T. ex accentibus* (Halle, 1786).

Tor. em. תורת אמת. See Pref. p. v.

Man. du Lect. Manuel du Lecteur,—a name given by J. Derenbourg to a compendium of grammar and masora, published by him (Paris, 1871), taken from Ox. 1505. Fragments of what seems to be the original Arabic of this treatise are in the Bodleian and Cambridge University Libraries, and will, I am informed, be also edited by M. Derenbourg.

Dikd. hat. ספר דקדוקי הטעמים לרבי אהרן בן משה בן אשר עם מסורות עתיקות אחרות, edited by S. Baer and H. L. Strack (Leipzig, 1879). This Work contains, with other matter, the rules assigned to Ben-Asher on the accents.

N.B. I beg my readers to notice that when referring to any part of the present Work, I have generally given page and line: thus 80. 14 is p. 80, l. 14.

---

[6] Of this ed. only two copies are known, one in the Library of the Dutch Jews' Seminary, Amsterdam, and the other in that of the Jewish Theological Seminary, Breslau. (This latter copy belonged formerly to Dr. Beer, of Dresden.)

CONTENTS.

CHAP.		PAGE
I.	Introductory. The origin and design of the accentuation. Plan of the present work . . .	1
II.	The division, names, and signs of the accents . .	10
III.	The main dichotomy, its position, and the accents employed to mark it	24
IV.	The continuous dichotomy and rules for the same .	38
V.	Olév'yored—Rules for division of its clause and its *servi* .	54
VI.	Athnach ,, ,, ,,	58
VII.	Silluq ,, ,, ,,	65
VIII.	R'bhia mugrash ,, ,, ,,	74
IX.	Great R'bhia ,, ,, ,,	77
X.	Șinnor ,, ,, ,,	80
XI.	D'chi ,, ,, ,,	82
XII.	Pazer ,, ,, ,,	87
XIII.	Little R'bhia ,, ,, ,,	90
XIV.	L'garmeh and its *servus* .	91
XV.	Great and Little Shalshéleth	94
XVI.	Paseq	95
XVII.	Transformation of the accents .	98

APPENDIX:—

   α. Introductory 102

   β. Arabic text of the treatise, assigned to Ben-Bil'am, on the accents of the three Books . . 106

Index of Scripture passages . 118

CHAPTER I.

INTRODUCTORY.

FROM time immemorial the reading of the sacred books in the synagogue has been a kind of *cantillation*, or *musical declamation*[1]. This mode of recitation was propagated at first, and through many generations, by oral instruction and manual signs[2] alone. At length—probably towards the close of the seventh century of our era—the attempt was made to represent it by *written* signs, introduced into the text. The Greek and Syriac Churches had both by this time nearly perfected their systems of musical notation and interpunction[3]; and it was doubtless their examples—and particularly that of the Syriac Church—which stirred up the Jews in Palestine and in the farther East to make the attempt named. The introduction of these musical signs was, in all probability, simultaneous with that of the vowel-signs—an improvement in which, too, the Syrians had led the

---

[1] The earliest intimation of this cantillation is found in the Talmud, and it is there named נְעִימָה, 'melody:' עליו הכתוב אומר . . . כל הקורא בלא נעימה וגם אני נתתי להם חקים לא טובים (Megilla 32, end).

[2] These signs were made by the teacher, when giving instruction in the recitation. They are referred to by the Talmud, Berachoth 62ᵃ: מראה בימין טעמי תורה; and continued in use long after the written signs were introduced. Thus Rashi, in his comment on the above passage, says that he had seen them used by Readers who came from the land of Israel. Comp. Dikd. hat. 18. 1, and Man. du Lect. 108. 2, where examples are given. According to Sappir (אבן ספיר, I. 56ᵇ) this method of instruction is still practised by the Jews of Yemen. We may suppose that these signs, sketched in the air, were more or less reproduced in the *written* accentuation.

In the Greek Church, too, this mode of directing the singing was observed long before musical signs were noted in the text, and had the particular name of χειρονομία (Christ et Paranikas, Anthologia Græca carminum Christianorum, p. cxiv: *Manuum variis motibus, altitudinem, depressionem, flexus vocis significabant*).

[3] Tzetzes, Die altgriechische Musik in der Griechischen Kirche, pp. 19 and 20; and Martin, Histoire de la Ponctuation chez les Syriens, p. 103 seq.

way. The one notation fixed the traditional *pronunciation* of each word, the other its traditional *modulation*. The two together furnished the needful directions to the Reader for the correct recitation of the sacred text.

These musical signs, or accents (as we term them)[4], are marked, according to the Palestinian system,[5] in our printed texts. We find there two sets of signs,—representing, of course, different modes of recitation,—the one employed for the twenty-one (so-called) Prose Books, the other for the three Poetical Books, Job, Psalms, and Proverbs[6]. It is the accentuation of these three books that I propose to examine in the present treatise.

But what interest, it may be asked, have these musical signs for *us*? And it must be allowed that, regarded simply as *musical* signs, they have no interest or importance at all; for the Jews themselves allow that the musical value of the accents of the three Poetical Books is altogether lost[7]. Happily, however, they have *another* value. Those who arranged this system of musical recitation must have felt that they had something more important to do than merely to produce a melody pleasing

---

[4] They no doubt received this name from their indicating (which they do by their position) the *tone-syllable* of the word. But as musical signs they mean much more than this. Each Hebrew accent denotes an entire musical phrase, and, as such, embraces several notes. (The German Jews assign, in the present day, to the prose Athnach, three notes; to Pazer, seven; to M'huppakh, three; to Mer'kha, two; and so on.) And this must have been the case with the Syriac accents, from the small number of signs which we often find in a verse; and so the signs in use in the Greek Church, and the *neumes* (musical signs) of the Latin Church represented often two or more notes (Gevaert, Histoire et Théorie de la Musique de l'Antiquité, p. 394). To avoid the introduction of a new term, I shall use the word 'accent,' not only for the 'musical sign,' but for the 'modulation,' which the sign represents, and which was in use before the signs were invented.

[5] In the Babylonian system many of the signs are different.

[6] Often termed by Rabbinical writers אמ״ת, a *vox memorialis* formed from the initial letters of their names: איוב, משלי, and תהלים. Of Job, however, the prologue to iii. 2, and the epilogue from xlii. 7, are accented like the Prose Books.

[7] Such is the testimony of the European Jews. But according to Eben Sappir, 55ᵃ, the Jews of Yemen have still a particular melody for the three books.

to the ear. The text was to be so recited *as to be understood*. Above all things it was necessary to draw out its *meaning*, and impress it on the minds of the hearers. The music itself was to be made subsidiary to this end[8]. Hence the *logical* pauses were duly represented—and that according to their gradation—by *musical* pauses; and when no logical pause occurred in a sentence, then the *syntactical* relation of the words to one another and to the whole sentence decided which of them were to be sung together, and which were to be separated by a musical pause. In this way the music was made to mark not only the broad lines, but the finest shades, of distinction in the sense; and when its signs were introduced into the text, they were also the signs of *interpunction*; no others were needed. The value and importance of the accents from this point of view is at once apparent. They help us, in the most effective way possible, to the understanding of the text; they give us, that is, the meaning which tradition among the Jews assigned to it. On this account they have from the very earliest times been held in high esteem. The Talmud informs us that teachers were paid for giving instruction in the 'pausal system of the accents[9].' Indeed their very name, טְעָמִים, points to

---

[8] I think we may see a manifest advantage in the employment of a *musical system* at a time when written signs were not admitted into the text. The absence of vowel as well as interpunctional signs from the text necessitated careful and long-continued instruction on the part of the teacher. This instruction commenced in early years. Now if the teaching had been merely that of plain reading, it would have been hard for the teacher to make his pupils, in difficult and doubtful passages, remember the proper logical pauses. With a musical recitation it was much easier. The musical form was of itself a help to the memory. And what was learned in youth was retained, by constant repetition, in after years. The melody thus became a valuable help for preserving the meaning of the text; and probably not a verse was ever quoted *vivâ voce* without it.

[9] Nedarim 37ᵃ, שכר פיסוק טעמים. It is to be observed that it is not for instruction in their *melody*, נעימה, but in their *divisional value* that the teacher is said to have been paid. The two went together; but the latter appeared to the Talmudic authorities the more important. Comp. Chagiga 6ᵇ, where the פיסקי טעמים, 'the divisions made by the accents,' are referred to, as determining the sense. Later Rabbinical writers fully recognise this function of the accents. See Rashi, e.g. on Deut. xi. 30 and Ezek. i. 11. So in Kuzari ii. 72 the accents are said to be specially

the importance attached to them in this respect: they were so called because they were considered really to indicate the '*meanings*[10].' And so, in the present day, there is not a work which touches on the subject of the accents but lays special stress on this their *interpunctional* value.

If, now, this system had been only regularly carried out in practice, the Hebrew accentuation would be simple enough. But here, at the very outset, our difficulties begin. We find, when we come to examine the text for ourselves, words *united*, which ought from the sense or construction to be *separated*, and *separated*, where we should have expected them to be *united*. Nor do such instances turn up only here and there; they are, on the contrary, of very frequent occurrence. And such discredit have these and similar irregularities brought upon the whole system, that few scholars in the present day trouble themselves about the Hebrew accents, or give them more than a general and superficial consideration. Yet what if it be possible to find a fair and sufficient explanation of these irregularities? What if in some cases we can correct and remove them? What if in others (and those the great majority) we can trace laws which cross and modify the laws of logic and grammar, and co-operate in forming the system as it lies before us? In these latter cases we shall not indeed be able to restore the missing interpunction,

---

designed להבין העניינים, 'to make the meanings intelligible;' and in Man. du Lect. 71. 14, לא יתבארו עניני הפיסוק אלא בטעמים. Hence, too, Aben-Ezra's well-known rule (4[b] מאונים): כל פירוש שאיננו על פירוש הטעמים לא תאבה לו ולא תשמע אליו.

[10] Another explanation of the origin of the name is indeed possible; but, when we consider the marked importance which so old an authority as the Talmud assigns to the logical value of the accents, hardly probable. We may take, that is, the primary meaning of the word טַעַם, 'taste, flavour,' and consider that they were so called because the whole 'flavour' (as it were) of the recitation, in regard both to melody and meaning, depended on them. Comp. a note of Moscato's to Kuzari ii. 80 (quoted by Buxtorf, De Punctorum Antiq. p. 258), הטעמים לחיבות כתבלין לקדרה הן ליופי הקריאה הן לתועלת הענינים, *accentus sunt dictionibus, quod condimenta ollæ* (i.e. *cibis*), *cum ad pulchritudinem lectionis, tum ad commodum sensuum*. But even on this supposition there is an ultimate reference, in part at least, to their logical value.

but shall, at least, account for the accentuation as it stands; order will take the place of confusion; and, with due allowance for disturbing causes, we shall still be able to accept the accents as reliable helps for the exegesis of the text. The prospect of finding the needful explanations is not indeed very encouraging. It may almost seem like courting failure to renew an attempt which has met with so little success in the hands of the diligent and careful scholars who have preceded me. Still I venture to think that the difficulties are not insurmountable, and to hope that results which have satisfied my own mind will prove not less satisfactory to the minds of others. Of course a detailed examination of the anomalies in question will be necessary, for which the following general remarks are intended to prepare the way[11].

In the first place, it is clear that we must secure, as far as possible, *a correct text*. One fruitful source of perplexity has been the corrupt state of even our best and most carefully edited texts. Exceptions arising from this cause I have sought to eliminate by an extensive collation of MSS.[12]

Secondly, I take it for granted that we are willing to remove the unmeaning additions which the accentuators made to the original text, to their own perplexity as well as ours. I refer particularly to the superscriptions of many Psalms, not put apart by themselves—we might then have left the accentuators

---

[11] My readers will understand my dwelling upon this part of my subject; for all else that has to be established—the rules of sequence of the accents, &c.—is of very minor importance compared with it. It is only as guides to the meaning of the text that the accents have any value for us.

[12] But it is vain to hope to eliminate them all. Our oldest MS. does not come within three hundred years of the time when we suppose the accents were first marked. And most MSS. are far younger. Here then was ample time for many errors to have crept in. And when an eminent authority like Ben-Asher gave a false accentuation the sanction of his name, it became the recognised reading in a large class of MSS. for all time. It is most unfortunate for us that we have no Hebrew MSS. of any considerable age, as we have Syriac MSS. that reach up to the fifth century, and enable us to trace the Syriac punctuation back to its very first beginnings, and to watch its gradual development.

to their own devices—but made an integral part of the first verses; and to סֶלָה attached to the end of a verse. In such cases we may claim to have the text as it came from the poet's hands, and accentuate for ourselves accordingly[13].

The other cases, that occasion us difficulty, are mostly of quite another kind. We shall find in them an accentuation, which we have no reason to suppose is false, and for which an adequate explanation has (if possible) to be found. The following considerations will have here to be borne in mind:

A. The essentially *musical* character of the accentual system.

If, then, it *generally* adapts itself (as we have supposed above) to the logical and grammatical laws of the verse and its clauses, we may expect that at other times its purely *musical* character will make itself felt. And this we shall find to be often the case. Indeed, *most of the exceptional cases that occur are due to this cause.* But then they are referable to certain *definite laws,* so that we know beforehand *when* they will take place. Given certain conditions, the exception will follow.

B. The *rhetorical* character of the declamation.

A good public reader does not despise oratorical effect, as his main object is to *impress* what he reads on the minds of his hearers. Hence he may hurry over some words, to come to what he counts the pith and marrow of the sentence, to the part which appears to him most weighty and important; hence too he will introduce a pause here and an emphasis there. This liberty we must grant to the Hebrew Reader.

C. The peculiar *form* of composition, as exhibited in the *parallelismus membrorum.*

For not unfrequently the logical or grammatical division is passed over, that prominence may be given to this *form.*

---

[13] Take, for example, Ps. xi. 1, which, as it stands in the text, is so pointed: לַֽמְנַצֵּ֗חַ לְדָ֫וִ֥ד בַּֽיהוָ֨ה ׀ חָסִ֗יתִי אֵ֭יךְ תֹּאמְר֣וּ לְנַפְשִׁ֑י נ֝֗וּדִי הַרְכֶ֥ם צִפּֽוֹר׃. But here we require Olév'yored on חָסִ֗יתִי, where the main division in the sense occurs. We put the superscription on one side, and point: בַּֽיהוָ֨ה חָסִ֗יתִי אֵ֭יךְ תֹּאמְר֣וּ לְנַפְשִׁ֑י נ֝֗וּדִי הַרְכֶ֥ם צִפּֽוֹר׃. In De R. 1244 I actually found the words so accented.

By the application of these rules and principles, it is believed that most of the apparent irregularities of our texts will be either corrected or explained. A few cases will yet remain, which may perhaps be put under the heads of (1) *clerical errors*, which our MSS. do not enable us to correct; and (2) *accentual licenses*, which find their parallel in the metrical licenses, which poets of all ages have indulged in. In regard to these last—certainly not the most important—exceptions, my readers will probably agree with me, when we come to them: *De minimis non curat lex.*

One remark in conclusion. We must not attempt to force the accents to yield a meaning which they were not intended to represent. The meaning they give is that which had become traditional among the Jews. It may seem to us incorrect. But, when explaining the accents, we have nothing to do with the correctness or incorrectness of the sense they indicate. Let me cite an example. Ps. i. 3 admits of two interpretations[14], one which refers the last clause of the verse to the flourishing *tree*, and the other to the prosperous *man*. The accentuators chose the former, and the accents are to be explained accordingly. And so, in many other passages, the accentuation may be perfectly correct, though founded on a false conception of the meaning. In some cases, we find a double accentuation in the MSS. Of course, we are then at liberty to choose the one which seems to us the more suitable.

In the next chapter I shall give the names and signs of the accents; and I shall then proceed to examine the construction of the verse, and to analyse its several parts. In the course of the examination thus pursued, the exceptional cases, to which I have referred, will come under review.

Obs. The questions have often been asked, Why the three (so-called) Poetical Books—Psalms, Proverbs, and Job—have a different accentuation from the twenty-one Prose Books;

---

[14] See Targ. and Aben-Ezra's note.

and again, why—if there was to be a distinction—the poetical accentuation should have been *confined* to the three books above-named, when there are other books which, if their poetical character be regarded, seem equally to claim it[15]. There was clearly no *necessity* for any distinction at all, for we find the same portions, Pss. xviii and cv. 1–15, at one time marked with the poetical, and at another (see 2 Sam. xxii and 1 Chron. xvi. 8–22) with the prose, accents; and in the Babylonian system of punctuation, Psalms, Proverbs, and Job were accented in the same way as the other books[16]. We have then to do with a refinement peculiar to the Palestinian synagogues and schools,— a refinement (as it would seem) of a purely *musical* character. At least, we find the melody much more frequently interfering with the rules of the accentuation, as fixed by the logical or grammatical construction of the verse, than in the other books. The idea seems to have been to compensate for *the shortness of the verses* (which is a marked characteristic[17] of the greater

---

[15] We have ourselves added unnecessarily to the difficulty of the question by this distinction (as far as I have observed, quite a modern one) of *prose* and *poetical* books. That of *prose* and *metrical* (though older) is equally objectionable, for we have no *metre* here, in any true sense of the term. Rabbinical writers know nothing of such distinctions. They speak simply, and rightly, of the accentuation of the three books and that of the twenty-one books. If I might venture to propose terms which should indicate the difference in question, I would suggest 'plain' and 'musical' accentuation,—the former as designating the simpler cantillation of the twenty-one books, the latter the more finished melody of the three books. The accentuation of the twenty-one books was indeed also musical, but in *a less marked degree* than that of the three books. The latter might be termed 'musical,' κατ' ἐξοχήν.

It is interesting to notice that, in the Greek Church also, there were two systems of notation—the one for the rhythmical reading, e. g. of the Gospels; the other, of a more distinctly musical character, for the singing of Psalms, &c. (Tzetzes, ib., p. 130); and that, similarly, there was in the Latin Church the recitative (*Tonus prophetiarum, Tonus evangelii et epistolarum*), and the chant, of which the *neumes* were the notation.

[16] See a specimen, prefixed to Baer's edition of Job.

[17] Ben-Bil., I. 3, mentions it as a distinguishing mark of the three books, שהפסוקים שלהן קטנים; and R. Isaac (grandson of Rashi), in the Tosaphoth to Baba B. 14[b], names, in the same way, as one of their characteristics, מקראות קצרים (quoted by Baer, Torath emeth, p. 55 note).

part of these books) by a finer and fuller, more artificial and impressive, melody[18]. For the Psalms a peculiar melody was suitable enough, and it may not have been inappropriate when applied to the brief and pregnant verses of Job and Proverbs.

When and by whom this improvement in the cantillation of the synagogue was introduced, we are unable to say. By the help of the Talmud we can trace the accents to the first centuries of the Christian era; but the Talmud (Palestinian as well as Babylonian) gives no hint as to any variation in the accentuation of the several books. The *argumentum e silentio* may perhaps be allowed its weight here, particularly as Jerome also does not allude to having heard from his Jewish teacher a particular mode of reading for the three books, although he draws special attention to their other peculiarities,—metre (as it seemed to him) and stichical division in the writing[19]. Moreover, if this accentuation had been due to an *early* tradition, we should expect to find it represented in the Babylonian system of punctuation. I venture therefore to think that it had its origin in a comparatively recent period, the *terminus a quo* being the early part of the fifth century, at which time the Palestinian Talmud had been closed, and Jerome was dead; and that *ad quem*, the close of the seventh century, when, in all probability, written signs were first employed for the accents. It would not, on account of this its later origin, lose its interest for us, because it would still represent the traditional division and interpretation of the text.

---

[18] Moreover, it is a melody that suits *only* these short verses. When applied to longer (prose) verses, as Ps. xviii. 1, it is in danger of breaking down. Of course *every accent* will be affected by it. We must not suppose, because the accentual arrangement of a verse is short and simple, that the melody is not there.

[19] See his prefaces to Job and Isaiah.

CHAPTER II.

ON THE DIVISION, NAMES, SIGNS, ETC. OF THE ACCENTS.

THE meaning of the word טְעָמִים, the original name of the accents, has been already explained. The Arabic-speaking Jews introduced a name that had exclusive reference to their musical value, أَلْحَان, 'melodies, modulations[1];' and to this name corresponds the Hebrew נְגִינוֹת, as used by later Rabbinical writers[2].

The melody of the three books is, as has been stated, unknown in the present day. We observe only that even for the melody *pauses* were necessary, and that the accents admit of being divided into two classes, according to their *pausal* or *non-pausal* character[3]. By most writers on the accents the *pausal* accent is termed *disjunctive*, as separating by its pause its own word from the word following; and the *non-pausal* accent *conjunctive*, as connecting without a pause its word with the following. But if we employ these terms we must bear in mind (which is not always done) that they hold only for the *melody*. If applied to the accents as signs of *interpunction*, they are only *partially* true. The musical separation and connection do not always agree with the logical or syntactical.

The above-named distinction, which is obvious enough, has been adopted, as the basis of the accentual system, by most modern scholars. It did not, however, commend itself, as such, to Rabbinical writers on the accents, though, of course, they were aware of its existence. Ben-Asher[4] tells us of *conjunctive* accents (מחברים) and their opposites. In Man. du Lect. 71. 15, we read of an accent that

---

[1] This is the name used e. g. in the Arabic text of Ben-Bil'am.

[2] The word properly meant the notes produced by *striking* the lyre or other stringed instrument, and then came to be used for musical notes generally.

[3] It is to be noted that *every word* in the text has its accent, either pausal or non-pausal. The only exception is, that two or more words united by the hyphen, called Maqqeph, were regarded for the purposes of accentuation as constituting a *single* word. Thus כָּל־אַפְסֵי־אָרֶץ, Ps. xxii. 28, has only one accent, not three.

[4] Dikd. hat. 16. 7. Comp. מפסיק 28. 13.

makes a pause (פוסק), and of another that *joins* word to word (מחביר זו לזו). Whilst Moses Qimchi[5] gives us the lists of the *pausal* (מפסיקים 'ט) and *non-pausal* accents (ט' שאינם מפסיקים)[6]. But such notices are few and far between. Ben-Bil., in his formal treatise on the poetical accents, alludes only once, and that incidentally (8. 11), to this distinction. On the other hand, the principle, which lay at the foundation of the Rabbinical division of the accents, was the *weakness or strength, the dependence or independence*, of the modulations. Those accents, which could not stand alone, but only prepared the way for, and found their complete expression in, a final and fuller modulation, were called מְשָׁרְתִים, *servi*. Whilst the accents in which they merged, and on which they were clearly dependent, were regarded as the leading, ruling accents. These latter had not only a fuller and stronger modulation, which gave the tone to the melody of the verse, but they could occupy an independent position, could stand alone, with their modulation complete in itself. Hence the high-sounding title, by which they were distinguished, of מְלָכִים, Kings, or שָׂרִים, Princes[7]. This distinction is, however, insufficient, because it furnishes no indication of—what is to us the most important matter—the relation of the מְלָכִים to one another. Hence many modern writers have adopted the division of these accents into the several grades of Emperors, Kings, Dukes, Counts, etc.[8], to represent their relative pausal value and dependence one on the other. But this fanciful division we may also dispense with. I shall give hereafter the classification I suggest instead. The only title of those named above which I propose to retain is that of מְשָׁרְתִים, *servi*, a useful *terminus technicus*, as marking the *subordinate* position of the conjunctive accents.

Divided into the two classes above-named, the accents, with their usual names[9] and signs, are as follows:—

---

[5] מהלך 11ᵃ, ed. Hamb. 1785.

[6] Comp. Michlol 89ᵃ, ed. Fürth.

[7] The term טְעָמִים properly belongs to both these classes, but is often applied, κατ' ἐξοχήν, to the latter, as playing the more important part in the verse. In Greek Church music we have ἦχοι κύριοι, and τόνοι δεσπόζοντες, even ἡ διαφορὰ κατὰ διάζευξιν καὶ συναφήν (Tzetzes, ib. p. 56), but all in quite a different sense.

[8] First proposed by Sam. Bohlius, in his Scrutinium S. S. ex accentibus, 1636.

[9] The *names* of the accents, as handed down to us by the Jews of the Middle Ages, vary considerably, apparently according to the schools (of Tiberias, Jerusalem, etc.) in which they originated. Some of those given above are of more recent date. I have retained them, as they have become current amongst us, and it seemed better to avoid the confusion which would be caused by reverting to the older names. The *form* of the names is in some cases Aramaic, in others Hebrew. The *meanings* may be traced (see below) to their figure, position, or musical or pausal value.

NAMES, SIGNS, ETC. OF THE ACCENTS.

I. Pausal, or Disjunctive Accents.

1. ־ֽ Silluq (סִלּוּק), as in . . . . דָּבָֽר
2. ־֫ ־֥ Olév'yored (עוֹלֶה וְיוֹרֵד), as in . . . דָּבָ֫ר
3. ־֑ Athnach (אֶתְנָח), as in . . . . דָּבָ֑ר
4. a ־֗ Great R'bhîa (רְבִיעַ גָּדוֹל), as in . . . דָּבָ֗ר
   β ־֗ Little R'bhîa (רְבִיעַ קָטוֹן)[10], as in . דָּבָ֗ר
5. ־֭ R'bhîa mugrash (רְבִיעַ מֻגְרָשׁ), as in . דָּבָ֭ר
6. ־֮ Sinnor (צִנּוֹר), *postpositive*, as in . דָּבָ֮
7. ־֭ D'chî (דְּחִי), *prepositive*, as in . . דָּבָ֭ר
8. ־֡ Pazer (פָּזֵר), as in . . . . . דָּבָ֡ר
9. ׀ ־֓ Great Shalshéleth (שַׁלְשֶׁלֶת גְּדוֹלָה), as in . דָּבָ֓ר׀
10. a ׀ ־֨ Azla l'garmeh (אַזְלָא לְגַרְמֵהּ), as in . . דָּבָ֨ר׀
    β ׀ ־֤ M'huppakh l'garmeh (מְהֻפָּךְ לְגַרְמֵהּ) . . דָּבָ֤ר׀

II. Non-pausal, or Conjunctive Accents (*Servi*).

1. ־֥ Mer'kha (מֵירְכָא), as in . . . . דָּבָ֥ר
2. ־֖ Tarcha (טַרְחָא) . . . . . . דָּבָ֖ר
3. ־֨ Azla (אַזְלָא), as in . . . . דָּבָ֨ר
4. ־ֻ Munach (מוּנַח) . . . . . . דָּבָ֣ר
5. ־֬ Illuy (עִלּוּי) . . . . . . דָּבָ֬ר
6. ־֤ M'huppakh (מְהֻפָּךְ), as in . . . דָּבָ֤ר
7. ־֪ Galgal (גַּלְגַּל), as in . . . . דָּבָ֪ר
8. ־֓ Little Shalshéleth (שַׁלְשֶׁלֶת קְטַנָּה), as in . דָּבָ֓ר
9. ־֘ Sinnorîth (צִנּוֹרִית), *pretonic*, as in . . דָּבָ֘ר

The signs fall generally on the tone-syllable. The only exceptions are D'chî, Sinnor, and Sinnorîth, on which see below. Where there are two signs, the *second* marks the tone.

---

[10] Little R'bhîa is distinguished by its *position*, which is always immediately before Olév'yored. Anywhere else in the verse the accent will be Great R'bhîa.

The semantik, represented above, must strike one as being of a very simple character. And it becomes still more simple when we revert to the earliest and original forms. The elements into which it then readily resolves itself are the *point*, the *straight line*, and (in one case) the *curved line*.

From these elements the Greek grammarians derived their system of accentuation and interpunction; and to the same elements may be referred the musical notation of both the Greek and Latin Churches of the Middle Ages[12].

Remarks on the several Accents[13].

I. 1. סִלּוּק signifies 'cessation, close,' i.e. of the melody. Its sign is a perpendicular stroke[14] below the tone-syllable of the word. Ben-Asher's name is חֹזֵר[15].

The term סוֹף פָּסוּק, which is often used for Silluq, refers properly to the two points which mark the 'end of the verse,' but which have nothing to do (as their position alone shows) with the present system of accentuation[16]. As they always however immediately follow Silluq they became identified with it.

---

[12] For the former, see Tzetzes, ib., p. 129; for the latter, Coussemaker, Histoire de l'Harmonic au Moyen Age, p. 158.

[13] In these remarks, I have occasion to refer to lists of the accents found in the following MSS.:

Vat. 25.—In the Vatican Library (? 14th century).

Cas.—H. III. 13 in the Casanatensian Library, Rome (A.D. 1466).

De R. 333 and 1016.—Two of De Rossi's MSS., now in the Royal Library at Parma (A.D. 1392 and ? 14th century).

Ox. 125.—In the Bodleian Library, Oxford (? 14th century).

Pet. 123.—In the St. Petersburg Imperial Library (? 16th century).

(This last is the list referred to by Pinsker, Einleitung etc., p. 44.)

Ben-Asher's names of the accents I have taken from Dikduke ha-t°amim, p. 20; Chayyug's, from Nutt's edition of הניקוד 'ס, p. 129 (this part of the work is not, however, by Chayyug himself; see Nutt's remarks, p.xii); Eliezer Provenzale's, from a list, printed by him at the end of בשם קדמון, A.D. 1596 (a copy of this rare book is in the British Museum); and Lombroso's, from his edition of the Bible, A.D. 1639, p. 348.

Cod. Bab. is the famous MS. of the Prophets with the Babylonian accentuation (A.D. 916), photo-lithographed 1875.

[14] This stroke is often used (as we shall see) to indicate a pause.

[15] Apparently חָזֵר, 'returning,' 'recurring.' Whatever other accent fails (and they all fail in their turn) Silluq never does.

[16] These two points (or strokes, Dikd. hat. 18. 5) seem to be the relics of an earlier and simpler notation, in which a single point (or stroke) marked the cæsura at Athnach, and *two* the close of the verse. (So in Armenian, a sentence is divided by a single point, and closed by a double point; and in Sanskrit the half-verse is marked by a single stroke, the end of the verse by a double stroke.) When the

2. עוֹלֶה וְיוֹרֵד, so named from its 'ascending and descending' modulation (see chapter on Olév'yored). It is represented (in our texts) by a sign, like M'huppakh, *above*[17], and *before* the tone-syllable, and by a second, like Mer'kha, *below*, *with* the tone-syllable. The name I found in Vat. 25, Cas., and De R. 333, 1016. It is also used by El. Prov., Lombroso, and later writers on the accents. Ben-Asher's name is סָלֵק, 'ascending.'

Rabbinical writers generally regard this accent as dependent on, because it always follows, R'bhia or Zarqa, and have no other name for it than רודפי הרביע and רודפי הזרקא[18]! The name used by most Christian writers, *Merca Mahpachatum*, is altogether false. Ben-Bil. (8. 11) has long ago warned us that we have nothing to do here with *Mer'kha*. The lower sign in MSS. is just like the Silluq-sign, and designates Olév'yored as a pausal accent.

3. אָתְנָח, אַתְנָחְתָּא, אַתְנַחְתָּא or אֶתְנָח[19].

The name (Aram.) is derived from the inf. Aphel of תְּנַח[20], secondary form of נוּחַ, Properly it would mean 'the causing to rest;' then abstr. for concr. (comp. אַזְהָרָה in Heb.), 'what causes to rest or pause[21].' Ben-Asher has טָרֵף, 'breaking off;' Vat. 25, Cas., De R. 333, 1016, and El. Prov. חוֹנֶה, 'encamping,' = resting.

The form, as it occurs in Cod. Bab. (our oldest Cod.), is ⟨symbol⟩, which, by rounding off the angle, became ⟨symbol⟩, and then ⟨symbol⟩, as we find it in our printed texts.

---

present accent-signs were introduced, the two points were retained, as serving to mark clearly the limit between two consecutive verses, and then the simple stroke below was deemed sufficient for Silluq. Otherwise (as it seems to me) we should certainly have had a more prominent sign for this, the chief accent of the verse.

[17] Sometimes I have found, as in Ox. 15 and in Br. Mus. 1, a sign like Şinnorith for M'huppakh.

[18] According to them, it belongs neither to the מְלָכִים nor to the מְשָׁרְתִים,—not to the former because it is a *dependent* accent, and not to the latter because its word *stands apart* from the word following (as is seen by the Dagesh after a vowel). And so it is left out in the cold! They treated S'golta in the same way, in the prose accentuation.

[19] The vocalization, with Pathach in the first syllable, is unquestionably the traditional one. I have found it in Vat. 25, Cas., and Pet. 123, and in the Spanish and Italian Zarqa-lists. The German Jews alone, I believe, pronounce אַתְנַחְתָּא.

[20] This form occurs (as my friend Dr. Baer has pointed out to me) in the Talmud, Erubin 53ᵃ: נקיימא (or סימני) בני יהודה דדייקי לישנא ומתנחי להו סימנא תורתם בידם, 'the Jews, who are accurate in their speech, and set signs for themselves, their Law is established in their hand.'

[21] A similar *nom. verb.* is אַתְחַלְתָּא, 'beginning,' from תחל (Root, חלל). Müller, in his recent edition of Masechet Sopherim, p. 173, explains אתנחה as meaning 'sign of rest' (אות=אה). But such a form is, I believe, without analogy; and certainly one would expect, instead of נח, נחת or נוח.

The original form was (as it seems to me) ־֑־, a compound sign made up of Silluq and Ṭiphcha. This composition (like the mixing of wine with water) represents Athnach as an intermediate accent, neither so strong as the former, nor so weak as the latter (comp. 7 end). An exact parallel is furnished by the Syriac accentuation, where Tachtaya (=Athnach) ־֑־ is derived from the union of Pasûqa (=Silluq) and Samka (=Tiphcha). The origin of the sign was after a time forgotten, and the perpendicular stroke became inclined to the left, just as is often the case (in MSS.) with Silluq itself.

4. רְבִיעַ is represented by a point placed over the tone-syllable of the word. It is also called מְיוּשָׁב [22]. This latter name, ('settled, fixed,') is used technically to indicate a 'sustained' note [23]. The name R'bhîa therefore, 'resting,' (from Aram. רְבַע=Heb. רָבַע,) refers probably not to the *pause*, but to the *modulation* of the voice, as 'resting, dwelling' on one and the same note [24], neither ascending nor descending in the scale [25]. Ben-Asher's name is תָּקֵף, 'strong, firm,'=מְיוּשָׁב.

The R'bhîa-sign represents two accents—בִּשְׁנֵי דְרָכִים מְתַקֵּף (Ben-Asher),—which, however, are readily distinguished by their *position*. The ancients, and most modern writers on the accents, make no distinction (as far as name is concerned) between the two R'bhias. Lombroso was the first to propose the title רְבִיעַ גָּדוֹל. That of רְבִיעַ קָטֹן was added by the author of שערי נעימה (1765), whom Heidenheim and Baer have followed. This simple and necessary distinction I have also adopted.

So the Eastern Syrians, who had the same sign (a point above the word) for two different accents, distinguished between them, as ܡܙܝܥܢܐ ܪܒܐ and ܡܙܝܥܢܐ ܙܥܘܪܐ ('Great' and 'Little' M'zi'ana) [26].

5. There is a third accent, marked by the same sign as R'bhîa, but distinguished from it by a stroke (in MSS. a straight line) over the first letter and on its right hand, thus דָּ֜בָר. As this stroke resembles the Géresh-sign of the prose accentuation, the accent has been called רְבִיעַ מֻגְרָשׁ, *R'bhîa Gereshatum*. This is, however, quite a modern name (first employed by Lombroso), and quite inappropriate, for

---

[22] This name I found in Vat. 25, Cas., and De R. 333, 1016. It is also used by El. Prov.
[23] See Man. du Lect. 87. 6, ולשון מיושב שהמלה תצא בו בנעימה מיושבת לא למעלה ולא למטה.
[24] That this note was a *high* note, we learn from Chayyug, p. 129. 1.
[25] The name רביע is sometimes explained as *punctum quadratum*. But this form is not found in MSS., and where it occurs in printed texts is simply due to the fancy of editors.
[26] See Bar-Hebræus on Syriac Accents (Phillips' edition), p. 50, and Bar-Zu'bî (Martin's edition), p. 18.

Géresh is altogether unknown in the accentuation of the three books[27]. Rabbinical writers term our accent טִפְחָא, because it occupies the same position before Silluq, as Tiphcha does in the prose accentuation. Nay more, the stroke over the first letter is, no doubt, *the Tiphcha-sign itself*, transferred from below[28] (where there is no longer any place for it, as this sign *below* is, in the three books, used for quite a different accent). The placing of the two signs *apart* seems to indicate that each had its own modulation, although the intonation of the word was always with the second sign[29].

This accent appears only before Silluq. Ben-Asher calls it גֹּזֵר, 'cutting off;' and certainly no accent 'cuts off,' so often and so abruptly, the word on which it falls from the following word (e. g. חֶשְׁבֵּי רָעָתִי ; Ps. xxxv. 4) ; and *that*, because there is a musical necessity for its presence before Silluq.

6. צִנּוֹרִי, צִנּוֹר, or זַרְקָא. The form of this accent seems to point to a winding, meandering note; *circumflexione vocis gaudebat* (as an old writer says)[30]. Its *name* was taken from its *form*, which was likened to the meandering of a 'canal,' or 'water-channel[31],' such as were common in the East. Ben-Asher calls it מָתַח, 'drawing out,' because of its long-drawn form or tone. The former is very conspicuous in many MSS.

As regards *position*, it is (what is called) a *postpositive* accent (made so, to distinguish it from Ṣinnorith, which has the same form, but occurs at the beginning, or in the middle of the word, see p. 22). In correct MSS., when the tone falls on the penultimate, it is (at least, in all doubtful cases) *repeated*, to mark the tone and prevent the possibility of a mistake in the chanting, thus : בָּאָרֶל֘, בָּטַחְתִּי֘.

7. תְּ֘לִי is the Tiphcha which precedes Athnach in the prose accentuation, transferred to the first letter, and made *prepositive*. (It was made so, to distinguish it from the conjunctive Tarcha, which has the same form, but is placed under the *tone-syllable* of the word; see

---

[27] It has, however, become established among us, and I do not propose to change it. A suitable name (as it seems to me) would be רָבִיעַ מֻרְכָּב, 'compound R.'

[28] Just as R'bhia is transferred from *above*, in the prose accentuation, to form with Mer'kha the accent T'bhîr.

[29] Where the tone falls on the first letter, the two signs come together, as מִ֖י, חָ֖מּוּ. But this would not prevent the double modulation, as the Masora to Gen. v. 29 shews. Where two words are united by Maqqeph, both signs fall on the second word, as עֲלִי־צִיּ֘וֹן. In practice, the one or other of these signs is often dropped, through the carelessness of punctators and editors.

[30] Like the *Sinuosum* of the Latin neumes. (See Helmore, Plain-song, p. 6.)

[31] צִנּוֹר is used in this sense in the Talmud, and probably זַרְקָא had the same meaning. I do not find it (as Heidenheim, Mishp. hat. p. 6, states) in Chaldee; but in Arabic زِنَّق signifies 'rigole, saignée.' (See Dozy, Supplément aux Dictionnaires Arabes.)

p. 20)[32]. It is represented by a straight line, inclining to the right, and is, in many MSS., *repeated* when the tone falls elsewhere than on the first syllable, and there might be a doubt as to its position, thus, עֻזְרָה‎[33], גְּמַלְתִּי‎.

There are few accents that can boast of so many names. As representative of the prose Tiphcha, it is still, by some writers, named Tiphcha, or *Tiphcha præpositivum*. טַרְחָא‎ and דְּחִי‎ are synonyms of the prose Tiphcha[34]; hence Moses Qimchi and others have named it טַרְחָא‎[35]; Lombroso and those who follow him, דְּחִי‎. By Rabbinical writers generally it is known as יְתִיב‎, 'stationary, pausal[36],' in contradistinction to the *conjunctive* accent of the same form. Vat. 25, De R. 333, 1016, and El. Prov. name it יְמָנִית‎, from its position on the *right hand* of the word. In many MSS. I have found it, to my surprise, marked like the prose accent תְּבִיר‎, and Cas. *names* it so. This sign— as made up of R'bhia and Mer'kha—would represent it as an intermediate accent, neither so strong as the former, nor so weak as the latter[37] (all three, as we shall see, appear regularly before Athnach). With this form it ceases to be *prepositive*.

8. פָּזֵר‎ derives its name from its modulation, הוּא הַקּוֹל יְפֻזַּר‎ (Man. du Lect. 73. 23). It was a 'shake' or 'trill.' Hence it is named in Cas., De R. 333, 1016, and by El. Prov. מַרְעִיד‎, 'making to tremble.' Similarly, in Greek church music the trill was designated τρομικόν. Ben-Asher calls it נֶצַח‎, 'conspicuous,' 'clear,' in reference, no doubt, to its sharply-defined tone.

---

[32] When two words are united by Maqqeph, D'chî is placed before the first letter of the *second* word, thus: שִׁבְטֵי־יָהּ‎, בְּכָל־לַיְלָה‎.

[33] Baer (following Ben-Bil. 6, below) makes the second sign here Métheg. MSS. vary. The Métheg-sign has the advantage of preventing confusion with Tarcha, see the ex. p. 32.

[34] For Tarcha this is well known. For D'chî see Chayyug 127. 1, and a list at the end of the first Bomberg Bible. דְּחִי‎ properly signifies 'thrust back,' in reference to the backward inclination of the sign. In Pinsker, p. 43, this accent is called in Arabic دَحِي‎, 'thrusting back,' viz. its sign. The name דְּחִי‎ is appropriate enough for us, seeing that the sign is 'thrust back' from its proper position on the tone-syllable to the first letter of the word.

[35] The name is found first so used in Dikd. hat. 26. 5. But in his list of the accents of the three books, Ben-Asher calls this accent חֶרֶץ‎, apparently because of its *straight, undeviating* course. It is always the forerunner of Athnach (or of Athnach's representative), whereas the other pausal accents *vary* in their sequence.

[36] So in the prose accentuation Y'thibh is 'stationary, pausal,' in opposition to the conjunctive M'huppakh, and so also Pashta is often (e. g. in Man. du Lect. 76. 9) called יָתִיב‎, in opposition to אוֹלָא‎, 'going on,' not pausing.

[37] The same explanation applies to תְּבִיר‎ in the Prose Books. See Derenbourg's note, Man. du Lect. 219.

To explain the *form*, we must go back to the prose system, where it occurs constantly as a somewhat greater pause, in the same clause with Géresh. Luzzatto[39] regards it as a mere substitute for Géresh. However that may be, I do not doubt that its *form* is derived from Géresh, viz. by the addition of the pausal stroke, thus, ֜[40], which, with the sharp angle rounded off, becomes the Pazer, ֡, of our texts[41].

9. שַׁלְשֶׁ֓לֶת׀. This zigzag line represents the musical character of the accent. (Comp. the similar sign sometimes used in modern music for a trill.) Shalshéleth was an *ascending shake* or trill. It belonged to the same class as Pazer. Hence the two are often confounded in MSS., and where Ben-Asher has the one, as in Ps. cxxv. 3, לְמַ֓עַן, Ben-Naphtali has the other, לְמַ֡עַן. Hence, too, Shalshéleth is described in Cas., De R. 333, 1016, and by El. Prov. as מַרְעִישׁ, a term of the same meaning as that used by them for Pazer above. There must, of course, have been a difference between the two; and, no doubt, Shalshéleth was the more extended and emphatic trill[42]. It occurs far less frequently than Pazer.

Ben-Asher's name for this accent is רְתָק, which has the same meaning as שַׁלְשֶׁלֶת, 'chain' (comp. Heb. רַתּוֹק and רְתֻקוֹת)[43]. The name 'chain' has by some been referred to the succession of tones, 'in linked sweetness long drawn out,' which characterized this accent,—making it perhaps like the *trillo di catena* of the present day; but see note.

The stroke on the left hand is the pausal sign, Paseq, which distinguishes it as a pausal accent from the conjunctive of the same form and name. Lombroso was the first to apply to these two accents the distinctive titles of גְּדוֹלָה and קְטַנָּה.

10 and 11. ׀ לְגַרְמֵהּ, 'by itself,' 'independent,' = Heb. לְנַפְשׁוֹ. Like Shalshéleth, M'huppakh and Azla become independent pausal accents,

---

[39] In Torath emeth, p. 61.

[40] A form still found in some MSS. It must be remembered that the sign for Géresh is properly a *straight line* inclined to the right.

[41] So Zaqeph gadôl ֔ is from Zaqeph qatôn ֕, by the addition of the pausal stroke.

[42] Ben-Asher says of it: לֹא בִמְהֵרָה יִנָּתֵק, 'it is not quickly broken off.'

[43] In Cod. Bab. Amos i. 2, we find the original form of the accent ׃. Here the points one above another were taken to represent the several rings of a pendent 'chain,' whence the name Shalshéleth. They were probably originally meant to symbolize the several ascending notes of the trill. It is observable that the *Quilisma*, or trill of the Latin neumes, has also 'the form of several dots hanging one on the other' (Helmore, Plain-song, p. 10). With this form of Shalshéleth may be also compared the Syriac accent ܫܝܫܠܐ, 'chain,' with two points, one above the other, ܀ (Zeitschrift für die Kunde des Morgenlandes, i. p. 206), and the vowel-sign R'bhaṣa, with its two points, called also ܫܫܠܬܐ, 'chain' (Merx, Gram. Syr. p. 30).

by the addition of Paseq. Ben-Asher names the former שׁוֹפָר הָרַב, and Cas. פּוֹנֶה נַרְמֵי. Neither mentions the latter; nor do other Rabbinical writers distinguish between the two. It is convenient, however, to do so (as Heidenheim and Baer have done) by the names of the accents (M'huppakh and Azla) from which they are derived.

II. 1. The usual names of this accent, מַאֲרִיךְ, מַאֲרְכָא, and מֵירְכָא, or מֵרְכָא, are all from the same root (מֵירְכָא like מֵימְרָא and מֵיכְלָא), and indicate it, as *prolonging* the modulation. Comp. the Arabic name in Pinsker, p. 42 מָד, 'lengthening out,' 'prolonging.' By Ben-Asher it is termed יוֹרֵד, from its *descending* tone : לְמַטָּה טַעֲמוֹ (Dikd. hat. 24. 12). Hence the further Arabic name in Pinsker, p. 43 حَاطَة, 'descending.' In MSS. it is generally represented by a straight line, turning more or less to the left hand.

2. טַרְחָה or טַרְחָא[44], a name first used by M. Qimchi (in Mah^alakh 11^b). By the older grammarians (with the exception of Ben-Asher), it is divided into three accents—each, of course, with its own modulation[45]— a sign that it is one of the most important of the conjunctives :

α. מָאִילָה or מָאִילָא when it occurs before Silluq. Unquestionably the Arabic مَائِلَة, 'inclined[46],' and so written in Pet. 123, מָאִילָה *maylé* (modern Arabic pronunciation), not as it is usually pronounced מָאִילָה. This derivation is confirmed by the name נְטוּיָה[47], 'inclined,' given to this accent in Man. du Lect. 74. 6.

β. דְּחוּיָה when it occurs before Athnach[48]. For the meaning of the term, see D'chî, note 34 : (דָּחוּי and נָטוּי are used as synonyms, Ps. lxii. 4.)

γ. שׁוֹכֵב when it occurs before R'bhia mugrash. שׁוֹכֵב is *recumbens, se inclinans* = נְטוּיָה above[49].

---

[44] A synonym of the pausal Tiphcha in the prose accentuation (derived from טָרַח, *laboravit*, 'labouring, heavy, slow'), but here applied to a *conjunctive* accent. Yet the name is perhaps not so inappropriate, for the employment of the *sign* seems to imply a similar *slow* modulation.

[45] So in the prose system, Munach, Illuy, and M'kharbel have all the same sign, but different modulations. Ben-Bil. (Oxford MS.) has the following remark on the intonation of two of the above accents : הדחויה יציאתה בכובד ושוכב יוצא רפה בלא כובד, i. e. the enunciation of D. was *pesante*, that of Sh. *leggiero*. But if the intonation before Athnach was *pesante*, much more (we may be sure) must it have been so before Silluq.

[46] See Man. du Lect. 96, Derenbourg's note. Even in the old MS., Cod. Bab., I find a form derived from the Arabic, מסלסלין, Masora to Amos i. 2.

[47] נטויה refers to the *sign*, not to the *tone*, as is clear from the expression נטויה לאחור, 'inclined backwards,' 77. 19.

[48] Or before R'bhia mugrash, when it takes the place of Athnach.

[49] Derenbourg, in Man. du Lect. 74. 6, has made the sign of שׁוֹכֵב like Galgal, but in the original MS. it is שׁוּכָב, i. e. שׁוֹכָב; the double accentuation, with Mer'kha

The sign of these accents is (in MSS.) a straight line, inclined to the right, and *under the tone-syllable*. D'chî has the same form, but is distinguished from them by being always placed outside the word before the first consonant. Ben-Asher, like ourselves, has only one name for the three accents, בֵּ֫, which points to the position *between* the letters of the word, as דָּבָ֫ר. El. Prov. and other moderns employ the name Tiphcha, since the form and position is the same as that of Tiphcha, in the prose accentuation.

3. אַזְלָא, a name taken from the prose accentuation, and first employed by Lombroso. (On its meaning see note 36.) The older writers call it simply מַקֵּל (Ox. 125 עצא, i. e. عَصًا), 'rod, stroke[50];' Ben-Asher מַעֲלֶה, from its ascending tone[51].

Its sign is a straight line, inclined to the left, over the tone-syllable.

The next three accents belong to the Shophar-class, so called because of their fancied resemblance to the שׁוֹפָר, 'trumpet,' used by the Jews on certain festival days[52].

4. שׁוֹפָר מוּנָח. The form is two lines, inclined at a right (in MSS. often an acute) angle to one another, and placed *under* the tone-syllable. The name here given is that adopted by most writers. Chayyug has שׁוֹפָר נָחַת[53], 'Shophar of rest' (=מוּנָח). Lombroso, and others since his time, make it שׁ׳ הוֹלֵךְ, the name of the prose Munach in the Spanish Zarqa-list. Often it is מוּנָח מִלְּמַטָּה, *Munach inferius*, to distinguish it from the following sign. Sometimes, as the leading representative of the Shophar-class, it is called simply שׁוֹפָר[54].

---

and Tarcha, pointing to the *variations in MSS.;* some, with Ben-Naphtali, having Mer'kha, and others, with Ben-Asher, Tarcha. In Chayyug's list, and in Ox. 125, we meet with the strange names תלישא רבה and חלישא ועירה ('Great and Little T'lisha') for α and γ (β and γ), a lame attempt (as it would seem) to introduce the prose nomenclature into our accentuation.

[50] Comp. ῥάβδος, *virgula*, as used by Greek grammarians (Osann, Anecdotum Romanum, p. 133), and the *virga* or *virgula* of the Latin neumes (Helmore, Plainsong, p. 4). In the musical notation of the Greek Church this sign was called κέντημα, 'goad' (Christ and Paranikas, Anthologia Graeca, p. cxxv), the דָּרְבָּן of Man. du Lect. 90. 1.

[51] Dikd. hat. 22. 9.

[52] This trumpet (as I have seen it) is made of a straight (flattened) horn, somewhat more than a foot in length, turned up a few inches at the end. A good representation may be seen in Stainer's Music of the Bible, fig. 75, p. 127.

[53] For so, no doubt, we must point, not with Hupfeld, נֹחַת, 'descending.' In Ox. 125 we have the Arabic name שופר וצֹע, where وَضْع, *positio*, *depositio*, is evidently the rendering of נַחַת.

[54] In Cas. and De R. 333 occurs the name קִלְקֵל; according to Chayyug 128. 15 a synonym of מְכָרְבֵּל. But there is no reason for the introduction of מְכַרְבֵּל here! El.

But the correct designation of this accent is, no doubt, that used by Ben-Bil. and those who follow him, שׁוֹפָר עִלּוּי[55], a name given it because of its *ascending* tone[56], answering to that of the accent of the same name in the prose system[57]; whereas מוּנָח implies an *equal, sustained* tone (לֹא לְמַעְלָה וְלֹא לְמַטָּה)[58]. Ben-Asher has a similar name, עוֹלֶה, 'ascending.' These fine musical distinctions have, however, no meaning for us. I have therefore retained the common name Munach, and then the name עִלּוּי will be employed for the following accent.

5. שׁוֹפָר עִלּוּי. This name is convenient enough for us, as descriptive of the position of the accent, *above* the tone-syllable of the word. It was first used (I believe) by Lombroso. Ben-Asher has a similar name, תּוֹלֶה, 'suspended.' Others use the term מוּנָח מִלְמַעְלָה, *Munach superius*.

But the best authorities introduce us here to a *new* accent (the counterpart of which is not found in the prose system), שׁוֹפָר שָׁבוּר, an accent, the modulation of which (from its name) must have been of a broken character, and was probably a plain shake—shake on one note[59]—the Greek πεττεία. It is easy to see how it might thence get the name (which is found in Man. du Lect. 74. 5) of מְפַזֵּר 'שׁ, 'the tripping Shophar' (2 Sam. vi. 16). In this note we have one of the musical refinements of the three books[60].

Prov. (whom Norzi follows) has made confusion worse confounded by changing (as it would seem) this name into גַּלְגַּל !!

[55] In the original Arabic, and in Pet. 123, רפע 'שׁ, i. e. رَفْع, 'Sh. of elevation.'
[56] See Dikd. hat. 24. 12, and Baer's note there.
[57] See Man. du Lect. 87. 5. The name used for עלוי there is מוּרָם.
[58] See Man. du Lect. 87. 5. For מוּנָח we have there מְיוּשָׁב (a name used also by Chayyug, 128. 24). We thus ascertain the meaning of the term מוּנָח. It is the same as מְיוּשָׁב, 'settled,' unvarying, in its tone (see above, under R'bhia).
[59] In Man. du Lect. 102. 4, the term שָׁבוּר is opposed to מְיוּשָׁב, just as, in any dictionary of music, the *vibrato*, or plain shake, is opposed to a pure sustained tone. So Ben-Asher, Dikd. hat. 19. 7, tells us of מוּנָח 'שׁ, that its modulation is *not broken* (ניימתו בל תוסר), in accordance with the preceding note.
[60] In the printed text of Ben-Bil. (taken from the Paris Cod.) we find מונח instead of שבור. So that the strange phenomenon presents itself, of Ben-Bil.'s calling our Munach by the name of Illuy, and *vice versâ*. With regard to Illuy, I have already explained above; and as to Munach, it is simply, in the case before us, a correction of some early copyist, who missed an accent with which he was familiar in the prose accentuation. I say 'an early copyist,' because the correction is already found in Hadassi (A.D. 1148). It is also in the De Rossi Cod. (evidently from the same original as the Par. Cod.) and in the grammatical work of Samuel hanaqdan, Berlin Cat. No. 118. But in the original Arabic of Ben-Bil., and in Ox. 125,

6. שׁ׳ מַהְפָּךְ, שׁוֹפָר מְהֻפָּךְ, or שׁ׳ הָפוּךְ. This is the שׁוֹפָר, 'turned round[61],' properly (as in some texts) ֔. Ben-Asher, Vat. 25, Cas., and others term it פּוֹנֶה, which has the same meaning. Ben-Asher's description of the prose M'huppakh shews us that the modulations of the conjunctive accents played no unimportant part in the melody of the verse: 'It first descends, then mounts up, and keeps itself mounted up' (יוֹרֵד וְעוֹלֶה וּמִתְעַלֶּה).

7. גַּלְגַּל, 'wheel[62];' Ox. 125 הלִיל כבירה[63], i. e. هلال كبيرة, 'great new moon,' from its semicircular form. (In the prose list this accent is יָרֵחַ בֶּן־יוֹמוֹ, 'the moon a day old.') In Cas. and De R. 333, 1016, it is named מְנַדְנֵד, 'making to tremble,' a designation which must refer to the modulation, similar to that of Pazer, which it immediately precedes.

8. See Shalshéleth among the pausal accents. Little Sh. is of very rare occurrence.

9. צִנּוֹרִית—in Ox. 125 צִנּוֹרָה—has the same sign as צִנּוֹר, but צִנּוֹר is *postpositive*, whereas it is *pretonic*. It occurs only in an open

---

and Pet. 123, we have שופר תכסיר (i. e. تَكْسِير), Sh. *fractionis* = Sh. *fractus* ; and in the Ox. and Vat. texts of Ben-Bil., and in Simsoni, שבור 'ש. In Cas., De R. 333, 1016, and by El. Prov. the accent is not named. By Chayyug it is called simply שופר (שבור has probably fallen out).

[61] In the Arabic text of Ben-Bil., Ox. 125, and Pet. 123, שופר מקלוב, i. e. مَقْلُوب, 'turned about.' In the same sense, Greek and Latin grammarians used the terms ἀπεστραμμένος and *aversus*. Thus כ is Σίγμα ἀπεστραμμένον. We even find a sign just like ours, and called by the same name, < *aversa* (C. Suetoni Tranquilli Reliquiæ, p. 140).

[62] But this name and the form do not agree. Here we must once more recur to the prose accentuation. Galgal is there the servus of Pazer gadôl, usually represented by two T'lishas, ֒֝ the original form of which was ֝֒ (for so T'lisha appears in our oldest MS., Cod. Bab.) One of these T'lishas was then taken for the servus, ֬, as is clear from the name given to the servus in Man. du Lect. 89. 14, *T'lisha q'tanna*. The usual name is Galgal. We now understand why Galgal and Pazer, coming together, are described in the Masora as אופן ועגלה, 'wheel and waggon,' the single circle representing the wheel, and the double the waggon. By putting the part for the whole, we get the form usual in MSS., ֬, and with the ornamentation of printed texts, ֝. But it is questionable whether this particular *form* does not come from ֬, a form of the servus common enough in MSS., and corresponding to the form ֨ for Pazer gadôl, which latter is also frequent enough, e. g. all through Man. du Lect. Ben-Asher's name for Galgal is שכבל, of which nothing can be made. Baer proposes עגול, 'round.' I would suggest שכלל=משכלל, 'completing.' The wheel *completes* the waggon. The root of this form is used by Ben-Asher, in describing the prose Galgal, 19. 4 : 'A waggon with wheel *complete*' (כלולה).

[63] According to the pronunciation in most parts of Syria. See Wallin, Zeitschrift der Deutschen Morgenländischen Gesellschaft, xii. p. 669.

syllable *before* Mer'kha or M'huppakh, e. g. דָּבָר, דָּבָר[64]. Ben-Asher names it מְמַלֵּא, because it serves as a *complement* to these accents. Yet it had its own modulation, which must, to some extent, have resembled that of Ṣinnor. The form צְנוֹרִית seems to be the fem. of a *nom. rel.*, like יָמָנִית, p. 17.

On the pausal sign Paseq, which is no accent, for it has no modulation attaching to it, see special chapter.

In the above remarks, I have aimed at bringing together the various names used for the accents, and at explaining them and the corresponding signs. At the same time I have collected the scattered notices, as far as they seemed of an authentic character, relating to the musical character of the accents. The information submitted, although not of much practical value, has a certain literary and historical interest. The investigation could not have been passed over altogether, and having undertaken it, I have sought to make it,—even at the risk of some wearisomeness of detail,—as complete as possible.

The first step towards the accentuation was the arranging of the text in a number of small divisions, called פְּסוּקִים, 'sections[65],' or מִקְרָאוֹת, 'lections.' These are what we call 'verses.' Each of these sections or verses was recited separately, and each is to be regarded in tracing the laws of accentuation as an *independent whole*. Logically, a verse may be closely connected with the one preceding or following it; but musically and accentually no such connection exists. The individual verse is to be taken, and the relation of its accents to one another to be alone considered.

The fundamental tone ('key-note' perhaps we may call it) of the verse was furnished by the end-accent, Silluq. This was the only *constant* musical element; in other words, Silluq is the only accent that never fails. The other accents vary in character and number, according to musical laws which we have to determine. This is the task that lies before us in the following chapters.

---

[64] Two words joined by Maqqeph are regarded for the purposes of accentuation as *one* word. If, now, Ṣinnorith falls on the first of two such words, the Maqqeph is dropped; thus, הוּא יְ for הוּא־יְ. Ṣinnorith joins the words so closely together, that Maqqeph is no longer needed.

[65] פָּסוּק, 'cut off,' 'a segment, section.' These sections are mentioned in both the Mishna and Talmud, and in Kiddushin 30ᵃ, the number of them is given for certain books.

CHAPTER III.

THE DICHOTOMY.

ONE of the distinguishing characteristics of the Hebrew verse is what has been termed its DICHOTOMY.

As I use the term in the present chapter, I would be understood to mean that every verse in the three books is divided by a cæsura into *two* parts.

The lengths of these parts, and the accents that mark the cæsura, vary in different verses, but *the cæsura itself cannot fail*.

In the present chapter we have to determine—

First, the *position* of this cæsura, or chief musical division of the verse; and secondly, the *notation* that is employed to mark it.

I. Our main guide to the dichotomy of the verse will be the *parallelismus membrorum*, the characteristic of poetry, and of the higher style generally, in Hebrew composition.

1. In such simple cases as the following, it will be seen at once that the dichotomy can come nowhere else than between the members of the parallelism.

a. Synonymous parallelism:

> Jehovah, rebuke me not in thine anger, |
> Neither chasten me in thy hot displeasure (Ps. vi. 1).
> If thine enemy hunger, give him bread to eat, |
> And if he thirst, give him water to drink (Prov. xxv. 21).

b. Antithetic parallelism:

> There is that giveth himself out as rich, with nothing at all, |
> There is that giveth himself out as poor, with much wealth (Prov. xiii. 7).
> A soft answer turneth away wrath, |
> But a grievous word bringeth up anger (Prov. xv. 1).

2. But the parallelism is far from being always so exact as in these examples. Indeed, such verses would soon become wearisome by their monotony. The poets therefore allow themselves the utmost liberty in varying the form of the parallelism[1].

---

[1] I confine myself in what follows to examples of synonymous parallelism. The *principle* is all that it is necessary to establish.

The perpendicular line used above is, I need hardly say, meant to indicate the *position* of the dichotomy.

1. Sometimes it is *loose* and *general:*

> But in Jehovah's law is his delight, |
> And in His law doth he meditate day and night (Ps. i. 2).

> The precepts of Jehovah are right, rejoicing the heart; |
> The commandment of Jehovah is pure, enlightening the eyes (Ps. xix. 9).

2. Still more frequently it is *limited* and *partial:*

a. So an accessory part may appear in the *second* member, e. g.

> And Jehovah helpeth them, and rescueth them; |
> He rescueth them from the wicked and saveth them, because they trust in Him (Ps. xxxvii. 40).

Comp. Ps. xviii. 51; xxi. 12; xxvii. 11; cxli. 8.

β. But it is much more common in the *first.* Indeed, the *main idea* of the verse (and this it is important to notice) is often given in the first member, and the second member merely echoes *a part* —a word only, it may be—of the first, which it may, or may not, expand or add to:

> Ask of me, and I will give thee the heathen as thine inheritance, |
> And as thy possession the ends of the earth (Ps. ii. 8).

> Life he asked of thee; thou hast given it to him, |
> Length of days for ever and ever (Ps. xxi. 5).

> Cast it on Jehovah; let Him deliver him, |
> Let Him rescue him, seeing He hath pleasure in him (Ps. xxii. 9).

Comp. Ps. ix. 18; xviii. 8 and 12 (חשׁך); xxviii. 2; xxxi. 20; cxv. 14; cxxxv. 12; cxl. 13; Prov. i. 33; Job xx. 4; xxxvi. 5.

Such cases often come (as the examples given above shew) under C, p. 6. The verse is divided to exhibit the parallelism, and the logical division has to give way.

Some peculiar cases of partial parallelism must be here noticed.

γ. When two parallel expressions follow one another in the course of a continuous construction (*progressive parallelism* this has been termed) they are often separated by the cæsura, so as to produce *parallelismus membrorum.* Such cases come also under C, p. 6; but here it is the *syntactical,* more frequently than the logical division, which is passed over.

> The splendour of the glory of thy majesty, |
> And thy wondrous works,—will I consider (Ps. cxlv. 5).

E

> As I have seen, those who plough iniquity, |
> And sow trouble,—reap it (Job iv. 8).
> Therefore I came out, to meet thee, |
> To seek thy face,—and have found thee (Prov. vii. 15).
> There is no wisdom, and no understanding, |
> And no counsel,—against Jehovah (Prov. xxi. 30).

The other passages that come under this head are (as far as I have noted): Ps. xvi. 3; l. 4; lxvi. 14; lxxv. 7[2]; xc. 2; cvi. 37[3]; cvii. 17; cxxxix. 20; Prov. iii. 2; vii. 6, 12; viii. 2, 3, 25; xvi. 30; xxv. 3; xxx. 32; Job iv. 10; v. 15; xi. 10; xx. 17; xxxii. 8; xxxvii. 13.

δ. In a few instances, words occurring in the first part of the verse are *repeated*, for the sake of effect, before the grammatical construction is completed. Here there is necessarily a pause before the repetition, and so a suitable place is found for the dichotomy:

> How long shall the wicked, O Jehovah, |
> How long shall the wicked—triumph? (Ps. xciv. 3).

And so in Ps. xxix. 1[4]; lxxxix. 52; xciv. 1; xcvi. 7; cxiii. 1; and Job xviii. 13. Ps. lxx. 2 is similar.

3. Where the verse consists of three members, two of which exhibit parallelism, but the third contains a different idea, we should expect the dichotomy to come either after or before the parallelism, and this we find to be generally the case, e. g.

a. When the parallelism *precedes*:

> On thee have I stayed myself from the womb,
> From my mother's bowels, thou art my sufficiency; |
> Of thee is my praise continually (Ps. lxxi. 6).

> Hear, O my people, and I will speak;
> O Israel, and I will testify against thee: |
> God, thy God, am I (Ps. l. 7).

Comp. Ps. xxiv. 7; xxxix. 6; xl. 10; liv. 5; lv. 16; &c.

But here a certain amount of liberty is claimed. Sometimes the division comes *between* the members of the parallelism:

---

[2] Correcting the last part of the verse, thus: וְלֹא מִמִּדְבַּר הָרִים with the following Codd., B. M. 2; Cam. 13; De R. 732; Par. 80; Ber. 17, 51; &c.

[3] Pointing אֶת־גְּנֵיהֶם with Ox. 15, 17, 72; Erf. 1, 3; &c.

[4] Leaving out the superscription.

> For he shall hide me in his tabernacle, in the day of evil, |
> He shall conceal me in the concealment of his tent,
> > On a rock shall he exalt me (Ps. xxvii. 5).
>
> Jehovah reigneth, hath robed himself with majesty, |
> Jehovah hath robed, hath girt himself with strength,
> > The world also standeth fast, doth not move (Ps. xciii. 1).

Comp. Ps. xxxvii. 5; lxix. 5; cxvi. 16; and cxliii. 12[5].

In such instances, attention seems to be drawn to the close connection between the idea contained in the parallelism, and the new idea introduced by the third member. Thus, in Ps. xxvii. 5, 'He shall hide me in his tent, where I shall be safe as on a rock above the reach of mine enemies;' and in xciii. 1, 'Jehovah hath put on his might and majesty, and order is, in consequence, once more established in the world[6].' We have here merely instances of what we have already seen in a simpler form above, viz. of parallelism, *with addition in the second member*. This is a recognised principle in Hebrew verse, and need not occasion any difficulty. Such an addition often comes in, with marked effect, at the close of the verse.

b. Again, when the parallelism *follows*, it is generally marked off by the dichotomy, e. g.

> > I will exult and rejoice in thy mercy, |
> > That thou hast seen my affliction,
> > Hast regarded the distresses of my soul (Ps. xxxi. 8).
>
> > Thou wilt make me know the path of life; |
> > Fulness of joys is with thy presence,
> > Pleasures in thy right hand for evermore (Ps. xvi. 11).

Comp. Ps. xxiv. 8; xxxv. 10; lxvii. 5; lxxviii. 21, 50; &c.

But here, as before, and apparently for the same reason, *mutatis mutandis*, the dichotomy sometimes appears *between* the members of the parallelism:

> Yea! though I walk through the valley of the shadow of death, I will fear no evil,
> For thou art with me, |
> Thy rod and thy staff—they comfort me (Ps. xxiii. 4).
>
> > Cause me to go in thy truth, and teach me,
> > For thou art the God of my salvation, |
> > In thee have I hoped all the day long (Ps. xxv. 5).

Comp. Ps. iii. 8; iv. 3; vi. 7; vii. 6; xiii. 6; xxvii. 6; xxxviii. 13; xcv. 10; cxlviii. 13; Job ix. 21.

It is unnecessary therefore to propose—as commentators, who have failed to notice this peculiarity in the division of the verse, sometimes do propose[7]—to shift back the cæsura to the early part of the verse, so

---

[5] So also Is. liv. 1.

[6] That such is the connection of ideas may be seen by comparing xcvi. 10.

[7] E. g. Hupf. and Hitz. in Ps. xiii. 6, and Hupf. in xxv. 5. But, to be consistent, we must make the same change in cases like Ps. xii. 2; xxx. 2; lxviii. 2; and xcvii. 1; where, however, neither Hupf. nor Hitz. have thought of suggesting it.

as to make the musical agree with the logical pause. In reality, we have here merely instances of that *partial* parallelism, which we noticed on a smaller scale, under 2, 2 β. The sentiment of the verse is first given, and then comes an echo (as it were) of the *concluding words* of that sentiment. This too is an established principle of the Hebrew versification.

4. The verse may admit of division into *three* members, more or less parallel. Here the dichotomy will be found at the close of the first member, and rightly; for this is evidently the leading clause. It gives the sense of the verse, which the other two members merely echo and emphasize:

> Blessed the man, who hath not walked in the counsel of the wicked, |
> Nor stood in the way of sinners,
> Nor sat in the seat of scorners! (Ps. i. 1).

And so in Ps. vii. 15; xxviii. 4; lii. 7; cxv. 12; cxxxix. 12; cxl. 6[8]; and Job xxxi. 7.

5. Where the verse consists of two parts, *each* of which contains a parallelism, the dichotomy will of course come at the close of the first part:

> For my life is spent with grief,
> And my years with sighing; |
> My strength faileth, because of mine iniquity,
> And my bones are consumed (Ps. xxxi. 11).

Comp. Ps. ii. 2; xi. 4; xviii. 16; xxx. 6; li. 6; &c.

II. But often *parallelismus membrorum* fails altogether, as a guide to the division of the verse.

1. The main *musical* will then correspond with the main *logical* pause:

> I will not be afraid of ten thousands of the people, |
> Who set themselves against me round about (Ps. iii. 7).
>
> And I had said in my confusion :
> 'I am cut off away from thine eyes.' |
> Yet thou didst hear the voice of my supplications,
> When I cried unto thee (Ps. xxxi. 23).

Such instances abound in every page[9]. Of course where there

---

[8] See *corrigenda*, at the end of this chapter.

[9] Scholars generally, following Bishop Lowth, classify them as instances of *synthetic* parallelism. This classification does not, however, seem to be very suitable: nor could I use it without an explanation and examples, which, for the purpose of the

are two or more logical divisions, of equal strength, in a verse, e. g. in Prov. xxiii. 29, the accentuators exercised their own judgment as to the position of the dichotomy.

2. Where no logical pause exists, the position of the dichotomy will be fixed by what we may call the *syntactical* pause, i. e. the words will be formed into two groups, according to their connection in sense and construction, and the dichotomy will come between[10]:

       Yet have I set my King |
          On Zion, my holy mountain (Ps. ii. 6).

And give back to our neighbours sevenfold into their bosom |
  Their reproach wherewith they have reproached thee, O Lord (Ps. lxxix. 12).

And so in Ps. xxv. 22; xxxiii. 14; xlviii. 3, 8; lxx. 4; lxxiv. 6; cxvi. 15; cxxi. 4; cxxiv. 5.

Exceptional cases, where the dichotomy is not found at the logical (or syntactical) pause, may be brought under the two following heads:

(1) In the more *musical* accentuation of the three books, there is an apparent reluctance to place the main dividing accent after the *first*, or before the *last* word of the verse. In cases where, according to the logical (or syntactical) division, it would come there, it is generally[11] moved forwards or backwards to where a convenient resting-place is found for it. The musical equilibrium is thus better preserved.

שָׁקַדְתִּי וָאֶהְיֶה כְּצִפּוֹר בּוֹדֵד עַל־גָּג׃ (Ps. cii. 8)[12].

אָהַבְתִּי כִּי־יִשְׁמַע ׀ יְהוָה אֶת־קוֹלִי תַּחֲנוּנָי׃ (Ps. cxvi. 1).

And so in Ps. xlviii. 4; lxxii. 20; lxxiv. 5; cxix. 18; and cxxii. 3.

The instances of Athnach drawn *backwards* are:

גָּרְסָה נַפְשִׁי לְתַאֲבָה אֶל־מִשְׁפָּטֶיךָ בְכָל־עֵת׃ (Ps. cxix. 20).

אֶל־יְהוָה בַּצָּרָתָה לִּי קָרָאתִי וַיַּעֲנֵנִי׃ (Ps. cxx. 1)[13].

וְאַתָּה מָרוֹם לְעֹלָם יְהוָה׃ (Ps. xcii. 9).

רוּם עֵינַיִם וּרְחַב־לֵב נִר רְשָׁעִים חַטָּאת׃ (Prov. xxi. 4).

---

present investigation, are quite unnecessary. Those who choose to employ it can do so. The result will be the same.

[10] On the principles which regulate the division in these cases, see chapter IV.

[11] In a few cases, however, where it was considered that the removal would do too great violence to the logical construction, it does not take place, see p. 33 below.

[12] Properly Athnach should be on שָׁקַדְתִּי. Hupfeld is completely puzzled by its removal to וָאֶהְיֶה.

[13] Leaving out the superscription.

יָדֶיךָ עִצְּבוּנִי וַיַּעֲשׂוּנִי יַחַד סָבִיב וַתְּבַלְּעֵנִי׃ (Job x. 8).

Further, some of the examples given in 2, 2 γ, e.g. Ps. cxlv. 5; Job iv. 8, might be brought under this head.

(2) The verb אָמַר and cognate expressions—with more or less of addition—are not unfrequently found at the commencement of the verse, without at all affecting the division of the same. It is the *speech itself*, which the melody aims at marking and emphasizing. Such cases will come under B, p. 6.

>He hath said in his heart: God hath forgotten, |
>Hath hidden his face, hath never seen it (Ps. x. 11).
>
>Jehovah hath sworn (and will not repent): Thou art a priest for ever, |
>After the order of Melchisedek (Ps. cx. 4).
>
>He will sing before men, and say: I had sinned and perverted what was right, |
>And it was not requited to me (Job xxxiii. 27).

These cases are common enough. See Ps. xii. 5; xvi. 2; lx. 8; lxxxiii. 13; lxxxix. 20; Job xxxiii. 24; xxxiv. 9 [14].

Such are the rules for the dichotomy of the verse in the three books. The principles here laid down suffice (I believe) to meet all requirements, and to remove the difficulties that have suggested themselves to scholars. The rules are simple enough, and a beginner will soon learn to apply them to the various cases, as they arise.

The *position* of the dichotomy fixed, we have next to enquire *what accent* is employed to mark it.

As the accentuators have fixed their rules,—

i. Olév'yored will occur in the *sixth* word [15] from Silluq, or further;

ii. Olév'yored or Athnach in the *fourth* or *fifth* word; and

iii. Athnach in the *first, second*, or *third* word:—

i.e. near to Silluq, Athnach will be employed; at a distance from Silluq, Olév'yored; and in an intermediate position, sometimes Athnach and sometimes Olév'yored.

We have clearly here to do with *musical* reasons. Athnach is, under any circumstances, bound to appear as a preparatory note to

---

[14] The same tendency is very common in the Prose Books, see Gen. iii. 16; iv. 23; xx. 6; &c.

[15] I observe again, that when two or more words are united by Maqqeph, e.g. פֶּן־אַסְפִּי־אֶרֶץ, אִם־בְּתוּלַת, they are counted, for the purposes of melody, as *one* word.

Silluq. But owing to the limited number of accents which the laws of melody allow (so different, in this respect, from those of the Prose Books), between Athnach and Silluq, the former cannot be removed further back than the *fifth* word. Hence the necessity for another dividing accent. That Olév'yored trespasses on the *fourth* and *fifth* word, which we should have expected to be reserved for Athnach, is due (as we shall immediately see) to the same cause.

I may observe, in passing, that owing to the *shortness of the verses* in the three books, Athnach divides the verse more than ten times as often as Olév'yored[16].

i. This rule is strictly carried out. There is not a single exception.

ii *a*. With the dichotomy on the *fifth* word, Olév'yored is usually—i. e. in about four cases out of five—employed.

I must here assume, what will be hereafter proved, that between the dichotomy and Silluq a musical pause must be introduced. This pause might fall on any of the intermediate words, but is almost always found (that so the rhythmical equilibrium might be better preserved) on the *second* or *third* word[17]. Now, with it on the *third* word, the only practically available accent for marking it was Athnach[18], and then of course Olév'yored had to be used for the dichotomy. Comp. Ps. vi. 3; vii. 9; viii. 3; ix. 7; &c.

But it might fall on the *second* word. Here the accentuators had their choice of two notations. They might mark the pause with R'bhia mugrash, and then Athnach would mark the dichotomy, as in Ps. xix. 8, 9; xxiii. 5; xxvii. 12; &c. Or they might prefer Athnach, for the sake both of the *melody*, and of the more effective division of the verse, according to the *sense*,—for Athnach in this position implies R'bhia mugrash following, and D'chî preceding. In three cases out of four they made the latter choice, and then, necessarily, Olév'yored preceded in the fifth place. See Ps. xiv. 2; xxvii. 5, 11, 14; xxviii. 3; and cxxv. 2.

---

[16] The proportion in the Books of Proverbs and Job is still greater. There, whole chapters occur in succession, without a single instance of Olév'yored. See chapters xi-xxii in Proverbs, iv-vi in Job, &c.

[17] There are, I believe, only three cases, Ps. xlii. 2; lxvi. 20; and cxxv. 3, where it falls on the *first* word; and two where it falls on the *fourth* word, viz. Ps. lxxix. 6 and Job xi. 6. And these five cases will admit, on the testimony of Codd. (as we shall see hereafter), of being reduced to *two*, with Olév'yored, as usual, on the fifth word. I take no notice of Ps. iii. 3; xxxii. 5; xlvii. 5; and liv. 5; which have קֶלָה for their last word, see p. 6.

[18] In four cases only does a different accent appear, viz. R'bhia mugrash in Ps. xviii. 31; lxviii. 19 (a doubtful instance); and Prov. xxv. 1; and Shalshéleth in Ps. lxxxix. 2. These accents properly follow immediately after Athnach. Here they occur with a servus between them and Athnach.

ii *b*. On the other hand, with the dichotomy on the *fourth* word, Athnach is generally—in something like ten cases out of eleven—employed.

This is the case, whether the subordinate pause before Silluq fall on the first, second, or third word. In the great majority of cases it falls on the second word,—we notice again the *rhythmical* effect,—and is made by R'bhîa mugrash. See Ps. iv. 4; ix. 5; x. 9, 13; xiii. 4, 5; &c.

The advantage of admitting Olév'yored into the fourth place is, as before, that it allows an *emphasis* (of melody and sense) to be thrown into the words following—by the employment of Athnach and R'bhîa mugrash[19]—above what is possible, when Athnach occupies the fourth place, and only R'bhîa mugrash can follow; see Ps. ix. 15; xviii. 13; xxxii. 10; lxii. 5; lxix. 4; &c. At the same time in the short clause, —of only four words—which here follows the dichotomy, it was not thought necessary to introduce this more emphatic accentuation often. To us it is a drawback that it is so frequently effaced, e. g. in Ps. i. 2, by the law of transformation.

iii *a*. When the dichotomy falls on the *third* word Athnach maintains its position.

See Ps. i. 5, 6; ii. 3, 7, 9, 10, 12; &c.[20]

iii *b*. So also, on the *second* word, as in Ps. ii. 1, 2, 4, 5, 6, &c. Only here, under certain circumstances, Athnach must be transformed into R'bhîa mugrash[21], e. g.

(Ps. lvii. 9). עוּרָה כְבוֹדִי עוּרָה הַנֵּ֫בֶל וְכִנּ֑וֹר אָע֖ירָה שָּֽׁחַר׃

iii *c*. On the word immediately preceding Silluq, Athnach is always transformed into R'bhîa mugrash.

Such cases are however, in the original text, of rare occurrence. To the poet himself a certain measure of rhythmical equilibrium must have seemed necessary. We have noticed above the tendency to rhythmical effect even in the minor sections of the verse. We need not therefore be surprised to find that in only a

---

[19] There are only two passages in our texts, Ps. iv. 7 and lv. 23, where there is not room for these two accents after Olév'yored. And here D'chî and Athnach, if there had been no transformation, would have come instead. As before, I pass over lxviii. 20, with סֶֽלָה as last word.

[20] So in Ps. cxxx. 1, שִׁיר הַמַּעֲלוֹת is marked with Athnach, whereas in all the other 'Songs of Degrees' it has Olév'yored.

[21] See chapter on Transformation.

few instances—notwithstanding the large number of *short* verses—does the main pause fall on the word *immediately preceding* Silluq[22]. Beside the passages already given in p. 29—in which the dichotomy has been moved back by the accentuators,—I have noted only Ps. xxxiv. 8; xxxv. 24; cxix. 52; cxxxvii. 9; and Prov. viii. 33[23]. In these cases, it did not seem possible to them to change the position of the dichotomy; it consequently remains on the word before Silluq, marked by R'bhîa mugrash.

The first verses indeed of a few Psalms, if we remove the additions prefixed to the original text, have the dichotomy immediately before Silluq, e. g. : הָרִיעוּ לֵאלֹהִים כָּל־הָאָרֶץ (Ps. lxvi. 1). But I have no doubt that these short clauses, consisting of only *three* words, belong properly to the verses following: (1) because verses of only three words *do not occur elsewhere* in the text proper[24]; and (2) because in one case, Ps. lxxxvii. 1, we should be reduced to a verse of *two* words. The other instances are xviii. 2; c. 1; cix. 1; cxx. 1; and cxlvi. 1.

The dichotomy has been further introduced in the word preceding Silluq in the following cases:

(1) The last verses in Pss. civ–cvi, cxiii, cxv–cxvii, cxxxv, and cxlvi–cl, which all end with הַלְלוּיָהּ (doubtless a liturgical addition to the original text).

(2) The verses heading the speeches in Job, like

וַיַּעַן אֱלִיפַז הַתֵּימָנִי וַיֹּאמַר : (iv. 1)[25].

And (3) the superscriptions of some Pss. containing only three words, e. g. מִזְמוֹר לְדָוִד לְהַזְכִּיר : (xxxviii. 1), and so in lx, lxix, lxxxi, lxxxiii, and cviii. In these cases, R'bhîa mugrash has been transformed, according to rule, but in שִׁיר מִזְמוֹר לִבְנֵי־קֹרַח : (xlviii. 1) it must be retained, with most Codd. and with Ben-Bil. 10. 10, although in opposition to the *Masora magna* to Ps. lxxxiii. 1.

Lastly, after what has been said above, we should not expect to find the chief logical (or syntactical) pause on the *first* word of the verse. Indeed, so few are these cases, that no provision was

---

[22] In the prose system it is otherwise, see Gen. i. 3, 7; v. 5; &c.

[23] Ps. lxxvi. 5 and Prov. viii. 23 I propose to correct, by dropping the Maqqeph between the two last words, and introducing a conjunctive accent instead. This pointing I have found in some Codd. (Comp. lxxx. 11ᵇ and Job v. 10ᵃ.) Others *move back* the dichotomy a word.

[24] In the prose text we have such verses, e. g. Gen. xxvi. 6; xliii. 1; but not in the poetical. Verses with *two* words occur only in the Decalogue (Ex. xx. 13-15).

[25] Most Codd. and edd. point these verses with *R'bhîa simplex*, by a common mistake, see chapter on R'bhîa mugrash at end.

F

made for the dichotomy occurring there. *It was contrary to the rules of melody of the three Books that either Olév'yored or Athnach should be admitted on the first word*[26]. And we have seen, p. 29, that the main musical pause, when due there, was moved forward to where a suitable resting-place could be found for it.

What then was to be done, when, by the accentuation of the superscriptions and other additions prefixed to the original text, the main pause came on the *first word ?* The accentuators had to make shift, as best they could, with substitutes for Olév'yored and Athnach. For the former they chose Azla l'garmeh, for the latter Pazer! Thus,

a. לְדָוִד ׀ the first word of Pss. xxvi, xxvii, xxxv, xxxvii, ciii, cxxxviii, and cxliv[27]; לִשְׁלֹמֹה ׀ of lxxii; and ׀ הַלְלוּיָהּ of cvi, cxi-cxiii, cxxxv, and cxlviii-cl. And

b. וַיֹּאמַר Ps. xviii. 2 (comp. וַיֹּאמֶר 2 Sam. xxii. 2); לְדָוִד xxv. 1[28]; מִזְמוֹר xxx. 1[28]; and הַלְלוּיָהּ cxlvi. 1[29].

(We could wish that they had confined this anomalous accentuation to the instances given, but in three cases they have introduced it into the original text, viz. in Ps. xlv. 13 ׀ וּבַת־צֹר[30]; cxlvii. 1 ׀ הַלְלוּיָהּ[31]; and Prov. i. 10 בְּנִי[32]. Otherwise, they kept to the traditional division, as laid down in p. 29.)

---

[26] It is otherwise in the prose accentuation, see Gen. xv. 8; xxxiv. 31; &c. Ordinary edd. indeed have Athnach sometimes on the first word, as in Ps. cxix. 84; Prov. vii. 9; but correct texts avoid such mistakes.

[27] Fixed by the *Masora magna* to Ps. xxvi. 1.

[28] ,, ,, to this verse.

[29] In Ps. xxviii. 1 and xcviii. 1, Pazer is used to mark the dichotomy on the first word, *although Athnach follows* in the verse! (It is fixed by the *Masora* to Ps. xxv. 1 and xxx. 1.) L'garmeh ought to have been employed here, and the accents following in xxviii. 1 to have been modified accordingly. Other instances of inaccurate accentuation are to be found in xviii, xxxiv, xlv, lxv, and lxviii. I believe that in the pointing of the superscriptions generally,—both in Psalms and Job,—we may trace not only a later but a less careful hand than that which fixed the accentuation of the text. Such mistakes are, however, of the very smallest moment to us.

[30] That we have not L'garmeh proper here will be seen when we come to the chapter on D'chî. The original accent was probably R'bhîa.

[31] Here undoubtedly this word belongs to the original text. Olév'yored is chosen (instead of R'bhîa) for the sake of agreement with Pss. preceding and following. (See a above.)

[32] Here Codd., B. M. 4, Ox. 5, Erf. 1, Hm. 7, K. 198, 599 have R'bhîa. Comp. xxiii. 15 with D'chî.

We must here notice, that where the verse containing the superscription consists of only *three* words, Pazer is dropped, and R'bhía mugrash[33] employed instead. This suits better the proximity of the pause to Silluq, which always claims (if possible) this latter accent before it, e. g. לַמְנַצֵּ֥חַ מִזְמ֥וֹר לְדָוִֽד׃ (Ps. xiii. 1), and so in the superscriptions of Pss. xix, xx, xxi, &c.[34]

N. B. In the superscriptions of eight Pss., viz. xxxvi, xliv, xlvii, xlix, lxi, lxix, lxxxi, and lxxxv, we have the strange accentuation of Silluq, preceded *by two Illuys*, e. g. לַמְנַצֵּ֥חַ לִבְנֵי־קֹ֥רַח מִזְמֽוֹר (xlvii. 1). And this accentuation has the support of most Codd.[35] Yet I have noted many which point regularly[36], as Ox. 1, 5, 71, 72, 98, &c., for the example just given: לַֽמְנַצֵּ֥חַ לִבְנֵי־קֹ֖רַח מִזְמֽוֹר. And so I have found ample authority for R'bhia mugrash on the first word, in Pss. xxxvi, xliv, xlix, and lxxxv. For the remaining three examples, we require R'bhia mugrash (transformed) on the word before Silluq, thus לַמְנַצֵּ֥חַ עַל־נְגִינַ֥ת לְדָוִֽד׃ (lxi. 1), with Codd. Ox. 5, 72; Ber. 32; K. 157, 246; De R. 304; &c. For lxix and lxxxi there is like testimony.

In conclusion I would correct some passages in which the dichotomy has been falsely made, or in which it might have been better made. In all, the Codd. enable us to make the change which is necessary, or which seems advisable. The corrections (I venture to think) speak for themselves, and need no comment on my part.

---

[33] In Codd. and edd. mostly *R'bhía simplex* (see note 25). In one instance, Ps. xcii. 1, it occurs in a verse of *four* words, where Athnach might have stood.

[34] So ordinary texts are quite right in xl. 1 and lxx. 1, and the accentuation with two servi, introduced by Heidenheim and Baer, must be rejected. The *Masora magna* to lxx. 1, למנצח ב' בטעם, indicates R'bhia mugrash (and *not R'bhia simplex*, as Codd. generally point in other similar passages, see note above) as required here. And this is just what Ben-Bil. 10. 7 expressly lays down for these two passages, and Codd. and edd. generally exhibit. Comp. xli. 1.

[35] Not, however, of Ben-Asher, who without doubt pointed, although quite irregularly, לַֽמְנַצֵּ֥חַ ׀ לִבְנֵי־קֹ֖רַח מִזְמֽוֹר, &c. On the other hand, Ben-Naphtali has no Paseq, and seems to have given the accentuation, which has crept into our texts. Both accentuations probably originated in the fanciful notion of setting a peculiar mark on a number of superscriptions, that have the common characteristic of למנצח for their *first* word, and of a double word formed by Maqqeph for their *second!* Baer assigns the two Illuys to Ben-Asher. But in all the lists of the Varr., which I have been able to consult, I have found the first word pointed as above, with L'garmeh, and then the second will, according to rule, have Illuy.

[36] Just as Codd. and edd. do, in the similar case, xlii. 1.

Corrigenda.

Ps. xi. 6. Divide at נַפְרִיץ with B. M. 3; Ox. 13; Ber. 2; K. 240, 246, 250, 251; De R. 2; &c.

יַמְטֵר עַל־רְשָׁעִים ׀ פַּחִים אֵשׁ וְנָפְרִית וְרוּחַ זִלְעָפוֹת מְנָת כּוֹסָם׃

Ps. xix. 14. Divide at בִי with B. M. 1, 2; Ox. 71; K. 240; De R. 3, 34, 193; &c.[37]

גַּם מִזֵּדִים ׀ חֲשֹׂךְ עַבְדֶּךָ אַל־יִמְשְׁלוּ בִי אָז אֵיתָם וְנִקֵּיתִי מִפֶּשַׁע רָב׃

Ps. xlii. 5. This verse has been a *crux* to accentuologists. Ouscel, p. 46, says of it: *locus singularissimus, codicum fide et collatione dijudicandus*. The main division of the verse is clearly at נַפְשִׁי, which ought therefore to be marked (as B. M. 2, 4; Ox. 2332; Par. 4, 30; Ghet. 1; and De R. 2, 304, do mark it) with Olév'yored. אֱלֹהִים following will then necessarily have Athnach (with Ox. 2332; Par. 4). So that the pointing will be:

אֵלֶּה אֶזְכְּרָה וְאֶשְׁפְּכָה עָלַי ׀ נַפְשִׁי כִּי אֶעֱבֹר ׀ בַּסָּךְ אֶדַּדֵּם עַד־בֵּית אֱלֹהִים
בְּקוֹל־רִנָּה וְתוֹדָה הָמוֹן חוֹגֵג׃

Ps. xlii. 9. It is better to divide this verse, with Par. 30; Ber. 2, 32; Vat. 468; Ghet. 1; De R. 304, 350, at the end of the first clause (comp. xl. 4ª), thus:

יוֹמָם ׀ יְצַוֶּה יְהוָה חַסְדּוֹ וּבַלַּיְלָה שִׁירֹה עִמִּי תְּפִלָּה לְאֵל חַיָּי׃

Ps. lxvi. 12. Clearly the last clause here will come in with much better effect if it stand by itself, and if we point with B. M. 2, 4; Ox. 17, 2332; Ber. 17; De R. 372;

הִרְכַּבְתָּ אֱנוֹשׁ ׀ לְרֹאשֵׁנוּ בָּאנוּ בָאֵשׁ וּבַמַּיִם[38] וַתּוֹצִיאֵנוּ לָרְוָיָה׃

Ps. lxxi. 3. Divide at תָּמִיד with B. M. 7, 8; Par. 111; Erf. 3; Fr.; De R. 732; &c.

הֱיֵה לִי ׀ לְצוּר מָעוֹז לָבוֹא תָּמִיד צִוִּיתָ לְהוֹשִׁיעֵנִי כִּי־סַלְעִי וּמְצוּדָתִי אָתָּה׃

Ps. lxxvi. 8. Divide as follows with Par. 9, 30; Erf. 1, 2; Ber. 2; De R. 304; &c.

אַתָּה נוֹרָא אַתָּה וּמִי־יַעֲמֹד לְפָנֶיךָ מֵאָז אַפֶּךָ׃

Ps. xciii. 5. Falsely divided in all texts. The correct division is found in B. M. 5; Vat. 27; K. 192; De R. 35;

עֵדֹתֶיךָ נֶאֶמְנוּ מְאֹד לְבֵיתְךָ נַאֲוָה־קֹדֶשׁ יְהוָה לְאֹרֶךְ יָמִים׃

---

[37] Most of these Codd. indeed exhibit only the *lower* sign of Olév'yored. But the omission of the *upper* sign is very common.

[38] We must then deviate from the *Masora* here (פתח באתנח) and point with Qames, as our common edd. do.

Job x. 15. Divide at לְ with Ox. 19; Ber. 2; K. 166; De R. 380, 589, 847;

אִם־רָשַׁעְתִּי אַלְלַי לִי וְצָדַקְתִּי לֹא־אֶשָּׂא רֹאשִׁי שְׂבַע קָלוֹן וּרְאֵה עָנְיִי:

Job xx. 25. Divide at יַהֲלֹךְ with Ox. 19; Par. 6, 9, 36; Vat. Urb. 1; De R. 368, 380; &c.

שָׁלַף ׀ וַיֵּצֵא מִגֵּוָה וּבָרָק מִמְּרֹרָתוֹ יַהֲלֹךְ עָלָיו אֵמִים:

(Other texts, as B. M. 13; Ox. 100, 127; Erf. 2; Hm. 8; &c., point מִמְּרֹרָתוֹ יַהֲלֹךְ עָלָיו אֵמִים.)

Job xxviii. 3. Divide at לַחֹשֶׁךְ with K. 246, 251, 531; De R. 349, 847; Ghet. 3;

קֵץ ׀ שָׂם לַחֹשֶׁךְ וּלְכָל־תַּכְלִית הוּא חוֹקֵר אֶבֶן אֹפֶל וְצַלְמָוֶת:

Job xxxiv. 20. Divide at יָמֻתוּ, though I have found only two Codd., De R. 349, 715, that do so. (The subject of יָמֻתוּ is שָׂרִים, v. 19.)

רֶגַע ׀ יָמֻתוּ וַחֲצוֹת לָיְלָה יְגֹעֲשׁוּ־עָם וְיַעֲבֹרוּ וְיָסִירוּ אַבִּיר לֹא בְיָד:

Job xxxvii. 12. Divide at בְּתַחְבּוּלֹתָו with Ox. 19; Cam. 25; Par. 9; K. 251, 403, 531; De R. 847;

וְהוּא מְסִבּוֹת ׀ מִתְהַפֵּךְ בְּתַחְבּוּלֹתָו לְפָעֳלָם כֹּל אֲשֶׁר־יְצַוֵּם ׀ עַל־פְּנֵי תֵבֵל אָרְצָה:

Job xxxix. 25. Divide at הֶאָח with Ox. 18; Ber. 2; K. 528, 531; De R. 32, 587, 847; &c.

בְּדֵי שֹׁפָר ׀ יֹאמַר הֶאָח וּמֵרָחוֹק יָרִיחַ מִלְחָמָה רַעַם שָׂרִים וּתְרוּעָה:

Baer has already corrected Ps. xxii. 26; lxviii. 18; xcv. 7; cxl. 6; and Prov. xxx. 8; with full support (as I have found) from the Codd. On the other hand, his division of cxix. 57 is quite without MS. authority (he names indeed Fr., but by a *lapsus calami*); and in lxxxvi. 11 his correction must be rejected,—ordinary edd. are quite right.

The above are the only passages I have noted, as seeming to me to call for correction, in the matter of the dichotomy. There are a few cases besides—as Ps. i. 3; xvii. 7; xxii. 30; Job xxvii. 8—where the *sense* has been misunderstood (as may be seen from the Rabbinical commentaries on these passages), and the division is, in consequence, false. Generally speaking, however, the punctators have shewn correct taste and a due apprehension of the meaning of the text, in the bisection of the verses. Considering that they had to deal with several thousands of cases, a few mistakes on their part are excusable.

The importance of the law laid down in this chapter cannot be over-estimated. It furnishes the principle on which the whole system of the accentuation is constructed.

CHAPTER IV.

CONTINUOUS DICHOTOMY.

The two halves of the verse having been constituted by the main dichotomy, we have next to enquire how *they*, in their turn, are prepared for musical recitation.

And the answer is, that the same principle is further applied in detail. Each half of the verse—*supposing it to contain three or more words*—is treated in just the same way as the verse itself. Should there be in it a parallelism of parts, the dichotomy—in this its second stage—will come between. Failing that, it will be fixed by the logical or syntactical pause.

Nor does the musical subdivision stop even here. It proceeds to bisect each minor clause, into which the half of the verse has been divided, *supposing three words, at least, remain in it;* and so on continuously, with every new clause that is formed, so long as the condition just named be fulfilled.

This is what has been termed the CONTINUOUS DICHOTOMY[1]. In the following chapters it will be our duty to trace the application of this law,—with the modifications to which it is subjected,—in the clauses governed by the various accents.

When the dichotomy is fixed by parallelism, or a logical pause, there is no difficulty in accounting for its presence; but in almost every verse—owing to the minute subdivisions which the continuous dichotomy introduces—we have to deal with cases, where the *syntactical* relation of the words to one another and to the whole clause of which they form a part, alone decides its position.

---

[1] The first to start the hypothesis of a continuous dichotomy was (according to Spitzner) C. Florinus, in his Doctrina de accent. divina, 1667. The two writers to whom is assigned the credit of having done most to establish the principle are J. Francke, in his Diacritica Sacra, 1710, and A. B. Spitzner, in his Institutiones ad analyticam sacram textus Hebr. V. T. ex accentibus, 1786. The former of these works I have not been able to consult. The latter I have read carefully through. It relates chiefly to the prose accents, and contains some good hints, but nothing more. A satisfactory result is certainly not worked out.

And it is not always easy to see on what principle the dichotomy, in such cases, is made. It is, therefore, necessary to consider what *the relation is between syntax and the accentual division*[2].

With clauses consisting of only *two* words we have (as I have stated) no concern. Music, logic, emphasis may occasionally introduce a separation here, but it is clear that rhythm must have been destroyed altogether, if such separation had been made at all general. Concepts therefore—as subject and predicate, adverb and verb,—which are generally kept apart in longer clauses, are here constantly brought together, thus: יְהֹוָה מָלָךְ (Ps. xcvii. 1); נַפְשִׁי לַאדֹנָי (cxxx. 6); כְּחַסְדְּךָ חַיֵּנִי (cxix. 88). And, as words united by Maqqeph are regarded as constituting a single word, we meet with such combinations as: אֲבוֹתֵינוּ תִּדְרוֹשׁ־ (cxxx. 3); אִם־עֲוֹנוֹת תִּשְׁמָר־יָהּ (xliv. 2); סִפְּרוּ־לָנוּ רְשָׁעוֹ בַּל־תִּמְצָא: (x. 15).

But in sentences, consisting of three or more words, the dichotomy is, with certain recognised exceptions, regularly introduced. Here the first step is to notice which of the component parts of a grammatical clause—subject, object, verb, &c.—precedes.

I. The SUBJECT may precede, and—from its independent position[3]—is almost always followed by the dichotomy, e. g. הָאֵל | תָּמִים דַּרְכּוֹ (xviii. 31), 'God — perfect is His way;' הַשָּׁמַיִם | מְסַפְּרִים כְּבוֹד־אֵל (xix. 2), 'The heavens—they declare the glory of God;' רוּחֲךָ טוֹבָה | תַּנְחֵנִי בְּאֶרֶץ מִישׁוֹר (cxliii. 10).

The variations that occur come under the following heads:

(1) The *personal pronoun* is not always accounted of sufficient importance to stand by itself: אֲנִי שָׁמַרְתִּי | אָרְחוֹת פָּרִיץ (xvii. 4); אַתָּה רִצְצְתָּ | רָאשֵׁי לִוְיָתָן (lxxiv. 14); הוּא (xxv. 15; Job xxxvii. 12);

---

[2] The only scholar (as far as I am aware) who has treated this subject, has been Ewald, in an Appendix to his Lehrbuch der Hebräischen Sprache, pp. 869-873, but I cannot say that I have found his remarks of any service; as my readers will understand, when I mention, that he altogether discards the dichotomical principle.

[3] See Ges. Gr. § 144.

הֵמָּה (cvii. 24)¹. And so the *interrogative* מִי (iv. 7), and מָה (Job xvi. 6); and the *relative* אֲשֶׁר (Ps. i. 3; iii. 7).

(2) The dichotomy is sometimes found after the *second* member of the clause, when the subject with that member admits of being taken to form a proposition *complete in itself*, capable of standing alone, *without* the member that closes the clause, e. g. יְהוָֹה יֵשַׁע | בְּקֹרְאָי אֵלָיו (iv. 4); יְהוָה מֶלֶךְ | עוֹלָם וָעֶד (x. 16); עֵינַי דָּאֲבָה | מִנִּי־עֹנִי (lxxxviii. 10)⁵. (As for the closing member in such cases, it is necessarily merely *supplemental*,—a *Zusatz*,—most commonly an adverb, or preposition with its government.) On like conditions, the main dichotomy may come even after the *third* member, but then the subject must be marked off by a *minor* dichotomy, e. g. וַאֲנִי | נָסַכְתִּי מַלְכִּי | עַל־צִיּוֹן הַר־קָדְשִׁי (ii. 6)⁶. Only, when the second and third members are *united by Maqqeph*, this minor dichotomy is not required, as in חֲבָלִים נָפְלוּ־לִי | בַּנְּעִמִים (xvi. 6).

(3) The dichotomy is also transposed to the second member, when that member is the *vocative*, in such expressions as וְאַתָּה יְהוָה | מָגֵן בַּעֲדִי (iii. 4); כִּסְאֲךָ אֱלֹהִים | עוֹלָם וָעֶד (xlv. 7); and often⁷.

(4) In a few instances *assonance* has decided : יַבִּיעַ אֹמֶר | יוֹם לְיוֹם (xix. 3). So also in xlii. 8; cxlv. 4; Prov. xxvii. 17; Job xli. 8.

I have noticed no other variations, save such as are open to correction (see *Corrigenda*).

II. The OBJECT may precede; and as a certain emphasis is implied by its position at the commencement of the sentence⁸, it is marked off by the dichotomy : חֶרֶב | פָּתְחוּ רְשָׁעִים (Ps. xxxvii. 14); מַטֵּה עֻזְּךָ | יִשְׁלַח יְהוָה מִצִּיּוֹן (cx. 2).

The variations follow closely the lines laid down for the *subject*.

(1) Examples of the *pronoun* are indeed confined to מָה and אֲשֶׁר, as אֲשֶׁר אֲנִי | אֶחֱזֶה־לִּי (Job xix. 27). מַה־יִּתֶּן לְךָ (cxx. 3); The pers. pron. appears mostly as a *suffix*, and, in the few cases in which it occurs under the independent forms אֹתוֹ, אֹתִי &c., does not call for any remark. מִי too is rare in the accusative.

---

⁴ Or, where it must be marked off, we find an *inferior*, instead of the *main*, dichotomy employed, e. g. וַאֲנִי for וְאָנִי (lxxiii. 28).

⁵ Such cases are not, however, numerous; and where this division is adopted in one text, other texts often point regularly; comp. common edd. and Baer's text in xlviii. 15ᵇ; li. 5ᵇ; lxxxix. 37ᵇ; cxix. 142ᵃ. In Job xxx. 30 the position of the dichotomy varies in the *two halves* of the verse.

⁶ The main and minor dichotomy I indicate by d 1 and d 2 respectively.

⁷ The vocative also naturally takes the dichotomy at the *beginning* of a sentence, see iii. 2; v. 4; viii. 2; lxxxviii. 2.

⁸ See Ges. Gr. § 145.

CONTINUOUS DICHOTOMY.

(2) If we substitute 'object' for 'subject' in I. 2, we have the explanation of such instances as, שָׂמָם מָחִית | לְעוֹלָם וָעֶד (Ps. ix. 6); and נְדָרַי אֲשַׁלֵּם | נֶגֶד יְרֵאָיו (xxii. 26)⁹. It is very rarely that the *Zusatz* consists of *two* members, as in cxix. 65; Job xxxii. 29.

A peculiar class of variations is possible, under this head. A clause, syntactically complete, may be formed by the object, verb, and pronominal subject (latent in the verb); and then the real subject may follow supplementally. Thus in (Prov. v. 3) כִּי נֹפֶת תִּטֹּפְנָה | שִׂפְתֵי זָרָה, 'For honey do they drop—the lips of the harlot;' Ps. lxxv. 9ᵇ (where Hupf. alone translates according to the accents) and Job xxxi. 35ᵇ. This accentual arrangement brings with it a slowness and emphasis in the expression, which is not without effect. But it is quite uncommon.

(3) The *vocative* occurs, as in I. 3, e. g. דְּרָכֶיךָ יְהוָה | הוֹדִיעֵנִי (Ps. xxv. 4); and חַסְדְּךָ יְהוָה | מָלְאָה הָאָרֶץ (cxix. 64).

Other variations I have not observed.

III. Adverbs, adverbial expressions, and prepositions with their government, when at the beginning of a clause, derive (like the *object*) a measure of emphasis from their position, and are generally marked off by the dichotomy, e. g. יוֹמָם | יְצַוֶּה יְהוָה חַסְדּוֹ (Ps. xlii. 9); מְאֹד | עָמְקוּ מַחְשְׁבֹתֶיךָ (xcii. 6); בְּתוֹכָחוֹת עַל־עָוֹן | יִסַּרְתָּ | עָלֶיךָ | הִשְׁלַכְתִּי מֵרָחֶם אִישׁ (xxii. 11); (xxxix. 12); בְּרוּחַ קָדִים | תְּשַׁבֵּר אֳנִיּוֹת תַּרְשִׁישׁ (xlviii. 8).

The variations run parallel for the most part to those given above:

(1) Thus a preposition with *pronominal suffix*, or with the *pronoun* אֲשֶׁר or מָה, attaches itself readily to the word following, e. g. מִמֶּנּוּ בַּמֶּה יֵחָשֵׁב־ | עָלַי יִתְלַחֲשׁוּ | כָּל־שֹׂנְאָי (xli. 8); יָגוּרוּ | כָּל־יֹשְׁבֵי תֵבֵל (xxxiii. 8); לָמָּה־קֹדֵר אֶתְהַלֵּךְ | בְּלַחַץ אוֹיֵב (xliii. 2); לַאֲשֶׁר נַעַר | אֶת־אָרְחוֹ (cxix. 9); הֵבִיא אֱלוֹהַּ | בְּיָדוֹ (Job xii. 6).

(2) We have cases corresponding to those given in I. 2 and II. 2, e. g. מְאֹד נַעֲלֵיתָ | עַל־כָּל־אֱלֹהִים | וּבְתוֹרָתוֹ יֶהְגֶּה (Ps. i. 2); יוֹמָם וָלָיְלָה (xcvii. 9)¹⁰.

In xxv. 7ᵇ and xciii. 5ᵇ, the *Zusatz* consists of *two* members.

---

⁹ Here also Codd. often vary; thus some point אֲמָרַי | הַאֲזִינָה יְהוָה (v. 2), but our edd. with a better emphasis אִמְרַי הַאֲזִינָה | יְהוָה. So common edd. and Baer's text differ in x. 17; lvii. 7; cxix. 133, 149.

¹⁰ As before, Codd. vary; thus some have מֵאִתְּךָ | תְּהִלָּתִי בְּקָהָל רָב (xxii. 26), 'Of Thee | shall be my praise, in the great congregation;' others place the dichotomy after תְּהִלָּתִי, 'Of Thee shall be *my praise* | in the great congregation.' Common edd. and Baer's text differ in xxi. 13ᵇ; lxxviii. 40; cxxix. 7; Job xxiii. 14ᵇ.

(3) The *vocative* occurs as before, e. g. אֶקְרָא ׀ יְהוָֹה אֵלֶיךָ (xxviii. 1); לְמַעַן־שִׁמְךָ יְהוָה ׀ תְּחַיֵּנִי (cxliii. 11).

We notice that the vocative also sometimes claims the pause, even when no suffix of the second person precedes, e. g. ׀. עַד־אָנָה יְהוָה (xiii. 2); ׀ לְעוֹלָם יְהוָה (cxix. 89); ׀ עַד־מָתַי עָצֵל (Prov. vi. 9); ׀ וְעַתָּה בָנִים (v. 7). (The vocative in such cases comes in *parenthetically*, and the pointing is according to rule with a parenthesis[11].)

(4) Lastly, the rule is, as might have been expected, *relaxed*, in the case of the *common and less important* adverbs, which are often (*a*) joined to the word following, as אַף (Ps. li. 21); אַף (lxii. 2, 5); אֵיךְ (lxxiii. 19); כִּי (cxxiii. 2); שָׁם (xxxvi. 13); מָתַי (cxix. 84); עוֹד (Job xxxvi. 2); מָה (Ps. xlii. 12); הִנֵּה (xxxix. 6)[12]; or (*β*) marked by a *minor* pausal accent, instead of the main dichotomy of the clause, e. g. עַל־מֶה ׀ for עַל־מָה (x. 13); עַל־זֹאת for עַל־זֹאת ׀ (xxxii. 6); לָכֵן ׀ for לָכֵן (lxxiii. 10); שָׁם ׀ for שָׁם (cxxxii. 17); וְעַתָּה ׀ for וְעַתָּה (Job xxx. 1). In these minor matters the punctators claimed full liberty, and in consequence often differ among themselves: in Ps. i. 5 some have עַל־כֵּן ׀, others עַל־כֵּן; in ii. 5 some אָז, others אָז; and so on. Such variations were allowable, the only difference for us being that the stronger accent implies a fuller emphasis of the word on which it falls.

Other variations than those named are hardly to be found. In ׀ עַתָּה יָדַעְתִּי (xx. 7) and ׀ קֶדֶם יָדַעְתִּי (cxix. 152) the emphasis rests mainly on the *second* word, and therefore the dichotomy is rightly assigned to it. And similarly in Job xxviii. 3[b]; only there the adverbial expression has the *minor* dichotomy.

[If it be asked how, in the cases already considered, when we have marked off the first member, we are to proceed with the further division of the clause, the answer is very simple. We start *de novo* with the members remaining. Thus in an example like עוֹזֵר הָיִיתָ ׀[d2] אַתָּה ׀[d1] יָתוֹם (Ps. x. 14[b]) we first of all mark off the object יָתוֹם, next the subject אַתָּה, and then, as there are only two words remaining, the division of the clause is complete.

---

[11] Comp. for instance the parenthesis in Ps. xii. 6[b]; xl. 6[a]; cxxxii. 11[a].

[12] So יוֹם (Ps. lxxxviii. 2), in the sense of 'when,' is not counted of sufficient importance to be marked off by the dichotomy. And so I would account for the accentuation of מֵעֵת in Ps. iv. 8[b]. The clause must have been construed (as the old Verss. and comm. shew), 'From the time (i. e. *since*) their corn and their wine ׀ they increased,'—an unusual construction (it must be allowed), and altered in consequence by Ben-Bil. into מְעֵת רַבּוּ דְגָנָם וְתִירוֹשָׁם,—yet not quite without parallel. Comp. בְּטֶרֶם הָרִים ׀ הָטְבָּעוּ (Prov. viii. 25), 'Before the mountains ׀ they were sunk down.'

To take another instance: הָרִים ᵈ¹| כַּדּוֹנַג ᵈ³| נָמַסּוּ ᵈ²| מִלִּפְנֵי יְהֹוָה
(xcvii. 5), first the subject הָרִים is marked off, next the adverbial
expression כַּדּוֹנַג, and lastly the verb נָמַסּוּ, according to rule IV,
immediately following. And so in other cases.]

IV. When the VERB[13] precedes, we are introduced to quite
a different system of division. Then, supposing subject, object,
&c. follow, the first dichotomy will be *before the last member*,
the second before the last but one, and so on. Thus: שִׁיתָה
וִיבָרֵךְ כָּל־בָּשָׂר ᵈ²| שֵׁם קָדְשׁוֹ ᵈ¹| יְהֹוָה (ix. 21); ᵈ¹| מוֹרָה ᵈ²| לָהֶם
אִם־תִּכְתּוֹשׁ אֶת־הָאֱוִיל ᵈ³| בַּמַּכְתֵּשׁ ᵈ²| בְּתוֹךְ ᵈ¹|לְעוֹלָם וָעֶד (cxlv. 21);
הָרִפוֹת ᵈ¹| בַּעֲלִי (Prov. xxvii. 22).

The principle involved is a sound one. The first members of the
clause, which are already closely connected in grammatical construction, are kept together by the first dichotomy, and referred—for deter-
mination of their meaning—to the last member. Thus: 'Put, O Jehovah,
fear | in them;' and, 'Let all flesh bless His holy name | for ever and
ever.' These members are then taken *by themselves*, and—if they
contain three or more words—are again divided in the same way, and
on the same principle, 'Put, O Jehovah | fear;' 'Let all flesh bless |
His holy name.' It is very rarely that a *third* dichotomy, as in the
ex. given above from Prov., is necessary. In such a case as לֹא־יָקֻמוּ
רְשָׁעִים | בַּמִּשְׁפָּט (Ps. i. 5), a *single* dichotomy suffices. And in the still
simpler case, where there are only *two* members in the clause, the
dichotomy simply separates the one from the other, as תְּרֹעֵם | בְּשֵׁבֶט
בַּרְזֶל (ii. 9)[14].

The rule is most carefully observed. Such a case as תִּצְּרֵנוּ | מִן־הַדּוֹר זוּ
לְעוֹלָם (xii. 8),—a double *Zusatz* after the verbal predicate,—stands
(as far as I have observed) quite *per se*. יִגְמָר־נָא רַע | רְשָׁעִים (vii. 10)
is no exception, but must be rendered (with Aben-Ezra and Qimchi),
i. e. if we keep to the accents, 'Let evil make an end of the wicked'
(comp. xxxiv. 22). וּזְכָר־אֲנִי מֶה־חָלֶד (lxxxix. 48) is one of the very few
passages, which I propose to correct, without the authority of Codd.,

---

[13] It need hardly be mentioned that participles, infinitives, and verbal adjectives
follow, so far as they have verbal government, the same rule as the verb itself.

[14] It may be stated that the vocative is generally treated as a separate member
in this division, e. g. אֲמָרָה שָׂמְךָ | עָלְיוֹן (ix. 3); but sometimes not, when the suffix,
which refers to it, immediately precedes. Thus בְּתוֹכֵכִי מִצְרָיִם (cxxxv. 9) are kept
together by the accents.

thus זְכֹר ׀ אֲנִי מֶה־חָלֶד. In lxi. 6[b] and Job xxxi. 31[b], the sense was misunderstood (as the Targ., LXX., and Vulg. shew); hence the (for us) false accentuation. We find one exception, Ps. xxxiv. 8, due to the presence of the anomalous accent, Little Shalshéleth.

V. In nominal sentences, *when the predicate precedes*, the division will follow the same rule (and on the same principle) as in verbal sentences, e. g. מָגֵן (x. 5); מָרוֹם מִשְׁפָּטֶיךָ ׀ מִנֶּגְדּוֹ (xviii. 31); זֶה ׀ אֱלֹהִים אֱלֹהֵינוּ ׀ הוּא ׀ לְכֹל הַחוֹסִים בּוֹ עוֹלָם וָעֶד (xlviii. 15, 'Such a one is God, our God, for ever').

This rule is strictly carried out. Only when הָיָה follows, the dichotomy falls not on *it*, but on the predicate[16], e. g. בְּהֵמוֹת ׀ הָיִיתִי אָח ׀ הָיִיתִי לְתַנִּים (lxxiii. 22); זְמִרוֹת ׀ הָיוּ־לִי חֻקֶּיךָ (cxix. 54); עָפָר (Job xxx. 29); עָמְדוֹת ׀ הָיוּ רַגְלֵינוּ (Ps. cxxii. 2).

In Prov. xxv. 7, כִּי טוֹב אֲמָר־לְךָ ׀ עֲלֵה־הֵנָּה, there is a slight license—the division should properly have been at טוֹב, as in xxi. 19—for the purpose of bringing out with effect *the words spoken*. Just so in our modern punctuation.

VI. Lastly, the CONJUNCTIONS, as אֲשֶׁר, אוֹ, אִם, אַף, גַּם, יַעַן, כִּי, לוּ, לְמַעַן, עַד, פֶּן, the NEGATIVES לֹא, בַּל, אֵין, בְּלִי, and forms compounded from them, as אִם לֹא, כִּי לֹא, עַל כִּי, כִּי אִם, &c., need not detain us. They are, from their character, generally *joined*, either by a conjunctive accent or Maqqeph, to the word following. It is unnecessary to give examples, as they may be found in every page. It may however be noted that these particles often affect the division of the clause, thus כִּי שֶׁמֶשׁ ׀ וּמָגֵן (Ps. lxxxiv. 12), where, without the כִּי, there would be no dichotomy; and so אֲשֶׁר רָאִיתָ ׀ אֶת־עָנְיִי (xxxi. 8); וְלֹא אָמְרוּ ׀ הָעֹבְרִים (cxxix. 8), &c.

But, sometimes on musical grounds, sometimes with a view to

---

[15] K. 156 has זכר מה־חלד אני, a very good correction (comp. xxxix. 5[b]), but more violent than is necessary.

[16] In reality this word is, as we learn from the Arabic, in the *adverbial accusative*. The passage from Job is rendered in the Polyglot Vers. أَخًا كُنْتُ لِأَوْلَادِ ٱلْوُحُوشِ. And עָמְדוֹת הָיוּ רַגְלֵינוּ answers to قَآئِمًا كَانَ رَبّ (Wright, Arab. Gr. ii. p. 109). We see then in the accentuation a fine appreciation of the grammatical construction.

emphasis[17], even these unimportant words, which have so little claim to an independent position, are found marked with a pausal accent, thus : אַף (cxix. 3) ; אֲשֶׁר ׀ (cix. 16) ; כַּאֲשֶׁר (xxxiii. 22) ; גָּם (cxxix. 2) ; יָעַן (cix. 16) ; כִּי ׀ (xvi. 10) ; לָמָּה (lx. 7) ; לֹו (lxxxi. 14) ; בְּלֹא (xvii. 1) ; בְּלִי (xix. 4) ; בַּל (xxxii. 9) ; עַל (Job xvi. 17) ; אַל־נָא (xxxii. 21) ; תַּחַת (Prov. i. 29), &c.

Thus far, we have had to do with the division of the *clause* into its several members, but there is a further point that requires consideration, and that is, the division, in certain cases, of the *members themselves*. Every member of a clause—subject, object, &c.—will be either *simple*, consisting of one word, or *compound*, consisting of two or more words. And such compound members introduce a new element into the dichotomy of the verse, about which it is necessary to say a few words.

(α) Two nouns in *apposition* are almost always kept together by the accentuation : כְּאִישׁוֹן בַּת־עָיִן (Ps. xvii. 8) ; אַתָּה שִׁמְךָ (lxxxiii. 19) ; דָּוִד עַבְדּוֹ (cxliv. 10) ; בֶּסֶף מְחִירָה (Job xxviii. 15).

The punctators did not, however, tie themselves to rule. Sometimes the dichotomy comes, with a certain emphasis, *between* the two nouns, e. g. אֲרַחֶמְךָ יְהוָה ׀ חִזְקִי (Ps. xviii. 2).

But, if *three* nouns occur in apposition, the dichotomy becomes *necessary*, as יְהוָה ׀ אֶל אֱלֹהִים (l. 1) ; or if one of the members of apposition consists of two words, as יְהוָה ׀ אֱלֹהֵי יִשְׂרָאֵל. In particular cases we may even require a *second* dichotomy, as in the compound subject : הַר־צִיּוֹן ׀ יַרְכְּתֵי צָפוֹן ׀ קִרְיַת מֶלֶךְ רָב (xlviii. 3).

(β) Two nouns in the same construction, and united by the conjunction *and*, are joined by the accentuation : מִשְׁפָּטֵי וְדִינֵי (ix. 5) ; לְדֹר וָדֹר (x. 6) ; שָׁמַיִם וָאָרֶץ (lxix. 35) ; גָּדוֹל וְנוֹרָא (xcix. 3)[18].

Yet not unfrequently the punctators emphasize two such words, particularly when they shew parallelism, by placing the dichotomy *between*, e. g. וְשֵׂיבָה ׀ וְעַד־זִקְנָה (lxxi. 18) ; כָּלָה שְׁאֵרִי ׀ וּלְבָבִי (lxxiii. 26) ; אֱלֹהִים ׀ וְאָדָם (Prov. iii. 4). That they held themselves quite free in this respect is shewn by the different grouping of the words in the *same* verse, : מְחֹרָף וּמְנַדֵּף מִפְּנֵי אוֹיֵב ׀ וּמִתְנַקֵּם ׀ מָקוֹל (Ps. xliv. 17).

But when *three* nouns come together the dichotomy cannot fail : חֶרְפָּתִי וּבָשְׁתִּי ׀ וּכְלִמָּתִי (lxix. 20). And so, if for one of the nouns, we have a nominal expression containing two words, as חָמָס וְאֹהֵב ׀ רָשָׁע (xi. 5).

---

[17] It was left to the taste of the Reader to *discriminate* between these two cases, and to give emphasis, where emphasis was due.

[18] Occasionally the two nouns stand ἀσυνδέτως, as צִנִּים פַּחִים (Prov. xxii. 5) ; and עֶלְיוֹן נוֹרָא (Ps. xlvii. 3).

(γ) The *substantive* and its qualifying *adjective* are necessarily taken together: מֶלֶךְ גָּדוֹל (xcv. 3); רוּחַ טוֹבָה (cxliii. 10). The *participle* also is generally joined to its substantive, as עַם נִבְרָא (cii. 19)[19].

Instead of the adjective, we may have an adverb, a preposition with its government, or a verb (with the relative understood), e.g. מָגֵן בַּעֲדִי (iii. 4); צוֹרְרִי רֵיקָם (vii. 5); שָׂחַד עַל־נָקִי (xv. 5); אֹיְבַי בְּנֶפֶשׁ (xvii. 9); מֶלֶךְ לְעוֹלָם (xxix. 10); אָדָם בִּיקָר (xlix. 21); מַלְכִּי מִקֶּדֶם (lxxiv. 12); דָּבָר בְּעִתּוֹ (Prov. xv. 23); שְׁאוֹל מָטָּה (ib. 24); עַם לֹא־יָדַעְתִּי (Ps. xviii. 44)[20]. But the connection in such expressions is not so close as that between substantive and adjective, and the punctators were quite at liberty to bring in the dichotomy *between* the words, if the constitution of the clause allowed, and they meant an emphasis (more or less) to rest on the words. So we meet with זָכַרְתִּי יָמִים | מִקֶּדֶם (xvi. 4); | בַּל־אַסִּיךְ נִסְכֵּיהֶם | מִדָּם מִקֶּדֶם (cxliii. 5). Comp. l. 4ᵃ; lxxx. 14ᵃ; lxxxv. 5ᵇ; Job xxxi. 28ᵇ[21].

When however *two* adjectives or participles follow, the dichotomy must appear, e. g. אַרְיֵה | טֹרֵף וְשֹׁאֵג עֻזּוּז וְגִבּוֹר | יְהֹוָה (Ps. xxiv. 8); צָרוֹת רַבּוֹת | וְרָעוֹת (xxii. 14). (Sometimes *between* the adjectives, as כָּל־הוֹן | יָקָר וְנָעִים (lxxi. 20); (Prov. xxiv. 4).) And so, when in any other way, the qualifying expression consists of two or more words, as הָאֵל | הַנּוֹתֵן נְקָמוֹת לִי (Ps. i. 3); | בְּעֵץ שָׁתוּל עַל־פַּלְגֵי־מָיִם (xviii. 48); נָגִיד | חֲסַר תְּבוּנוֹת וְרַב מַעֲשַׁקּוֹת אִישׁ־שְׁלוֹמִי | אֲשֶׁר־בָּטַחְתִּי בוֹ (xli. 10); (Prov. xxviii. 16).

Exceptions are exceedingly uncommon. In the difficult passage כֶּסֶף צָרוּף | בַּעֲלִיל לָאָרֶץ (Ps. xii. 7), the sense was misunderstood (as we may gather from the old Verss. and Rabb. comm.) In עֹבֵר מִתְעַבֵּר (Prov. xxvi. 17), the two words have probably been kept together, for the sake of the *assonance*. A slight laxity, perhaps due to emphasis, has crept into Prov. vi. 18: 'Feet that are *eager* | to run to evil;' and in אִישׁ־עֵנָה (xxv. 18) and אִישׁ־שֹׁחַד (Job xv. 16) the compound expressions seem loosely treated as the simple particles עֵנָה and שֹׁחַד. For Job iii. 3ᵇ see the explanation p. 44, l. 16.

(δ) The union by means of the *status constructus* is of the very closest description; but here also, if *two* words with this construction follow one another, the first is marked off by the dichotomy, as referring

---

[19] Yet sometimes it stands with good effect *apart*, as in Ps. lxviii. 26: 'In the midst of damsels | (who are) playing the timbrel,' and Prov. xxx. 20, 'So is the way of a woman | (who has been) committing adultery.' Such cases come under η below.

[20] The preposition with its noun may even *precede*, as in בִּדְמָעוֹת שָׁלִישׁ (lxxx. 6; where Hitzig is, no doubt, right in translating: *Ein Becher, in Thränen bestehend*) and בַּצִּיּוֹת נָהָר (cv. 41), 'a river in the desert.'

[21] Of course the punctators often differ, as in Ps. xviii. 19ᵇ (comp. 2 Sam. xxii. 19); cviii. 13ᵃ; cxix. 142ᵃ; Job vi. 25ᵇ; xxxi. 28ᵇ (above); xxxiii. 10ᵇ; &c.

to the *compound idea* expressed by the second and third words, thus: עֵת ׀ לָדַת ׀ יַעֲלֵי־סָלַע ׀ (xx. 2); שֵׁם ׀ אֱלֹהֵי יַעֲקֹב ׀ (Ps. ii. 12); אַשְׁרֵי ׀ כָּל־חוֹסֵי בוֹ (Job xxxix. 1); אֵת ׀ יוֹם יְרוּשָׁלָ͏ִם ׀ (Ps. xcvii. 5); even מִלִּפְנֵי ׀ אֲדוֹן כָּל־הָאָרֶץ ׀ (cxxxvii. 7); עַל ׀ אַדְמַת נֵכָר ׀ (ib. 4); כֹּל ׀ יְמֵי חַיָּיו ׀ (cxxviii. 5)[12]. And so, when the words following contain a compound idea, formed in some other way, the dichotomy will be equally due, e. g. עֵט ׀ סוֹפֵר מָהִיר ׀ (xlv. 2); וְאַשְׁרֵי ׀ דְּרָכַי יִשְׁמֹרוּ ׀ (Prov. viii. 32). בַּעֲבוּר ׀ דָּוִד עַבְדֶּךָ (cxxxii. 10); Sometimes it comes *between,* מִפִּי ׀ עוֹלְלִים ׀ וְיֹנְקִים ׀ (Ps. viii. 3); comp. β.

Exceptions I have not noticed, save cxxxvii. 8[b], 9[a]; in the former of which verses, a slight license has been admitted, for the sake of rhythm; and in the latter the clause has been thrown out of gear by the introduction of Little Shalshéleth.

(ε) *Adverbial expressions* like עוֹלָם וָעֶד (x. 16); יוֹמָם וָלָיְלָה (lv. 11); מִבֹּקֶר לָעֶרֶב (Job iv. 20); מֵחַיִל אֶל־חָיִל (lxxxiv. 8); מִיָּם עַד־יָם (lxxii. 8); are properly held together by the accents. And so, generally, the punctators are careful to keep the several parts of one and the same adverbial phrase together, e.g. בְּתוֹכָחוֹת עַל־עָוֹן (Ps. xxxix. 12); בַּחֲלוֹם מֵהָקִיץ (lxxiii. 20); although of course, where there are three or more words, the minor dichotomy must appear, as בְּהִתְעַטֵּף עָלַי ׀[d2] (xxvii. 2)[23]. בִּקְרֹב עָלַי ׀[d3] מְרֵעִים ׀[d2] לֶאֱכֹל אֶת־בְּשָׂרִי ׀[d1] רוּחִי ׀ (cxlii. 4);

(ζ) With regard to the *Verb*, we have to notice—
(1) That the *infin. absol.* is united with the corresponding *verb. fin.,* as קַוֹּה קִוִּיתִי (xl. 2); הָלוֹךְ יֵלֵךְ (cxxvi. 6); שִׁמְעוּ שָׁמוֹעַ (Job xxi. 2).

(2) That two verbs, joined in the same construction, are generally also united accentually, as אֱלֹהִים ׀ יְחָנֵּנוּ וִיבָרְכֵנוּ ׀ (Ps. lxvii. 2); וִישִׁישִׁים ׀ קָמוּ עָמָדוּ (Job xxix. 8); אָכְלוּ וַיִּשְׁתַּחֲווּ ׀ כָּל־דִּשְׁנֵי־אֶרֶץ ׀ (Ps. xxii. 30); מַהֵר עֲנֵנִי ׀ יְהוָה ׀ (cxliii. 7).

But sometimes the dichotomy appears *between:* יָדֶיךָ עִצְּבוּנִי ׀ וַיְעַשּׂוּנִי ׀ (Job x. 8); אֶרֶץ יְרָאָה ׀ וְשָׁקָטָה ׀ (Ps. xxxvi. 4); חָדַל לְהַשְׂכִּיל ׀ לְהֵיטִיב ׀ (lxxvi. 9). We find variation, even in the *same* verse: הֵמָּה ׀ כָּרְעוּ וְנָפָלוּ ׀ וַאֲנַחְנוּ קַּמְנוּ ׀ וַנִּתְעוֹדָד׃ (xx. 9).

If, however, either of the verbs receives an *addition* of any kind, a minor dichotomy must be introduced: יִזְכְּרוּ ׀[d2] וְיָשֻׁבוּ אֶל־יְהוָה ׀[d1] כָּל־ אַפְסֵי־אָרֶץ (xxii. 28); לֹא יָדְעוּ ׀ וְלֹא יָבִינוּ ׀ (lxxxii. 5). And so when *three* verbs occur in sequence, פִּצְחוּ וְרַנְּנוּ ׀ וְזַמֵּרוּ ׀ (xcviii. 4).

(This is all analogous to what we saw with the noun, β.)

---

[22] But these small words, which are so used to Maqqeph, constantly appear with it, in this construction. See עַל־ (cvi. 17); עִם־ (cxx. 5, comp. 4); כָּל־ (vi. 9); אֶת־ (lx. 2).

[23] As these adverbial expressions begin with an infinitive, they are divided as *verbal* clauses.

(3) In a few cases, two verbs are brought together, which a strict regard to syntax would have kept apart: לְכוּ חֲזוּ | מִפְעֲלוֹת יְהֹוָה (xlvi. 9); הַרְפּוּ וּדְעוּ | כִּי־אָנֹכִי אֱלֹהִים (ib. 11); comp. lxvi. 5, 16; lxxxvi. 9. The punctators were here quite right in deciding that the first verb has not sufficient importance to claim the dichotomy. It is merely introductory to the second, on which the main stress and emphasis lies. Syntax therefore has to give way. On the other hand, they rightly separate לְכוּ | נְרַנְּנָה לַיהֹוָה (xcv. 1); and הֶרֶב | כַּבְּסֵנִי מֵעֲוֺנִי (li. 4).

(η) The *relative* clause, in whatever form it appears,—with or without אֲשֶׁר, or as a participle or verbal adjective,—is constantly treated as a separate and independent member, even when the substantive precedes, to which it properly belongs. (It is so in our own punctuation.) Thus אַשְׁרֵי הָאִישׁ | אֲשֶׁר יָגֹרְתִּי ; הֶעָבֵר חֶרְפָּתִי | אֲשֶׁר יָגֹרְתִּי (cxix. 39); יְמָאֲסוּ כְמוֹ־מַיִם | יִתְהַלְּכוּ־לָמוֹ (i. 1); אֲשֶׁר לֹא הָלַךְ בַּעֲצַת רְשָׁעִים (lviii. 8); כֵּן יְבָרַךְ גָּבֶר | יְרֵא יְהֹוָה (lxix. 32); וְתִיטַב לַיהֹוָה מִשּׁוֹר פָּר | מַקְרִן מַפְרִיס (cxxviii. 4). On the other hand, זִכְרוּ | נִפְלְאֹתָיו אֲשֶׁר עָשָׂה (cv. 5). Baer's text and ordinary edd. differ in ix. 12; xvi. 7; lxxix. 6; cxli. 9; Job xxiii. 5.

Such are the laws for the accentual division of a syntactical clause,—laws of no little importance, for they enable us to decide, in many a doubtful case,—where Codd. differ,—what the true accentuation is[24]. In applying them however we have to make allowance for other musical rules,—particularly that of transformation,—which will be given in due course. The student will understand that, till he is familiar with these additional rules, he must not attempt to apply for himself the laws laid down above. But these rules mastered, he will be surprised to find how strictly the laws (so modified) are carried out, and how simple and easy the accentual analysis becomes, under their guidance.

We must now for a moment retrace our steps. It has already been noticed that the principle of *parallelism*—which is our chief guide for the main dichotomy of the verse—shews itself also in the minor divisions. Here also it may be *complete*

---

[24] These laws may, for the most part, be traced in the prose accentuation as well, but undergo such very different modifications, that it is impossible to consider the two systems together. The accentuation of the three Books seems to me much the simpler, so that the study of it may well serve as an introduction to that of the other.

(e.g. Ps. lxiii. 2ᵇ), *general* (v. 11ᵃ), or *partial* (xviii. 7ᵃ); and under the last-named head, *progressive* (xi. 4ᵇ), or simply *repetitive* (xciii. 3ᵃ)[25]. It may occur at the beginning (lxiii. 2ᵇ), the middle (xxxi. 3ᵇ), or the end (ib. 11ᵃ) of a clause, and is particularly common at the *end*. It is marked in the finest detail, being often confined to the smallest possible limits of *two words* (lxxi. 18ᵃ). Of course, we have to make allowance for it, when dividing according to our rules; and in most cases an *additional dichotomy* will be necessary, to separate the members of the parallelism from one another; for instance in Ps. xxxi. 3ᵇ:

הָיָה לִי ׀ᵈ¹ לְצוּר מָעוֹז ׀ᵈ¹ לְבֵית מְצוּדוֹת ׀ᵈ¹ לְהוֹשִׁיעֵנִי:

where, without the parallelism, we should have had

הָיָה לִי ׀ᵈ² לְצוּר מָעוֹז ׀ᵈ¹ לְהוֹשִׁיעֵנִי:

This additional dichotomy is the only modification of our rules which parallelism introduces. We may indeed notice a distinct tendency to *emphasize* the parallelism, as though the punctators felt that the poet, in introducing it, did not do so without a meaning, but had intended, by the repetition of the idea, that a certain *stress* should be laid upon it. When therefore there was a choice, we find them constantly selecting the stronger and more important accent for the parallelism. Thus, in the ex. given above, הָיָה לִי is not marked (as it might properly have been) with *d* 2, but this division was reserved for the members of the parallelism. Hence too such cases as

כִּי לֹא יָבִינוּ ׀ᵈ¹ אֶל־פְּעֻלֹּת יְהוָה ׀ᵈ² וְאֶל־מַעֲשֵׂה יָדָיו (xxviii. 5);

הֵן הִכָּה־צוּר ׀ᵈ¹ וַיָּזוּבוּ מַיִם ׀ᵈ² וּנְחָלִים יִשְׁטֹפוּ (lxxviii. 20);

תֹּסֵף רוּחָם ׀ᵈ² יִגְוָעוּן ׀ᵈ¹ וְאֶל־עֲפָרָם יְשׁוּבוּן: (civ. 29).

I draw attention to these cases, because, had not the punctators decided to mark and intone the parallelism, *d* 1 would, in accordance with the syntactical or logical division, have come where *d* 2 now stands, and *vice versa*[26]. We have here, on a smaller scale, the same principle which we noticed (25. 14) under the main dichotomy, viz. the main idea first given, and then an echo following of a *part* of the same,—the part to which attention was to be specially drawn.

---

[25] Comp. pp. 24–26.
[26] Baer has indeed (following Heid.) adopted this division for the second of the examples given above; but with very slight MS. authority.

Lastly, there is another principle of division, which we have already noticed in 1. 2; II. 2, &c. The part of the clause, which follows the dichotomy, is often not parallel, but *supplemental*. The main idea is given, in the first part of the clause,—in a form, syntactically complete,—and then comes what is explanatory, qualifying, amplifying, &c. Of course the division is here often according to our rules, but not always. Thus, instead of 'How long | shall I be forming plans in my soul?' (xiii. 3), we find 'How long shall I be forming plans | in my soul?' instead of 'When I was silent, | my bones wasted away through my roaring all the day' (xxxii. 3), we have 'When I was silent, my bones wasted away | through my roaring all the day.' And so,

> If I did not believe to look on the goodness of Jehovah | in the land of the living! (xxvii. 13).
> Hope thou in God, for I shall yet praise Him | the help of my countenance and my God (xlii. 12).
> El, Elohim, Jehovah hath spoken, and called the earth | from the rising of the sun to the going down thereof (l. 1).
> And they shall know that God ruleth in Jacob | to the ends of the earth (lix. 14).
> By the rivers of Babylon, there we sat, and wept too | as we remembered Zion (cxxxvii. 1).

In such cases the supplemental part belongs properly to the *latter* part of the clause preceding. Here also the division may be regarded as more or less *emphatic*.

If now it be asked, What is the *meaning* of the continuous dichotomy, the rules of which have been investigated in the present chapter? What *principle* underlies it? I can only give the answer, which I have given before, with regard to the general objects of the accentuation. The principle was clearly twofold—primarily *melody*, and secondarily (as far as the laws of melody allowed) *development of the sense*. Whatever the melody may have been, the succession of pauses, which the continuous dichotomy introduced, afforded ample opportunity for the production of *musical effect*, e.g. with the trills, of which Eastern music is so fond; whilst all *monotony* was avoided by the change of accentuation, which the varying lengths of successive verses and their divisions rendered necessary. (The accents themselves, I presume, see p. 2, note 4, supplied in full measure that rising and falling of the voice—the *arsis* and *thesis* of the Greeks—on which the melody of public recitation so largely depends.)[27] With regard to the second object of the accentuation, we have seen that the continuous dichotomy not only takes note of the *logical* divisions, but aims at keeping apart for distinct enunciation the several members of a *syntactical* clause—i. e. whenever the length of the clause seems to make such separation necessary—at the same time giving *emphasis*, where emphasis is due. The accentuators thus did their best to assist both reader and hearers in apprehending what seemed to them the true meaning of the Sacred Text. And this is for us the recommendation of their system.

Some corrections of the *textus receptus* are necessary, in accordance with the rules laid down in this chapter. I shall then proceed to apply these rules to the clauses governed by the several disjunctive accents.

Corrigenda[28]

(arranged according to the order of the rules, pp. 39–44).

SUBJECT. Ps. xxix. 7. קוֹל יְהֹוָה חֹצֵב לַהֲבוֹת אֵשׁ׃ with B. M. 2, 6, 8, 13; Erf. 2.

Ps. xcv. 7. וַאֲנַ֫חְנוּ ׀ עַם מַרְעִיתוֹ וְצֹאן יָדוֹ with Ox. 109; Par. 9, 30; Ber. 32; De R. 304; Ghet. 1.

Prov. xiv. 6. וְדַעַת לְנָבוֹן נָקָל׃ with Ox. 5, 17, 72; Erf. 1; Par. 4; K. 157.

Prov. xiv. 13. וְאַחֲרִיתָהּ שִׂמְחָה[29] תוּגָה׃ with B. M. 1; Ox. 15, 17, 111, 2322; Pet. Comp. v. 22ᵃ.

Prov. xv. 31. אֹ֫זֶן שֹׁמַעַת תּוֹכַחַת חַיִּים with Ox. 5, 6, 15, 17, 96; Pet.

---

[27] On these points of detail I desire to speak with all diffidence, as I have no knowledge of music.

[28] Some instances I have, for special reasons, reserved for the chapters following. It was not necessary to give them there and here too.

[29] Munach stands here, by transformation (as will be hereafter shewn), for R'bhia mugrash.

Prov. xxii. 3. Better עָרוּם רָאָה רָעָה וְנִסְתָּר with Par. 30; Ber. 1, 32; De R. 304, 518; Vat. 3. Comp. b. So also in xxvii. 12.

Job xxii. 18. וְהוּא מִלֵּא בָתֵּיהֶם טוֹב with B. M. 5, 8, 14; Ox. 1, 19, 2323.

Job xxxvii. 23. Better שַׁדַּי לֹא מְצָאנֻהוּ שַׂגִּיא־כֹחַ with Ox. 19; Erf. 2; Fr.; K. 157; De R. 593, 737.

Job xxxix. 13. אִם־אֶבְרָה חֲסִידָה [30] וְנֹצָה׃ with B. M. 1; Par. 17, 30; Erf. 1, 4; Fr.

OBJECT. Job xxxviii. 32. וְעַיִשׁ עַל־בָּנֶיהָ [30] תַנְחֵם׃ with B. M. 14; Ox. 18; Vi. 4, 8, 11. Comp. Hos. x. 14[b].

ADVERB, &c. Ps. iv. 9. בְּשָׁלוֹם יַחְדָּו אֶשְׁכְּבָה וְאִישָׁן, though I have found only two Codd., Erf. 1 and K. 538, that point so. The punctators generally seem to have adopted the rendering, which we find in Aben-Ezra and Qimchi, that יַחְדָּו=עמהם, 'with them,' my enemies!

Ps. xxxv. 7. כִּי־חִנָּם טָמְנוּ־לִי שַׁחַת רִשְׁתָּם with Ox. 71, 2332; Erf. 2.

Ps. xliv. 25. לָמָּה פָנֶיךָ תַסְתִּיר with B. M. 4, 8, 13; Ox. 5, 71; &c. So also correct Job xiii. 24.

Prov. xiv. 14. מִדְּרָכָיו יִשְׂבַּע סוּג־לֵב with Ox. 1; or מִדְּרָכָיו יִשְׂבַּע סוּג לֵב with B. M. 5, 7, 8, 12, 13; Ox. 5. Comp. xviii. 20.

Job vi. 14. לַמָּס מֵרֵעֵהוּ חָסֶד with B. M. 4; Ox. 1, 17, 71; Erf. 2, 3.

Job xvii. 15. וְאַיֵּה אֵפוֹ [31] תִקְוָתִי with B. M. 3; Ox. 19; Fr.; K. 445; De R. 2, 589.

Job xvii. 16. אִם־יַחַד עַל־עָפָר נָחַת׃ with B. M. 3, 4; Ox. 13, 72, 101; Fr. Comp. xxi. 26.

Job xxix. 25. כַּאֲשֶׁר אֲבֵלִים יְנַחֵם׃ with Ox. 19, 72; Ber. 2; Fr.; De R. 349, 368. Comp. Ps. lvi. 7[h].

VERB. Ps. v. 3. הַקְשִׁיבָה ׀ לְקוֹל שַׁוְעִי. See Norzi's note: בספרים מדוייקים כן הוא בטעם גרמיה.

Ps. xi. 1. If we take the reading of the K'thibh, we have necessarily the pointing

אֵיךְ תֹּאמְרוּ לְנַפְשִׁי נוּדוּ הַרְכֶם [30] צִפּוֹר׃

The Q'ri (as it seems to me) can only be rendered:
    'Flee thou! Off to your mountain, ye birds[32]!'

---

[30] See p. 51, note 29.
[31] אֵפוֹ, as is well known, attaches itself to the word preceding.
[32] It must be borne in mind that the accentuation is always *according to the Q'ri*.

Ps. xxxii. 5. אוֹדֶה ׀ עֲלֵי פְשָׁעַי לַיהוָה with Par. 9; Fr.; K. 188, 403; De R. 350; or אוֹדֶה עֲלֵי־פֶשַׁע with Par. 21, 24, 30; K. 157, 246; &c.

Ps. lxxxix. 6. וְיוֹדוּ ³³שָׁמַיִם פִּלְאֲךָ יְהוָה with B. M. 1; Ox. 13, 15, 2323; Erf. 3; Bomb. 2.

Ps. cxix. 138. צִוִּיתָ צֶדֶק עֵדֹתֶיךָ with Ox. 1, 6; Par. 4, 30; Erf. 2; Fr.

Job ix. 30. וַהֲזִכּוֹתִי ³³בְּבֹר כַּפָּי with Ox. 96; Par. 17, 36; Ber. 52; De R. 2, 596. Comp. Ps. lxxiii. 13.

Job xv. 22. לֹא־יַאֲמִין שׁוּב מִנִּי־חֹשֶׁךְ with B. M. 3, 4; Ox. 1, 7, 19, 96.

Job xix. 21. חָנֻּנִי חָנֻּנִי אַתֶּם רֵעָי with Ox. 1, 5; Erf. 3, 4; K. 157, 606; Sonc.

Job xxiv. 9. יִגְזְלוּ ³³מִשֹּׁד יָתוֹם with Ox. 1, 72; Cam. 28; Fr.; K. 224; De R. 380.

Job xxxi. 15. וַיְכֻנֶנּוּ בָּרֶחֶם ³⁴אֶחָד with B. M. 14, 16; Ox. 101; Ber. 32; Hm. 8, 21.

Job xxxi. 16. אִם־אֶמְנַע מֵחֵפֶץ ³³דַּלִּים with B. M. 6; Ox. 18; Erf. 2; Hm. 15, 32; Vi. 8. Comp. xxxviii. 15.

Job xxxix. 10. הֲתִקְשָׁר־רֵים בְּתֶלֶם ³³עֲבֹתוֹ (taking עֲבֹתוֹ as *accus. instrumenti*) with B. M. 11; Ox. 9, 2437; Erf. 1; Hm. 8; Cop. 4.

Job xl. 2. הֲרֹב עִם־שַׁדַּי ³³יִסּוֹר with B. M. 12; Ox. 1, 5, 19, 100, 101.

NOM. PREDICATE. Ps. xc. 1. The simplest correction of our texts would be אֲדֹנָי מָעוֹן אַתָּה הָיִיתָ לָּנוּ בְּדֹר וָדֹר, but no Cod. points מָעוֹן with R'bhia, whereas many—B. M. 4, 8; Ox. 4, 13, 72, 97, &c.— have מָעוֹן אַתָּה, which removes all difficulty, as far as the accents are concerned: 'O Lord, a refuge art THOU; Thou hast been for us (comp. הָיָה לָנוּ cxxiv. 1) in generation and generation.'

Job xxix. 15. עֵינַיִם הָיִיתִי לַעִוֵּר with B. M. 7, 8; Ox. 5, 7, 15, 19.

Many other similar corrections have been made in the text by Heidenheim and Baer, which I shall have occasion to refer to hereafter.

---

[33] Munach stands here, by transformation, for D'cht.
[34] See p. 51, note 29.

CHAPTER V.

WE saw, in chapter III, that every verse is divided into two parts by either Olév'yored or Athnach. These parts have now to be taken *separately*. Each has its own musical arrangement, which makes it so far independent of the other. In this chapter and the next I purpose considering the *first* part, as closed by Olév'yored and Athnach. I shall then proceed to the examination of the *second* part, lying between the one or other of these accents and Silluq.

OLÉV'YORED[1].

We have already noticed (34. 2) that this accent cannot come at the *beginning* of the verse; in other words, Olév'yored's clause cannot consist of a *single word*.

I. When it contains *two* words, Little R'bhia is always required in the first, e. g. אֶל חֹק אֲסַפְּרָה (Ps. ii. 7); רְגֹזוּ וְאַל־תֶּחֱטָאוּ (iv. 5).

---

[1] The name of this accent was doubtless chosen to indicate its twofold melody, in the chanting of which the voice first *ascended* (עלה) and then *descended* (ירד) in the scale. In support of this derivation, it may be mentioned that Ben-Asher (Dikd. hat. 20. 16) employs these same terms עולה and יורד for the accents Munach and Mer'kha, of which he distinctly states (24. 12), that the former has an *ascending*, and the latter a *descending* melody; and that in the *Mas. magna* to Num. xxxvi. 3, we find the terms סלק ונחת (=עולה ויורד) used of the *ascending* melody of Azla, followed by the *descending* melody of Mer'kha. Did we know more of the accentual melodies, we might perhaps find that the commencing melody of Olév'yored *resembled* the melody of M'huppakh, and that *that* was the reason why M'huppakh was chosen to represent it. The lower sign is (as has been stated) in MSS. like Silluq,—קוּ וְקוּף El. Levita calls it,—and designates Olév'yored as a *pausal* accent. (The same stroke is also used, to indicate a *pause*, for Paseq and Méthcg.)

With regard to the *position* of the first sign, I have found in the Codd. that—
a. If the tone be on any other than the first syllable, it is placed over the preceding syllable, as רְשָׁעִים (i. 1); חָפְצוֹ (i. 2). Similarly, if the tone be on the first syllable, and Sh'va precede, as מְצָא (xxxii. 6); שְׁמוֹ (lxviii. 5). It will be remembered that two words joined by Maqqeph are counted as one word; we might then expect that עַל־פְּלַגֵּי־מָיִם (i. 3), אֶל־חֹק (ii. 7) would be so pointed, but the Maqqeph is in such cases dropped, as no longer necessary. β. If the tone be on the first syllable—and Sh'va do not precede—the M'huppakh-sign is transferred to the last syllable of the preceding word, supposing that syllable is unac-

Such verses are not, however, numerous,—if we except the superscriptions, hardly 20 in the whole of the three Books,—and when we examine them, we find that the poet, in dividing his verse so near to its beginning, has taken care that the words should be *emphatic* in their character; so that the accentuators decided rightly in insisting on a *pausal*, instead of a conjunctive accent, here[2]. The additional pause gives a weight to this short half of the verse.

II. When the clause contains three or more words, the position of the dichotomy will be fixed by the rules laid down in the preceding chapter, and the accents employed to mark it will be as follows[3]:

1. Little R'bhia, if the dichotomy fall on the *first* word before Olév'yored, e. g. אֲנִי שָׁכַבְתִּי וָאִישָׁנָה (iii. 6), p. 47. l. 28[4]; הַמְּאֹות אָהֲבוּ אֶת־יְהוָה כָּל־חֲסִידָיו (xxxi. 24), 43. 22; אִם־אֵלֵךְ ׀ בְּקֶרֶב נְעוּרַי ׀ וּפְשָׁעַי אַל־תִּזְכֹּר (xxv. 7), 40. 23; צָרָה תַחְתֵּינִי (cxxxviii. 7), 38. 11.

2. Sinnor, on the *second* word[5]: יְהוָה יָדִין עַמִּים (vii. 9), 39. 20; חֶרֶב ׀ בְּיֹום צָרָתִי אֲדֹנָי דְּרַשְׁתִּי (lxxvii. 3), 41. 17; תְּשִׁיתֵמֹו ׀ פָּתְחוּ רְשָׁעִים וְדַרְכֵי קָשְׁתָּם (xxxvii. 14), 38. 9; כְּתַנּוּר אֵשׁ לְעֵת פָּנֶיךָ (xxi. 10), 43. 5.

In such cases, the first word will almost always have the *servus* Galgal. But Little R'bhia is musically admissible, and we find it

---

cented, as כְּיֹוב מִי־יִרְאֵנוּ (iv. 7); פָּעֲלֵי אָוֶן (xiv. 4). But if it is accented, then the sign remains on the first syllable, as שׁוּב נָא (lxxx. 15); וְיָשָׁר אָתָּה (Job viii. 6). Some Codd. adopt this pointing even in the former case, thus מִי־יִרְאֵנוּ כְּיֹוב, פָּעֲלֵי אָוֶן. (Comp. R'bhia mugrash, p. 16, note 29.)

Not unfrequently the one or other of these signs is dropped in Codd. In particular, the upper sign often falls away, when the tone is on the first syllable, as יֹום ׀ יֹום (Ps. lxviii. 20). So too R'bhia mugrash often loses one of its signs.

[2] They have, however, in one case, hardly caught the division intended by the poet. The first two words of cxliv. 14 belong clearly (see Hupf.) to the previous verse, which must then, in its turn, be otherwise divided. On Job xxxii. 12 see Delitzsch's remark.

[3] The three accents, named in 1, 2, and 3, furnish a sufficient musical variety before Olév'yored.

[4] Here, at the beginning, I refer in each case to the page and line, where the rule is to be found.

[5] This is by far the most common division of Olév'yored's clause.

introduced, apparently for the sake of emphasis, in a few passages of the *textus receptus*, viz. Ps. xxii. 15; xxxv. 10; xxxix. 13; Prov. xxiii. 35; xxx. 9. Perhaps in the Codd. other examples might be found; but the matter is not of any moment.

3. Great R'bhîa, on the *third* word or further, e. g. אַשְׁרֵ֥י הָאִ֗ישׁ אֲשֶׁ֤ר ׀ לֹ֥א הָלַךְ֮ בַּעֲצַ֪ת רְשָׁ֫עִ֥ים (i. 1), 48. 14; וְהָיָ֗ה כְּעֵ֤ץ (i. 3), 43. 23; שָׁת֪וּל עַֽל־פַּלְגֵ֫י מָ֥יִם יְהוָ֗ה מִשָּׁמַ֥יִם הִשְׁקִ֖יף עַל־ עַתָּ֣ה יָ֭דַעְתִּי כִּ֤י הוֹשִׁ֥יעַ ׀ יְהוָ֗ה מְשִׁ֫יח֥וֹ בְּנֵֽי־אָדָ֑ם (xiv. 2), 39. 20; (xx. 7), 42. 22.

In such cases, we have to notice that there are three or more words left between Great R'bhîa and the end of the clause. These words then will claim a minor dichotomy. And the same accents will be employed (i. e. the same musical notes will be required) before Olév'yored, as above under 1 and 2. If this minor dichotomy fall on the *first* word, it will be marked by Little R'bhîa; if on the *second*, by Ṣinnor[6].

The above rules are simple enough. One class of exceptions alone has to be noted. The two R'bhîas cannot, from musical reasons, occur in too close proximity. At least, *two* words, with their respective accents, must intervene[7]. Where this is not the case, Ṣinnor is employed instead of Great R'bhîa[8], as in the following examples:

---

[6] Further back than the second word this minor dichotomy does not come, save in one passage, where Olév'yored's clause is of unusual length, and an additional dichotomy becomes necessary, which is made by the *repetition* of Ṣinnor: מְפָתַ֨ים יָדְךָ֤ ׀ יְהוָ֗ה מִֽמְתִ֣ים מֵחֶ֣לֶד חֶלְקָ֥ם בַּֽחַיִּים֮ וּֽצְפוּנְךָ֮ תְּמַלֵּ֪א בִטְנָ֥ם (xvii. 14).

[7] Similarly, in the prose Books, a certain interval must occur between two consecutive R'bhîas; otherwise one of them is changed into Pashṭa. The rule is modified in the three Books, for here two Great R'bhîas (as we shall see under Athnach) can stand together, but a suitable interval must separate the two *different kinds* of R'bhîas. No writer on the accents has (as far as I am aware) noticed this peculiarity.

[8] I have observed only one passage, cxxxiii. 2, in our texts, at variance with this rule. But here Codd. vary much. Some, as Ox. 13, Par. 4, K. 192, De R. 593, have יֹרֵ֖ד עַל־הַזָּקָ֑ן ; whilst many—B. M. 2; Ox. 6, 111; Fr.; K. 155, 598; &c.—drop Olév'yored, and have D'chi instead, יֹרֵ֖ד עַל־הַזָּקָ֑ן. Either of these pointings does away with all difficulty. In xxviii. 7 we have a solitary ex. of Ṣinnor with *two* words between it and Little R'bhîa, but these words may be joined by Maqqeph, with B. M. 4, 7; Par. 20, 21, 25, 30; &c. The punctuation of common edd., and not that of the Heid.-Baer text, must be taken for xv. 5; xxxii. 4; li. 6; and lii. 9.

OLÉV'YORED. 57

כִּי הֶחֱלַ֣ט נַפְשִׁ֑י מִמָּ֖וֶת ; (xv. 5) ; בַּסָּפ֣וּ ׀ לֹא־נָתַ֣ן בְּנֶ֑פֶשׁ וְשַׁ֣חַר עַל־נָקִ֣י לֹֽא־לָקָ֑ח
הֲלֹ֣א רַגְלֵ֣י מְדֻחֶ֑י (lvi. 14). Comp. xiii. 6; xxvii. 9; xxxii. 4; xxxv. 10;
xl. 6, 15. On the other hand Great R'bhîa can remain in xx. 7; lii. 9;
cxxvii. 5; cxxxix. 14.

When the dichotomy of Olév'yored's clause is thus completed,
Great and Little R'bhîa, and Sinnor will often be left with clauses
of their own, containing three or more words. For the accentuation of such subordinate clauses I must refer to the chapters
reserved for these accents.

SERVUS OF OLÉV'YORED.

The servus of Olév'yored is (as we have seen) Galgal. In two
passages it comes, instead of Métheg, in the same word with Olév'yored,
מִמַּעֲצ֣וֹתֵיהֶ֑ם (v. 11) and יְבַהֲל֑וּן (civ. 29)[8].

EXCEPTIONS: (1) In three passages, where Paseq intervenes, Galgal
is changed into M'huppakh, thus י֣וֹם ׀ י֣וֹם אֲדֹנָ֣י בָּר֣וּךְ (lxviii. 20); and
so in lxxxv. 9 and Prov. xxx. 15. (Paseq fails here in common edd.)[9]

(2) In two passages Mer'kha comes as servus between Little R'bhîa
and Olév'yored: יְהוָ֥ה מִ֣י כָמ֑וֹךָ (Ps. xxxv. 10) and וְאָמַ֗רְתִּי מִ֥י יְהוָ֥ה
(Prov. xxx. 9)[10].

Olév'yored has never more than *one* servus.

---

[8] In lv. 22; lxxviii. 38; civ. 29; cvi. 47; cxl. 4; Prov. i. 22; and Job xxiv. 13,
Galgal is wanting in our texts. For lv. 22 point וְקָרֵ֣ב (see Norzi's note). In cvi.
47 I would propose to make R'bhîa and Sinnor change places. The other instances
have been already corrected by Heid. and Baer.

[9] Some Codd. and Ben-Bil. (8. 9) make this change, when the tone is on *the first
letter* of the word, e.g. מִ֣י זֶ֥ה מֶ֖לֶךְ הַכָּב֑וֹד (xxiv. 8). Common edd., with their
usual inconsistency, point sometimes with Galgal (xii. 3; xvi. 11), sometimes with
M'huppakh (vi. 3; xxiv. 8). The former was Ben-Asher's punctuation, the latter
Ben-Naphtali's. Of course, Codd. generally follow Ben-Asher.

[10] We shall see elsewhere, in the Masoretic text, Mer'kha taking (exceptionally)
the place of Maqqeph, which is here (at least for the passage in Prov.) retained by
Ben-Naphtali (see Ginsburg's Masora, vol. i. p. 588). In this use of Mer'kha, I believe that we have simply an instance of Masoretic trifling. Thus there are just these
two cases of מִי before Olév'yored, and so they are made to pair off, with an abnormal
accentuation! (Comp. p. 63, notes 23 and 24.) Mer'kha in Ps. xlii. 5 I have already
corrected, p. 36. In xv. 5 introduce Maqqeph with Heid. and Baer.

CHAPTER VI.

Athnach.

Athnach, like Olév'yored, is never found in the *first word* of the verse (34. 3).

I. When Athnach's clause consists of *two* words (and such cases are very common), the first has generally the servus Mer'kha[1], as לֹא־כֵן הָרְשָׁעִים (i. 4), but sometimes D'chî, as נִנְתְּקָה אֶת־מֽוֹסְרוֹתֵימוֹ (ii. 3).

We may suppose that the original intention was to reserve D'chî for cases of *pause* or *emphasis*, like כִּֽי־אָמַרְתִּי פֶּן־יִשְׂמְחוּ־לִֽי (xxxviii. 17); שִׁמְעוּ־זֹאת כָּל־הָעַמִּים (xlix. 2). But this rule is far from being always observed in our printed texts. For a matter of so little consequence, I have not thought it worth while to examine the Codd.[2], with the view of correcting exceptional cases.

II. When Athnach's clause consists of *three or more* words, the rules for the dichotomy are applied, just as in the case of Olév'yored, and the accents employed to mark it are:

1. D'chî, when the dichotomy falls on the word immediately preceding Athnach, e. g. שָׁמַע יְהוָה תְּחִנָּתִי (vi. 10); אָמַר בְּלִבּוֹ בַּל־אֶמּֽוֹט (x. 6).

2. D'chî also, when it falls on the *second* word before Athnach (for here we have no accent answering to Ṣinnor before Olév'-yored), e. g. שׁוּבָה הַקְשִׁיבָה לְקוֹל שַׁוְעִי מַלְכִּי וֵֽאלֹהָי (v. 3); יְהוָה חָלְצָה נַפְשִׁי (vi. 5)[3].

But not unfrequently Great R'bhîa appears instead, e. g. הוֹשִׁיעָה אֶת־עַמֶּךָ וּבָרֵךְ אֶת־נַחֲלָתֶךָ (xxviii. 9); הַשָּׁמַיִם מְסַפְּרִים כְּבוֹד־אֵל (xix. 2).

---

[1] *After Olév'yored* Mer'kha is always employed, as in vii. 1; xviii. 36; xxv. 7. I have observed only three exceptions, lxii. 11; Prov. xxx. 17; and Job xxxiii. 9, which are corrected in Codd.

[2] I have noticed, however, incidentally that they often vary, as in viii. 5; xxvi. 4; xxxvii. 13, 24, 29; Job xxi. 15, 22; xxxvii. 13.

[3] This is by far the most frequent division of Athnach's clause.

R'bhia, when contrasted with D'chi, marks a *greater pause* (logical or syntactical). This principle is however—for such clauses as those before us—only partially carried out in our texts. D'chi occurs where we should have expected R'bhia and *vice versa*. The point is not of any importance to us, for the *sense* is not appreciably affected, whichever accent be employed [4].

Generally, when R'bhia occupies this position, the first word has Mer'kha (as above), but in a few instances D'chi. The examples are Ps. xlv. 5; l. 1; lix. 8; lxxviii. 31; lxxxii. 1; cxliv. 3; Job xiii. 4; xxxii. 11; xxxiv. 25. The appearance of D'chi in these cases is parallel to that of Little R'bhia between Ṣinnor and Olév'yored (55. 22).

3. Great R'bhia, when the dichotomy falls on the *third* word or further, e.g. שָׁאַל מֵעִמִּי וְאֶתְּנָה גוֹיִם נַחֲלָתֶךָ (ii. 8); אַל־תֹּאמַר כַּאֲשֶׁר עָשָׂה־לִי כֵּן אֶעֱשֶׂה־לּוֹ (Prov. xxiv. 29); הֲיָדַעְתָּ עֵת לֶדֶת יַעֲלֵי־סָלַע (Job xxxix. 1). Great R'bhia divides in the same way (as we have seen) Olév'yored's clause.

But here we notice that, with R'bhia on the third word (or further), three words (or more) remain between it and the end of the clause. These words then will require a second dichotomy, which, in the examples given (as falling on the first or second word, see 1 and 2), is marked by D'chi. But, what if this second dichotomy itself fall on the third word (or further), where D'chi cannot be employed to mark it [5]? Then, *R'bhia is repeated* [6], and D'chi comes in for the third dichotomy, which has now become necessary. Thus חַטָּאתִי ׀ אוֹדִיעֲךָ וַעֲוֹנִי לֹא־כִסִּיתִי אָמַרְתִּי אוֹדֶה ׀ עֲלֵי פְשָׁעַי לַיהוָה (Ps. xxxii. 5). The other examples (as far as I have noted) are l. 21; lxxviii. 4; lxxxix. 20; xcv. 10; xcvii. 5; cii. 25; Prov. xxvii. 10; and Job vii. 4 [7].

---

[4] On this point the Codd. themselves exhibit no little variation. Thus שְׁוֹעִי and שַׁוְעִי (v. 3); יְהֹוָה and יְהוָה (vi. 2); סָבִיב and סָבִיב (xii. 9); רִגְּתִי and רִגָּתִי (xvii. 1); &c.

[5] It is a fixed rule that D'chi *cannot occur further back than the second word from Athnach*. Hence such mistakes, as in Ps. cxxxv. 4, Prov. xx. 4, Job xvi. 19, in common edd., must be at once corrected.

[6] Just as, under similar circumstances, R'bhia is repeated in the prose Books. It is clear, from the nature of the case, that the second R'bhia has a *less pausal value* than the first.

[7] In Ps. xvii. 1, xli. 7, xlvi. 5, lix. 6, Prov. iv. 4, Job xxiv. 24, xxxiii. 23, a second R'bhia appears, but merely as a substitute for D'chi (see II. 2 above).

(R'bhîa is not repeated more than once; in other words, the division of Athnach's clause does not proceed beyond the third dichotomy, and only in the few passages just named, beyond the second.)

Such are the simple rules for the analysis of Athnach's clause. Of course, the clauses closed by R'bhîa and D'chî may have (as in the last ex.) their own subordinate pausal accents, the rules for which will be considered in the chapters on Great R'bhîa and D'chî. One point only remains to be noticed, and that is the frequent change of D'chî—when due, from the dichotomy, in the first word before Athnach—into a *servus*. This change is, of course, simply musical, and is occasioned by the *shortness* of that part of Athnach's word which precedes the tone. When it contains two (or more) syllables, or one long syllable, followed by vocal Sh'va, D'chî can stand. Otherwise, a servus must come instead. Thus we have לְךָ־אֲנִי הוֹשִׁיעֵנִי (cxix. 94); but אֲבַדּוֹן וָמָוֶת אָמְרוּ (Job xxviii. 22); but אֱמוּנָתְךָ וּתְשׁוּעָתְךָ אָמְרָתִי (Ps. xl. 11). This law of *transformation* (as it has been termed) mars, in no slight degree, for us, here and elsewhere, the order and symmetry of the accentual system.

In connection with this transformation, I explain such cases as כִּי אֵלֶיךָ ׀ יְהוָה (lxxiii. 28) and שַׁתִּי ׀ בַּאדֹנָי יְהוִה מַחְסִי אֲדֹנָי עֵינָי (cxli. 8), where L'garmeh comes in the third word before Athnach[8]. At first sight, it often appears as if we had

---

[8] In Ps. v. 5 L'garmeh appears on the *fourth* word; but the explanation is the same. On the other hand, in Ps. lxii. 11, where it comes *immediately before* Athnach, it must be dropped (with B. M. 3; Ox. 13, 17, 27; Erf. 2; Fr. &c.). And so in Prov. xvi. 10 (see Baer's note). Further, I would correct Ps. xiv. 5,—where our edd. place it in the *second* word,—thus שָׁם ׀ פָּחֲדוּ פָחַד with B. M. 2; Par. 4, 9, 29, 30; Ber. 32; &c. And in Job xxxviii. 2, if we divide with Athnach, as various Codd. and Baer do, we must point either מִי זֶה ׀ מַחְשִׁיךְ עֵצָה with B. M. 3; Hm. 8; De R. 349; or מִי זֶה מַחְשִׁיךְ ׀ עֵצָה with B. M. 14; Ox. 18; K. 403. (In xxxvii. 1, cvi. 1, cxxxviii. 1, cl. 1, L'garmeh stands for Olév'yored (34. 12) and does not come into consideration here.)

here a substitute of R'bhîa, but such a substitution would be quite inexplicable; whereas, if we take L'garmeh as the pausal accent in D'chî's clause, *which remains, when D'chî is transformed,* all is clear. A comparison of Job xxvii. 13 with xx. 29 shows, beyond all possibility of doubt, that this is really the case. Other examples are Ps. xviii. 50 (compared with 2 Sam. xxii. 50); xxxi. 15; xliv. 24; cxxii. 5; Job iv. 5; xxxi. 2. Once, Ps. xix. 15, Pazer—the other pausal accent in D'chî's clause—is employed in the same way[9]. (But some Codd. point here with R'bhîa.)

This L'garmeh is very rarely wanting in its proper place. That the distinguishing Paseq now and then fails, will surprise no one who has any acquaintance with the Codd. Thus it must be supplied to ׀ הִנֵּה in Ps. lxxxvii. 4; cxxvii. 3; Prov. i. 23; Job xxxii. 12 (as I have found in various Codd.); and so Prov. xvii. 12 must be corrected פָּגוֹשׁ ׀ דֹּב שַׁכּוּל בְּאִישׁ; and xxi. 29 הֵעֵז ׀ אִישׁ רָשָׁע בְּפָנָיו [10]. I have noticed no other exceptions.

Servi of Athnach[11].

Athnach has often one, two, and three servi, rarely more than three.

1. One servus. This is (a) Munach, after D'chi, e. g. תִּרְעֵם בְּשֵׁבֶט בַּרְזֶל (Ps. ii. 9); יְהֹוָה מָלָךְ יִרְגְּזוּ עַמִּים (xcix. 1); (β) Mer'kha in all other cases, i. e. after Olév'yored[12] or R'bhia, or at the beginning of the verse, e. g. אֲפָפוּנִי חֶבְלֵי־מָוֶת (xviii. 13); יַצִּילֵנִי מֵאֹיְבִי עָז (ib. 18); מִנֶּגֶד נְגִדוּ עָבְיוּ עָבְרוּ (ib. 5)[13].

EXCEPTIONS. Munach (under a) is changed into Mer'kha, *when Paseq follows,* thus אָמְרוּ הֶאָח ׀ הֶאָח (xxxv. 21). This change is sup-

---

[9] The passages, Ps. xlv. 8, lxviii. 5, cix. 16, where Pazer appears in the *second* word before Athnach, are manifest mistakes, which are already corrected in the Heid.-Baer text.

[10] No Cod., however, in these two passages, gives Pascq, though many have M'huppakh. If, therefore, we wish to keep to the testimony of Codd., we must point שָׁכוּל דֹּב־שַׁכּוּל (with De R. 2; K. 166; Vat. 468), and הֵעֵז אִישׁ־רָשָׁע (with B. M. 12; Par. 30; Ber. 32; Vi. 2; K. 250). This accentuation is equally correct.

[11] I take no notice of the endless mistakes of common edd., as they are corrected in Baer's texts.

[12] In xxxvii. 1, cxxxviii. 1, cl. 1, Mer'kha comes after L'garmeh, but L'garmeh is here the representative of Olév'yored (34. 12).

[13] A strange exception occurs in Prov. vi. 3, where Ben-Asher has וְהִנָּצֵל כִּי בָאתָ בְכַף־רֵעֶךָ. Here we must take Ben-Naphtali's pointing, which is regular, כִּי־בָאתָ.

ported by the analogy of Paseq with two servi (below), and by the testimony, more or less regular, of Codd.[14]

2. Two servi. These are both Munachs, as: עָבְדוּ אֶת־יְהֹוָה בְּיִרְאָה (ii. 11),—properly עָבְדוּ אֶת־יְהֹוָה (see p. 60). Indeed, in *all* cases, where Athnach has two or more servi, the servus adjoining Athnach stands, by transformation, for D'chi. It is important (with a view to the sense) to bear this in mind. Without the operation of the law of transformation, Athnach, like Olév'yored, *would never have more than one servus*.

EXCEPTIONS. When Paseq comes after the second servus, it is changed into Mer'kha, and the preceding Munach into Tarcha, e. g. נָאֵין ׀ רָשָׁע אֱלֹהִים (x. 13). Comp. xliv. 24; lxvi. 8; lxvii. 4. This rule is laid down by Ben-Bil. (5. 5) and is fully borne out by the Codd.[15]

3. Three servi. The two adjoining Athnach are, as before, Munachs, —or, with Paseq, Tarcha and Mer'kha[16]. The first servus will be M'huppakh or Illuy, according to the following rules[17]:

a. M'huppakh, when the tone is on the *first* syllable, e. g. אָז יְדַבֵּר אֵלֵימוֹ בְאַפּוֹ (ii. 5); יְהִי כְבוֹד יְהֹוָה לְעוֹלָם (civ. 31). In one instance, the first and second servi come in the same word, שָׁאַל (cxlvi. 5, comp. 3).

β. M'huppakh also, when the tone is on the *second* syllable, supposing vocal Sh'va does not precede, e. g. אַתָּה פּוֹרַרְתָּ בְעָזְּךָ יָם (lxxiv. 13). The other examples are: שִׁוַּעְתִּי (xvi. 8); הַטֵּה (lxxxvi. 1); אַתָּה (lxxxix. 11); תִּקְרָב (cxix. 169); תִּכָּוֹן (cxli. 2); בַּקֵּשׁ (Prov. xiv. 6); וְרָעֵם (Job xxi. 8).

---

[14] Ben-Bil. (4. 30) lays down a further class of exceptions, by pointing Mer'kha, instead of Munach, after D'chi, when the servus falls on the *first letter* of the word, e. g. רְשָׁעִים וְגוֹ שִׁדּוּנִי (xvii. 9). But Ben-Asher does not agree. Ps. lxxxiii. 13 furnishes a test-passage. There all the lists of the Varr. I have seen assign to him the regular pointing: אָמְרוּ נִירְשָׁה לָּנוּ. And it need hardly be added that Codd. generally follow him, there and elsewhere. (Of course, an occasional variation may occur. Thus, in Ps. i. 1, Bomb. 2,—followed by subsequent edd.,—has brought in Mer'kha, לֹא עָמָד; but the older edd. and Codd. have לֹא עָמָד. And elsewhere Bomb. 2 has regularly Munach.) It is therefore to be regretted that Baer has adopted Ben-Bil.'s pointing, all through his texts. We have already seen (p. 57, note 9) that Ben-Bil. is wrong in a similar change before Olév'yored; and certainly, the fewer exceptions we have to our rules, the better.

[15] Ben-Bil. (5. 8) gives two passages, Job v. 27, xxxiii. 31, as marked by these accents, *although Paseq is wanting*, and Codd. are found, which agree with him. But many point regularly, and we may well follow their example.

[16] There are only two cases of these accents, Ps. v. 5 and lxxxix. 52.

[17] This servus is, in reality, the first servus of D'chi, which remains, when D'chi is transformed. In fact, when transformation takes place, Athnach takes over all D'chi's accents, conjunctive and disjunctive.

γ. Illuy, when the tone is on the second syllable, vocal Sh'va preceding[18],— or when it is on the *third* syllable, e. g. נָתְנוּ רְשָׁעִים פַּח לִי (cxix. 110); הֵנַפָּה מָן לֶאֱכֹל (Job iv. 2); וַיַּמְטֵר עֲלֵיהֶם כֶּעָפָר דָּבָר אֵלֶיךָ תִלְאֶה (Ps. lxxviii. 24, comp. 27). The other examples are: לַעֲשׂוֹת (xl. 9); וָיְהִי[19] (xciv. 22); טָפְלוּ (cxix. 69); הֲפַכְפַּךְ (Prov. xxi. 8); and לֹא־יַחְשֹׁב (Ps. xxxii. 2); כִּי־אַתָּה (lxxxiii. 19); וְאַל־תַּצֵּל (cxix. 43).

δ. M'huppakh with Sinnorith, when an open syllable directly precedes the tone, e. g. לֹא נָתַן לוֹ וְלֹא־נֶגֶד אוֹדְךָ יְהוָה מְאֹד בְּפִי (cix. 30); בְּעַמּוֹ (Job xviii. 19, where Sinnorith, as usual, displaces the Maqqeph). The other examples are: וַיְהִי[20] (Ps. ix. 10); גָּדוֹל (xlviii. 2; cxlv. 3); יְהוָה (lxx. 20); עָנִי (lxxxviii. 16); וְיוֹדוּ (lxxxix. 6); זָכַרְתִּי (cxix. 55); לַעֲשׂוֹת (cxxxvi. 4); וְנַעַר (ib. 15); אֲבָל (Prov. xxv. 27); הַאִם[21] (Job vi. 13); נֶדֶר (xv. 23); הָאַף[22] (xxxiv. 17).

Exceptions. The servi are irregular in יִשְׂאוּ הָרִים שָׁלוֹם לָעָם (Ps. lxxii. 3); לִוְיַת חֵן הֵם לְרֹאשֶׁךָ (Prov. i. 9); הָיְחִתָּה אִישׁ אֵשׁ בְּחֵיקוֹ (vi. 27); all (it will be observed) with Shalshéleth, the melody of which naturally affected the accents adjoining.

4. The following are the only examples in which Athnach has more than three servi: כִּי גָּדוֹל יְהוָה וּמְהֻלָּל מְאֹד[23] (Ps. xcvi. 4); כִּי אֶת אֲשֶׁר יֶאֱהַב יְהוָה יוֹכִיחַ[24] (Prov. iii. 12); and one with Shalshéleth, לְךָ דֻמִיָּה תְהִלָּה אֱלֹהִים בְּצִיּוֹן (Ps. lxv. 2).

---

[18] Vocal Sh'va is here, for the purposes of accentuation, counted as a syllable, so that the tone is really on the *third* syllable.

[19] On the vocal Sh'va here, see Olsh., § 82 a. (Common edd. have, as often, *Munach inferius* for *superius*; but the more correct edd. of Opit., Jabl., and Mich. are right.)

[20] No Cod. (as far as I have observed) has Baer's accentuation וַיְהִי.

[21] So I point with Ox. 15, Par. 3, K. 446, De R. 1261 (other Codd. have הַאִם, Sinnorith, as often, failing). The pointing of edd. הַאִם cannot stand. Better הַאִם, with Par. 6, Cop. 16, Vi. 12, which emphasizes the question with good effect.

[22] So B. M. 1; Ox. 15; Par. 42; De R. 1022, 1261. Edd. have here also Illuy. B. M. 4; Par. 80; Hm. 19; De R. 349, 596; Bomb. 1, point הָאַף. Comp. 40. 8.

[23] Common edd. have כִּי with Maqqeph, which is the regular pointing. But the Masora to Ps. cxliii. 3 has fixed Mer'kha. There are just two cases (here and in Job xxxiv. 37) of כִּי before Sinnorith and M'huppakh in Athnach's clause; so they are made to pair off, marked with an anomalous accentuation! The Masora joins with them two similar cases of כִּי in L'garmeh's clause!

We may note that מְאֹד in this verse is made by the accents to refer to גָּדוֹל, as well as to מְהֻלָּל. Otherwise, we must have had D'chi with יְהוָה. The same clause is accented in the same way in 1 Chron. xvi. 25.

[24] On this verse see Baer's note (p. 55 of his ed. of Prov.). Yet surely, we must

Corrigenda.

Ps. ix. 14. חָנְנֵנִי יְהוָה רְאֵה עָנְיִי מִשֹּׂנְאָי, with B. M. 1; Par. 3; De R. 350, 661, 865, 1261. Comp. Norzi's note.

Ps. lxii. 12. Better שְׁתַיִם זוּ שָׁמָעְתִּי with B. M. 4, 5; Ox. 1, 5, 7, 109.

Ps. lxxiii. 8. יָמִיקוּ וִידַבְּרוּ בְרָע עֹשֶׁק with Par. 30; Ber. 32; De R. 304; Ghet. 1.

Ps. xciv. 12. Better אַשְׁרֵי הַגֶּבֶר אֲשֶׁר־תְּיַסְּרֶנּוּ יָּהּ with Ox. 1, 7, 111; Par. 4, 20, 30.

Prov. xxviii. 23. מוֹכִיחַ אָדָם אַחֲרַי חֵן יִמְצָא with B. M. 8; Ox. 71; K. 170; De R. 304, 308, 518. 'He that reproveth a man shall afterwards find favour' (as Vulg., Ewald, Hitz., &c.)[25].

Other corrections have been made by Heid. and Baer, which generally have the full support of Codd.[26] But in xlviii. 5, xlix. 13, liv. 9, lxxix. 12, lxxxviii. 1, their emendations must be cancelled. Common edd. are right.

---

at least point אֶת אֲשֶׁר (comp. אֶת גָּאוֹן xlvii. 5 before Silluq), *Munach superius* having been confounded, as is often the case, with *Munach inferius*. אֶת is fixed by the Masora to this passage. This is the only instance in which אֶת precedes the third servus in Athnach's clause. It pairs off with a similar אֶת before Silluq (Ps. xlvii. 5)! The true accentuation is indicated, in part at least, by Ben-Naphtali בְּי׳ אֶת־אֲשֶׁר.

[25] The accentuation of *text. rec.* represents the view of the Talmud, Aben-Ezra, and others, that אַחֲרַי means '*after me*,' God or Solomon being supposed to be the speaker (see Delitzsch's Comm.). Some Jewish commentators (whom Delitzsch himself follows) render: 'He that reproveth a man *who is going backwards*,' &c.; but that would require מוֹכִיחַ ׀ אָדָם אֲחֹרַי, which no Cod. exhibits.

[26] It may interest some of my readers to examine these corrections for themselves. They refer, first (this arrangement of them is my own), to cases in which the (main or minor) dichotomy has been falsely introduced in common edd., Ps. ix. 9, lxxiii. 7, lxxviii. 66, cii. 23, Prov. xxiii. 26, xxxi. 17, Job xiv. 19, xxiii. 8, xxiv. 8, xxxi. 27, xxxiii. 12, 17, xxxv. 9, xxxviii. 36, xl. 9, xli. 26; and secondly, to cases in which the dichotomy fails, Ps. xviii. 42, xxxv. 19, lxxx. 9, lxxxvi. 6, ci. 6, cv. 11, cxix. 142, 150, Prov. ii. 7, 13, iii. 4, xiv. 10, xvii. 11, xxi. 19, xxix. 14, Job x. 17, xxi. 18, xxiv. 15, xxxi. 37, xxxviii. 38. (The corrections are by Heid. and Baer for the Pss., by Baer alone for Prov. and Job.)

CHAPTER VII.

SILLUQ.

HAVING completed (as far as is necessary for the present) our examination of the *first* half of the verse;—whether closed by Olév'yored or Athnach,—we proceed next to consider the *second* half, lying between the one or other of these accents and Silluq, the part of the verse, which may be regarded as specially under Silluq's control.

I. We take first the case when Olév'yored divides the verse.

The most important point to notice here is, that Athnach is still due between Olév'yored and Silluq. It marks the chief dichotomy in Silluq's clause; and its position is fixed, by the rules with which we are now familiar. Thus it may separate the members of a *parallelism:* וּבְדֶרֶךְ חַטָּאִים לֹא עָמָד וּבְמוֹשַׁב לֵצִים לֹא יָשָׁב׃ (Ps. i. 1). Or it may mark any other kind of *logical* pause, as in רְפָאֵנִי יְהוָה כִּי נִבְהֲלוּ עֲצָמָי׃ (vi. 3). Or (less frequently) it may simply note a *syntactical* division, e.g. בַּל־יוֹסִיף עוֹד לַעֲרֹץ אֱנוֹשׁ מִן־הָאָרֶץ׃ (x. 18).

The position of Athnach determined, we have only to consider the clause lying between it and Silluq. But this is just the consideration before us, *when Athnach divides the verse*. For our further investigation then the two cases merge into one[1].

II. To arrive at the various forms that the clause lying between Athnach and Silluq may assume, the simplest course will be to take *seriatim* the various possible positions of Athnach. Here, at every step, we shall find that we have to deal with a *musical* system.

---

[1] As for Athnach's own clause, the rules for the pausal accents and servi (ch. VI) hold equally good, whether Athnach marks the main dichotomy of the verse, or only the dichotomy of the second half, after Olév'yored. There is just one point that may be mentioned. Athnach cannot stand in the first word of the *verse*, but it may stand in the word immediately following Olév'yored. The instances are: Ps. iii. 6; iv. 7; v. 13; xxix. 9; lviii. 3; lxxvi. 12; lxxix. 6; Job xxvii. 5; xxxvii. 12 (p. 37).

1. Athnach may be due on the *first* word before Silluq. In this case, the clause vanishes altogether. But such instances are rare. A regard for rhythm prevented their frequent occurrence. With Olév'yored preceding, I have noticed only iii. 3; xviii. 51; xxxi. 3; xlv. 8; lv. 23; lxviii. 20; cix. 16; cxxv. 3; Prov. viii. 13. The few cases without Olév'yored have been already given, p. 33.

Moreover the melody does not allow Athnach to *remain* here, but changes it into R'bhîa mugrash, e. g. וְעָשָׂה חֶסֶד ׀ לִמְשִׁיחוֹ שָׁפְטֵנִי כְצִדְקְךָ יְהוָה (Ps. xviii. 51)*²; לְדָוִד וּלְזַרְעוֹ עַד־עוֹלָם: אֱלֹהָי וְאַל־יִשְׂמְחוּ־לִי (xxxv. 24).

2. Athnach may come on the *second* word. Then R'bhîa mugrash is due, as Foretone to Silluq, in the first word, e. g. לָמָּה רָגְשׁוּ גוֹיִם (xl. 15)*; יִסֹּגוּ אָחוֹר וְיִכָּלְמוּ חֲפֵצֵי רָעָתִי: וּלְאֻמִּים יֶהְגּוּ־רִיק (ii. 1); and so often. Of course the pause made by R'bhîa mugrash in such cases is simply and purely *musical*.

3. Athnach may come on the *third* word. Three words will then remain between it and the end of the clause; and the rules for the dichotomy must be applied. The accent employed to mark it,—whether it fall on the first or second word,—is as above R'bhîa mugrash (the accent whose melody is best suited for Silluq following), e. g. יֵשְׁבוּ בָנִים וְהִנִּיחוּ יִתְרָם לְעוֹלְלֵיהֶם: (xvii. 14)* and יְהוָה מָה־רַבּוּ צָרָי רַבִּים קָמִים עָלָי: (iii. 2). Examples are found in every page.

4. Athnach may come on the *fourth* word. R'bhîa mugrash will still in most cases mark the dichotomy, as (α) when it falls on the *first* word, אָבוֹא בֵיתְךָ אֶשְׁתַּחֲוֶה אֶל־הֵיכַל קָדְשְׁךָ בְּיִרְאָתֶךָ: (v. 8); or (β) on the *second* word,—and this is by far its most frequent position,—וּבְדֶרֶךְ חַטָּאִים לֹא עָמָד וּבְמוֹשַׁב לֵצִים לֹא יָשָׁב: (i. 1)*; or (γ) on the *third* word, as עָלֶיךָ

---

² In the cases where an asterisk is marked, *Olév'yored precedes*.

מָלַךְ (x. 14)* and יַעֲזֹב חֶלְקָה יָתוֹם אַתָּה ׀ הָיִיתָ עוֹזֵר׃
(xlvii. 9). אֱלֹהִים עַל־גּוֹיִם אֱלֹהִים ׀ יָשַׁב ׀ עַל־כִּסֵּא קָדְשׁוֹ׃
But, when this is the case, three words are left between R'bhîa mugrash and the end of the verse, and *a further dichotomy becomes necessary*. In the instances given, this dichotomy falls on the *second* word from Silluq, and is marked by L'garmeh. (And such is the constant rule in all like cases³.) But how, if it fall on the *first* word⁴? Will the same accents be possible? For instance, can we so point : יְהוָה עֹז לְעַמּוֹ יִתֵּן יְהוָה ׀ יְבָרֵךְ אֶת־עַמּוֹ ׀ בַשָּׁלוֹם (xxix. 11)? This is the accentuation we should have expected. But we do not find it. And we can only suppose that such a juxtaposition of Silluq and L'garmeh was against the rules of melody, and that L'garmeh had, in consequence, to be changed into a servus. But this change necessitated another; for R'bhîa mugrash cannot (again we must suppose, on musical grounds) stand in the third place, with Ṭarcha following⁵. Nothing remained then but to provide a substitute for it; and the accent chosen was Great Shalshéleth. So that finally the melody, in the ex. before us, found rest in the form יְהוָה ׀ יְבָרֵךְ אֶת־עַמּוֹ בַשָּׁלוֹם׃. Such also is the accentuation in the other passages, where the same division of Silluq's clause is found⁶.

---

³ I give a list of these passages, as some of my readers may like to compare them: iii. 1; x. 14; xviii. 31; xx. 2; xlv. 2; xlvii. 9; lvi. 8; lxviii. 19; lxxiii. 20; lxxiv. 2; lxxxviii. 11 (so most Codd.); xcviii. 6; xcix. 4; cii. 20; civ. 8, 26; cv. 3; cxix. 69, 104; cxxvii. 1; cxlviii. 4; Prov. xix. 10; xxi. 29; xxv. 1, 28; Job iii. 13; xv. 24; xviii. 21; xxi. 28; xxxvi. 28; xxxvii. 14. Total 31. I have left out Ps. xviii. 7 (see *Corrigenda*). Heid. and Baer have brought in wrongly xix. 5, and unnecessarily xxx. 11.

⁴ See the contrast between Job xv. 23 and 24. And note the true rendering of xxxvii. 12. Verss. and Comm. all explain as if we had R'bhîa mugrash and L'garmeh.

⁵ Common edd. have indeed a few instances, iii. 5; iv. 7; xxxviii. 21; &c. And even Baer leaves xlvi. 8 (12). But all these exceptions are corrected in Codd., if not already in the better edd.

⁶ The following is a list of these passages: vii. 6; x. 2; xii. 8; xiii. 2, 3; xx. 8; xxix. 11; xxxiii. 12; xli. 8; xliv. 9; xlix. 14; l. 6; lii. 5; lxvi. 7; lxvii. 5; lxxvii. 4; lxxix. 2, 3; xciv. 17; cxxxi. 1; cxliii. 6, 11; cxlvi. 3; Prov. vi. 10 (xxiv. 33); Job xi. 6 (see *Corrigenda*); xv. 23; xvi. 9; xxxii. 6; xxxvii. 12; xl. 23. Again (if we reckon the repetition in Prov. as *one*, and add xlii. 2, see note 7) a total of 31. Is

5. Athnach may come on the *fifth* word. Here we have nothing that is new. All the cases come under the several categories of 4, the great majority,—e. g. xiv. 1; xix. 8, 9; xxiii. 5,—with R'bhîa mugrash on the *second* word. With it on the *first* word, there are only two doubtful examples, xlii. 2 and lxvi. 20[7] (if we drop xxxii. 5; xlvii. 5; liv. 5; all with סֶֽלָה at the end). With it or Shalshéleth, on the *third* word (a *servus* coming between them and Athnach), we have xviii. 31; lxxxix. 2; xcix. 4; cxxvii. 1; Prov. xxv. 1; and Job xxxvii. 12 (p. 37). Of the dichotomy on the *fourth* word there is no example.

6. Further back than the *fifth* word Athnach does not occur, save in the prose verse, Ps. xviii. 1 (on which see p. 76, note 8), and the hybrid verse,—half prose and half poetry,—Job xxxii. 6, in which Shalshéleth appears with two servi, but which does not otherwise present any difficulty.

The result then of the above investigation is to shew, that whenever the dichotomy is by rule required between Athnach and Silluq, R'bhîa mugrash is employed to mark it,—excepting only the few (clearly defined) cases, in which Great Shalshéleth appears as its substitute;—and that, when further a minor dichotomy is due between R'bhîa mugrash and Silluq, M'huppakh L'garmeh marks it. For the laws regulating R'bhîa mugrash's own clause, I must refer to the chapter next following.

The accentual division of Silluq's clause completed, it remains only to mention that, here as elsewhere, the law of transformation often comes in, and obliterates or changes the pausal accent,

---

this coincidence accidental? We should be glad to see Shalshéleth here and there, e. g. in Ps. lxviii. 32, Job xv. 16, where it fails. On the other hand, it will disappear from nine of the above passages, e. g. Ps. vii. 6, xliv. 9, and R'bhîa mugrash come instead, if we leave out סֶֽלָה at the end of the verse.

It is to be observed that this Great Shalshéleth appears only in the position above assigned to it. It comes therefore under quite different circumstances, and with a very different value, from Shalshéleth in the prose accentuation.

[7] Some Codd.—B. M. 3, 4, 7; Ox. 6, 71; K. 155—pointing xlii. 2 with Shalshéleth, and some introducing (with Ben-Bil. 1. 11) Maqqeph after אֲשֶׁר in lxvi. 20.

which the above rules have fixed. Were it not for the operation of this law, we should find R'bhîa mugrash introduced in every verse (except in the few cases where Athnach would come on the first word), as a subsidiary tone and necessary precursor to Silluq,—just as Tiphcha is in the prose Books. But owing to this law, it is more frequently *absent* than present. The conditions for its presence are the same as those already laid down for D'chî before Athnach (p. 60). Thus, it remains in : כְּאִמְרָתְךָ הַצִּילֵנִי (cxix. 170), but is transformed in : כִּדְבָרְךָ הֲבִינֵנִי (ib. 169); it remains in : וּמַלְאַךְ יְהוָה רֹדְפָם (xxxv. 6), but not in וּמַלְאַךְ יְהוָה דֹּחֶה : (ib. 5).

Athnach too, as well as R'bhîa mugrash, is affected by this law. We have seen that it is always transformed, when it falls on the *first* word before Silluq[8]; and it is not unfrequently so, even on the *second* word. When, namely, R'bhîa mugrash has been transformed in the first word, and this word is like Silluq's word (without two syllables, &c., before the tone), then Athnach must give way to R'bhîa mugrash, e. g. הַדְּבָרוֹת עַל־צַדִּיק עָתָק עוּרָה הַנֵּבֶל וְכִנּוֹר אָעִירָה שָּׁחַר : (xxxi. 19); בְּגַאֲוָה וָבוּז : (lvii. 9). Comp. i. 2, iv. 5, v. 7, vii. 10.

SERVI OF SILLUQ[9].

Silluq, like Athnach, has often one, two, and three servi, rarely four.

1. One servus. This is (*a*) Munach, when the tone is on the *first* syllable, e. g. : לֹא יָשַׁב (Ps. i. 1), : לְמַעַן חַסְדֶּךָ (vi. 5) ; (*β*) Mer'kha, when on any other syllable, e. g. : הַיּוֹם יְלִדְתִּיךָ (ii. 7), : אֲשֶׁר־תִּדְפֶנּוּ רוּחַ (i. 4). Here, if an open syllable precede the tone, it is marked in some Codd. with Ṣinnorith, e. g. : יוֹמָם וָלַיְלָה (i. 2) ; : יָפִיחַ בָּהֶם (x. 5)[10].

---

[8] In lxviii. 20, cix. 16, Prov. viii. 13, the R'bhîa mugrash, which should have represented Athnach in the first word, has been itself changed into a servus, but has left its pausal accents behind it unchanged. So that Silluq appears with Great R'bhîa or D'chî dividing its clause! Some Codd. point in the same way Ps. iv. 7, but see Baer's note.

[9] I need not say that I cannot undertake to notice the many inexcusable mistakes of our ordinary edd. Nor is it necessary, as Baer has already corrected them in his carefully prepared texts.

[10] The Codd. in which I have noticed this Ṣinnorith are B. M. 1; Ox. 15 ; Par. 3.

EXCEPTIONS. (a) When L'garmeh precedes (67. 6), the servus is always Illuy, e. g. : אֲנִי בְכָל־לֵב ׀ אֹצֵר פְּקוּדֶיךָ (cxix. 69). (β) In two passages, נָתִין ׀ יְהֹוָה: (lviii. 7) and יוֹם ׀ יוֹם: (lxi. 9), Munach is changed into Mer'kha, because of Paseq following[11].

2. Two servi. The first is Tarcha and the second Munach, e. g. וְכֹל ׀ אֲשֶׁר־יַעֲשֶׂה יַצְלִיחַ: (i. 3). The two servi have here a closer affinity to one another than the second one has to Silluq; and *that*, for the simple reason that this latter stands for R'bhia mugrash. Indeed, in *all* cases, in which Silluq has two or more servi, the servus adjoining Silluq stands, by transformation, for R'bhia mugrash. It is important (with a view to the sense) to bear this in mind. Without the operation of the law of transformation, Silluq would—as in the prose system—*never have more than one servus*.

Tarcha may take the place of Métheg in the *same word* with Munach (supposing always that R'bhia mugrash does not precede[12]), e. g. : רְעוּתֶיהָ מוּבָאוֹת לָךְ (xlv. 15); יְאַחֲזוּנִי יְמֵי־עֹנִי: (Job xxx. 16)[13]. This is, of course, a mere musical embellishment.

108; Erf. 3; K. 446; De R. 331, 350, 1261. It appears also in a few instances—Ps. x. 3, 5; xviii. 20; xli. 14; &c.—in common edd. Baer has therefore authority for marking it (as he has done) regularly in his texts. But it is questionable whether it was worth while to revive a sign, which had fallen into all but general disuse, and which for us has no meaning. Moreover there seems never to have been any general agreement as to its employment. Ben-Bil. found in the MSS. which he used, a *different* sign, which he terms מתיגה (in the original Arabic המוה), and which was like an upper Métheg, thus : קָיִם בָּהֶם. The musical value and meaning of this sign he discusses at length (6. 5 ff.), and it is plain that it was to him something quite distinct from Ṣinnorith. We have then here another instance of the חלופים that prevailed among the punctators. Some employed Ṣinnorith, others M'thiga, and others again no sign at all beside the Mer'kha. As to Ben-Bil.'s M'thiga, it is still more rare in Codd. than the Ṣinnorith, I have found it only in the old Cod. Erf. 3, and occasionally in Cam. 15. It appears indeed in the prose accentuation (see משפטי הטעמים 13[b]), but under quite different conditions.

[11] Three strange exceptions are claimed by Ben-Bil. (7. 21) and the Erf. Mas. (MS.), are found also in some Codd., and are introduced by Baer into the text, viz. וּמִמַּעֲמַקֵּי מָיִם: (lxix. 15); יַעַמְדוּ מָיִם: (civ. 6); and וַיַּחְפְּכוּ אֶרֶץ: (Job xii. 15). All with Tarcha! But there can be no doubt that common edd. are right in pointing with Métheg and Maqqeph. The Maqqeph (we may suppose) was dropped in some early and model copy, and the Métheg taken for Tarcha. (These signs are often alike in MSS. See note 13 and Man. du Lect. 90. 2.) Ben-Asher knows nothing of these exceptions; for he was bound to notice them Dikd. hat. § 25 (סִימָן סוּמִי הַפְּסוּקִים), had he recognised them.

[12] Because R'bhia mugrash cannot have Tarcha after it (67. 16).

[13] Common edd. have constantly such false punctuation as אָרְחוֹתֶיךָ (xxv. 4), וּשְׁנוּצָתִי (cv. 9), Tarcha having been mistaken for Métheg.

EXCEPTIONS. (α) Munach is changed into Mer'kha in : לֹא יִשְׁמַע ׀ אֲדֹנָי (Ps. lxvi. 18), because of Paseq following. (β) In three passages, the servi are irregular, because of the irregularity of the pausal accent preceding : אִישׁ־עָנִי וְאֶבְיוֹן (Ps. lxviii. 20) ; יַעְמָס־לָנוּ הָאֵל יְשׁוּעָתֵנוּ סֶלָה (Prov. viii. 13)[14]. וְדֶרֶךְ רָע וּפִי תַהְפֻּכוֹת שָׂנֵאתִי (cix. 16); וְכִאֵב לְבָב לְמוֹתֵת :
(γ) For the two Illuys, which are found in the superscriptions of certain Psalms, see p. 35[15].

3. Three servi. The second and third remain unchanged; the first is M'huppakh or Azla, according to the following rules[16] :

α. M'huppakh, when the tone is on the *first* syllable, e. g. כִּי לֹא־עֲזָבְתָּ דֹרְשֶׁיךָ יְהוָה : (Ps. ix. 11); אֲשֶׁר יִקְרָאֻהוּ בֶאֱמֶת : לְכָל (cxlv. 18). In cxlvi. 3, the first and second servi occur in the same word, שֶׁאֵין (comp. v. 5).

β. M'huppakh[17] also, when the tone is on the *second* syllable, and vocal Sh'va does not precede, e. g. : עַל־כֵּן יוֹרֶה חַטָּאִים בַּדָּרֶךְ (xxv. 8; xlv. 3). I have found only two other exx., הִנֵּה (lxxiii. 15) and מִפִּי (Job xx. iv).

γ. Azla, when the tone is on the second syllable, vocal Sh'va preceding,—or when the tone is on the *third* syllable, e. g. יְמַלֵּט נַפְשׁוֹ אֶבְחָנְךָ : מִיַּד־שָׁאוּל סֶלָה (lxxxix. 49); בְּאֶחָד אוֹתוֹ פְלִשְׁתִּים בְּנַת (lvi. 1); מְבַקְשֵׁי : עַל־מֵי מְרִיבָה סֶלָה (lxxxi. 8). The other exx. are, וַיַּעֲנֵנִי (iii. 5); כִּי־רָאִיתִי (lii. 7); וְשֵׁרֵשְׁךָ (ib. 8, 12); מִשְׁכַּב־לָנוּ (xlvi. 4); יִרְעֲשׁוּ (xxiv. 6); (lv. 10); כִּי־רַבִּים (lvi. 3); אַל־תָּחֹן (lix. 6); אֶחֱסֶה (lxi. 5); כִּי־אַתָּה (lxii. 13); אֶעֱשֶׂה (lxvi. 15); וְאַל־תֵּאָטַר (lxix. 16); אָנֹכִי (lxxv. 4); אִם־קָפַץ (lxxvii. 10); הַאֲזִינָה (lxxxiv. 9); וּבָנִיתִי (lxxxix. 5); הֶעָטִיט (ib. 46); וְאַתָּה (cxlv. 15); בִּהְיוֹת [18] (Prov. iii. 27); לַאֲשֶׁר (Job xii. 6); וּרְאֵה (xxii. 12)[19].

---

[14] On these examples see note 8.

[15] Baer would establish a still further class of exceptions, by the rule that, when the two tone-syllables come together, Mer'kha takes the place of Munach, e. g. בִּמְזִמּוֹת זוּ חָשָׁבוּ : (x. 2). Ben-Bil. does indeed say (7. 26) that, *according to some* (מקצתם), this is the case. But Ben-Asher expresses himself (Dikd. ḥat. 25. 30) as decidedly opposed to such a change (אם בראש התיבה או באמצע התיבה כולם בשופר), pointing the ex. just given : בִּמְזִמּוֹת זוּ חָשָׁבוּ. I need hardly add that Codd. (with rare exceptions) agree with him. See too Norzi's note to Ps. cxxii. 9.

[16] Observe, that if we substitute Azla for Illuy, the rules here are the same as for the corresponding servus before *Athnach* (pp. 62, 63).

[17] Ben-Bil. (8. 2) points with *Azla;* but the unvarying testimony of Codd. is in favour of M'huppakh. He is equally wrong in giving the first servus of Athnach (5. 29).

[18] On the vocal Sh'va here, see Olshausen, § 85 b.

[19] I may mention that I have, in every doubtful instance, found ample MS. authority for the pointing with Azla given in the above list.

δ. M'huppakh with Sinnorith, when an open syllable directly precedes the tone, e. g. חֻרְבָּתָם אֲשֶׁר חֲרֵפוּךָ ;(liv. 8) אוֹדְךָ שִׁמְךָ יְהוָה כִּי־טוֹב:
אֲדֹנָי (lxxix. 12). The other exx. are, [20] מֵעֵת (iv. 8); כִּי הוּא (xxv. 15); וּמְעוֹן (xxviii. 8); מֵאִישׁ (xliii. 1); אֱלֹהִים (xlviii. 9); מוֹצָאֵי (lxv. 9); יָאֵר (lxvii. 2); תָּבִין (lxviii. 11); הֲלִיכוֹת (ib. 25); יְנַאֵץ (lxxiv. 10); כָּנֵן (lxxvi. 4); צֵידָה (lxxviii. 25); מָתַי (cxix. 84); מֵאִיר (Prov. xxix. 13); וְאַתִּי (Job xiv. 3); תָּשִׁית (ib. 13)[21].

With the tone on the *third* syllable, the punctators were at liberty to follow either this rule or the previous one. Thus, we have חֻרְבָּתָם above, and on the other hand אָנֹכִי. Generally, as the examples given shew, they took the latter course.

4. Four servi. The following are the only examples : אֵין יְשׁוּעָתָה לּוֹ בֵּאלֹהִים (iii. 3); בֶּן נַפְשִׁי (xxxii. 5) וְאַתָּה נָשָׂאתָ עֲוֺן חַטָּאתִי סֶלָה:
אֶת־ [22] נְאֻם יַעֲקֹב אֲשֶׁר־אָהַב סֶלָה: (xlvii. 5); תַּעֲרֹג אֵלֶיךָ אֱלֹהִים: (xlii. 2); לֹא שָׂמוּ אֱלֹהִים לְנֶגְדָּם סֶלָה: (liv. 5). It will be observed that four of the above passages end with סֶלָה. If then we reject it (as the poet, if he were living, would require us to do), and point xlii. 2 with Great Shalshéleth (note 7), we do away with these examples altogether. The accentuation will then be as follows : אֵין יְשׁוּעָתָה לּוֹ בֵּאלֹהִים: (iii. 3); בֶּן נַפְשִׁי ׀ תַּעֲרֹג אֵלֶיךָ אֱלֹהִים: (xlii. 2); וְאַתָּה נָשָׂאתָ עֲוֺן חַטָּאתִי (xxxii. 5); אֶת־נְאֻם יַעֲקֹב אֲשֶׁר אָהַב: (xlvii. 5); לֹא שָׂמוּ אֱלֹהִים לְנֶגְדָּם: (liv. 5).

---

[20] So I point with B. M. 1; Par. 3. 6; Vat. 475; De R. 1261. All edd. have Illuy, which is the third servus of Athnach, not of Silluq. Ben-Bil.'s authority (8. 1) may indeed be quoted in its favour, but his rules here are otherwise false, as we have already seen, note 17. (Of course, I do not accept Baer's rule, Accentuationssystem, § 4, note 2, '*Die Präfixa* בוכלם *erhalten kein Zinnorith.*' The testimony of Codd. is against it.) כָּנֵן (lxxvi. 4), צֵידָה (lxxviii. 25), and מָתַי (cxix. 84) are pointed in the same way, but must be corrected, with various Codd.

[21] Our texts exhibit an exceptional accentuation for several of the examples given above, thus, תָּשִׁית, מֵאִיר, תָּבִין, יָאֵר, מֵאִישׁ,—an accentuation against all rule, and (as it seems to me) unmeaning, except as indicating a *diversity of practice,* viz. that some punctators employ Mer'kha, others M'huppakh,—as is really the case, for nothing is more common in the Codd. than to find Mer'kha, as servus to Silluq, instead of M'huppakh (or Azla). The latter was Ben-Asher's punctuation, and the former seems (as far as I can gather from the lists of Varr.) to have been Ben-Naphtali's. But many Codd. point these words with M'huppakh in the *ultima,* and some few add Sinnorith. I have therefore not hesitated to accent them regularly.

[22] אֶת (Mer'kha for Maqqeph) is fixed by the Masora to this passage. See p. 63, note 24.

Corrigenda.

Ps. xviii. 7. וְשַׁוְעָתִי לְפָנָיו תָּבוֹא בְאָזְנָיו׃ with Ox. 17; Par. 17; Ber. 2; K. 170; De R. 1244, 1252. Comp. the old Verss.; and see Delitzsch's note, who, however, has quite misapprehended the meaning of the ordinary punctuation.

Ps. xlix. 15. וַיִּרְדּוּ־בָם יְשָׁרִים לַבֹּקֶר וְצוּרָם לְבַלּוֹת שְׁאוֹל מִזְּבֻל לוֹ׃ Athnach with B. M. 8; Par. 4, 19; Ber. 2; K. 157, 224.

Ps. cxxv. 3. The accentuation with L'garmeh is against all rule. If there had been no transformation, the clause would have stood לְמַעַן לֹא־יִשְׁלְחוּ הַצַּדִּיקִים בְּעַוְלָתָה יְדֵיהֶם׃; and making allowance for the same, we may point regularly לְמַעַן²³ לֹא־יִשְׁלְחוּ הַצַּדִּיקִים בְּעַוְלָתָה יְדֵיהֶם׃ with B. M. 1; Par. 28; Vat. 12, 468, 482; K. 598. But the clause is long and heavy, and *that* no doubt was the reason why many punctators divided it with L'garmeh. If, however, we have a division at all, it ought to be made (as the melody requires) with R'bhia mugrash, לְמַעַן לֹא־יִשְׁלְחוּ הַצַּדִּיקִים. B. M. 2, 3, 4; Ox. 15; Fr.; K. 157, point so.

Job xi. 6. Here too the accentuation of our texts is altogether anomalous²⁴. I would point regularly thus: וְיַגֶּד־לְךָ ׀ תַּעֲלֻמוֹת חָכְמָה כִּי־כִפְלַיִם לְתוּשִׁיָּה וְדַע ׀ כִּי־יַשֶּׁה־לְּךָ אֱלוֹהַּ מֵעֲוֺנֶךָ׃. Many Codd.—B. M. 6; Ox. 19, 100; Hm. 1; De R. 847, 874; &c.—have Athnach; and Ox. 100, Par. 6, K. 155, 246, give the above pointing for the last words.

As before, I should have had many more corrections to propose, had not Heid. and Baer preceded me. Their corrections are for the most part necessary and made on good authority. Few, however, will agree with them in cxviii. 5 (see Baer's note); even Delitzsch does not. And in xxiv. 6 (with the substitution of Azla for Mer'kha), and xcvii. 3, the pointing of common edd. is to be retained.

---

²³ We shall then have a second instance of Pazer before D'chî (transformed). The other is xix. 15 (common edd.).

²⁴ There is no place for Athnach, Shalshéleth follows Olév'yored, and R'bhia mugrash Shalshéleth,— three violations of ordinary rules, not one of which is to be found elsewhere. The simplest correction would be וְדַע, leaving Olév'yored in its place; the anomalies would then all vanish together. But this I have not found in any Cod. Probably Athnach and Olév'yored would then have been brought too close together for the chanting,— with only Sh'va between them.

CHAPTER VIII.

R'bhîa Mugrash.

I TAKE this accent next, because of its intimate connection with those last considered — Athnach and Silluq.

In this chapter we regard it, — as we have regarded the preceding accents, — in its *independent* character, as set over a clause of its own, and determining other accents in that clause. Here all will depend on whether Athnach be present in the verse or not.

I. If Athnach be present, R'bhîa mugrash divides the clause between it and Silluq, and can have one, two, or three words in its own clause (pp. 66–68). The first two cases call for no remark. But when there are *three* words, as in הַצִּילֵנוּ וְכַפֵּר עַל־חַטֹּאתֵינוּ (Ps. lxxix. 9), the clause becomes subject to the rule for the dichotomy, and should be divided by a subordinate pausal accent, — in the ex. given, at הַצִּילֵנוּ (as the sense requires). This division, however, never takes place. Probably the musical relation between Athnach and R'bhîa mugrash was such that a break, or pause, in the melody between them would have produced an unmusical effect. For this or some other reason connected with the melody, *the dichotomy always fails in R'bhîa mugrash's clause, when Athnach precedes.* (The consequence is that, when R'bhîa mugrash is transformed, we have *three* servi between Athnach and Silluq (71. 8).)

II. If Athnach be *not* present, it is because R'bhîa mugrash has, by the law of transformation (69. 12), taken its place in the first or second word before Silluq. Athnach's clause has in consequence become transferred to R'bhîa mugrash. This transfer, however, does not in any way affect the *division* of the same. Great R'bhîa and D'chî appear, just as if Athnach were present. Take for instance, [1] וָאֶשָּׂא כַפַּי אֶל־מִצְוֹתֶיךָ אֲשֶׁר אָהָבְתִּי

---

[1] R'bhîa mugrash retains also (as this ex. shews) the *long vowel* due with Athnach. Sometimes, however, a *short* vowel is found. A list of these exceptional cases is

וְאָשִׂיחָה בְחֻקֶּיךָ׃ (cxix. 48); and comp. xxxi. 23; xxxv. 24; lvii. 9; lxxix. 3; cxv. 18; Job xxxiii. 24, 27 (where R'bhia is repeated). So D'chî, if it would be changed into a servus before Athnach (60. 15), is equally changed before R'bhia mugrash, e. g. גָּמֹל עַל־עַבְדְּךָ אֶחְיֶה (Ps. cxix. 17); and so too, subject to this change of D'chî, L'garmeh appears in the *third* word before R'bhia mugrash (60. 24), e. g. הוּא נֹתֵן ׀ עֹז וְתַעֲצֻמוֹת לָעָם (lxviii. 36)[2]. In short, R'bhia mugrash is the complete representative of the Athnach it has displaced. *The rules for the dichotomy of its clause are*, in consequence—in direct contrast to the practice under § I—*strictly carried out*.

Ons. So striking are the changes which the accent has here undergone in its pausal value, its functions, and (doubtless also) its melody, that the early punctators were misled to the notion that it could no longer be regarded as R'bhia mugrash (proper). The distinguishing sign therefore of R'bhia mugrash was dropped, and the R'bhia-sign alone left to represent it,—an accentuation, which is found in the oldest MSS., and is sanctioned by the Masora itself (see p. 35, note 34)[3]. We must not, however, assign it to the original accentuators, for it is impossible to suppose that, when they were selecting the accentual symbols, they should have designedly represented—in the short verses of the three Books—*three different accents by one and the same sign*. The awkward and confusing nature of such a notation is evident, and

---

quite as necessary as that of the פסוק וסוף באתנח פתחין, and is given (at least for the Pss.) in Ginsburg's Masora, vol. i, p. 653 (taken from the old Cod. B. M. 1). There is, however, one mistake in this list. For lvi. 14, (query) xlvii. 10 must be substituted. We shall no doubt some day find corresponding lists for Prov. and Job.

[2] But it cannot come in the word *immediately before* R'bhia mugrash, as our texts have it in lxxi. 21 and cix. 28. The former passage I point גְּדֻלָּתִי הֶרֶב with B. M. 4; Ox. 17; Par. 4, 30; Erf. 2; &c.; and the latter יַבֹּשׁוּ קָמַי with B. M. 9; Ox. 17; Par. 4, 30; Fr.; &c. L'garmeh in the *second* word, Job iii. 26, must be also corrected, thus: לֹא שָׁלַוְתִּי ׀ וְלֹא שָׁקַטְתִּי ׀ וְלֹא־נָחְתִּי with Ox. 5, 15, 98, 125, 2322, 2323, &c. *Pazer* in the second word, Ps. lviii. 3 (common edd.), has been already corrected by Baer. (Comp. Athnach, notes 8 and 9.)

[3] Ben-Bil. too, all through his treatise, uses this R'bhia, when Athnach fails. Of course common edd. do the same,—retaining, however, often R'bhia mugrash *after* Olév'yored, as in i. 2, contrary to the practice of Codd.

This R'bhia has a *name of its own*—shewing that it was counted quite distinct from the two other R'bhias—in Cod. B. M. 1, viz. סוּר. (See, beside the list referred to in note 1, another list, ib. p. 652.) We must suppose that the punctator, who prepared this Cod., had, like Ben-Asher, another name for *our* Pazer.

has been felt by many writers on the accents[1], indeed by some of the punctators themselves, for I have found R'bhia mugrash regularly marked in the following Codd.: B. M. 2, Ox. 1, Hm. 8, 12, 19, and De R. 2. Jablonski and Baer have introduced it into their texts. No doubt we have a *different kind* of R'bhia mugrash from that under § I (just as we have two different kinds of *R'bhia simplex*); but the essential (musical) character of the accent may well have been retained in the changes it underwent. As foretone to Silluq, it cannot be dispensed with.

Servi of R'bhia Mugrash[5].

R'bhia mugrash has often one and two servi, less frequently three.

1. One servus. This is always Mer'kha, e. g. כִּי אִם־פַּמּוֹ (i. 4); קִשְׁתּוֹ דָרַךְ (vii. 13). If an open syllable precede the tone, it is marked in some Codd. with Ṣinnorith[6], as וּבְמוֹשַׁב לֵצִים (i. 1); וּבְתוֹרָתוֹ יֶהְגֶּה (i. 2).

2. Two servi. The first is Tarcha, the second (as above) Mer'kha, e. g. עֲרִית יְהוָה נֶאֱמָנָה (xix. 8); פָּדִיתָ אוֹתִי יְהוָה (xxxi. 6)[7].

3. Three servi. The second and third remain unchanged; the first is M'huppakh on the first or second syllable,—M'huppakh with Ṣinnorith, if an open syllable precede the tone. The following are the only exx.: זָכַרְתִּי מִשְׁפָּטֶיךָ מֵעוֹלָם ׀ יְהוָה (lxxiii. 1); אַךְ טוֹב לְיִשְׂרָאֵל אֱלֹהִים (cxix. 52); and בְּיוֹם[8] (xviii. 1); כִּי (xlvii. 8); אֲשֶׁר (lxvi. 20); שֶׁלֹּא (cxxix. 7).

---

[1] Eliezer Provenzale (Tor. em. p. 1), Wasmuth (Tab. ii, nota β), Ouseel (p. 6), the author of שערי נעימה (p. 1), Spitzner (p. 210), and Baer (Tor. em. p. 58) all advocate the restoration of R'bhia mugrash to its proper place in the verse.

[5] As before, I refer to Baer's texts for correction of the mistakes of common edd. The most notable of those mistakes occur in Ps. xxxi. 22; lxvi. 20; lxxix. 3; cxvi. 19; Prov. vii. 7; in all which cases there is abundant MS. authority for the necessary corrections.

[6] On this Ṣinnorith see Silluq, p. 69, note 10. The remarks made there apply *mutatis mutandis* here.

[7] A curious distinction is observed in some of the best Codd., and has passed into our printed texts, that *when Athnach precedes* (as in xix. 8 above), *the servi are both Mer'khas*. But this is Ben-Naphtali's punctuation (as the lists of Varr. clearly shew). Ben-Asher has always Tarcha and Mer'kha. And the Masoretic text is bound to conform (as we have often had occasion to observe) to *his* rules. Heid. and Baer therefore have been quite right in discarding the punctuation with two Mer'khas. The old Cod. B. M. 1 does the same. No doubt the punctators who adopted it *imagined* that they were following Ben-Asher. Erf. 3, in a marginal note to xcvi. 2, expressly assigns it to him. *Humanum est errare*.

[8] I point the clause, which has given so much trouble to punctators and accentuologists, thus: בְּיוֹם הַצִּיל־יְהוָה אוֹתוֹ מִכַּף־כָּל־אֹיְבָיו. B.M.12, Ox. 96, and Fr. join מִכַּף with Maqqeph. All is then regular. But the case does not really concern us at all.

EXCEPTIONS. The three passages הִנֵּה מַלְאַךְ־יְהֹוָה סָבִיב לִירֵאָיו (xxxiv. 8); בְּפָרֵשׂ שַׁדַּי מְלָכִים בָּהּ (lxviii. 15); and אַשְׁרֵי שֶׁיֹּאחֵז וְנִפֵּץ אֶת־עֹלָלָיִךְ (cxxxvii. 9); where the first servus indeed is regular, but the introduction of Little Shalshéleth has necessitated a change in the servus immediately preceding R'bhia mugrash.

CHAPTER IX.

GREAT R'BHÎA[1].

GREAT R'BHÎA may stand alone—as indeed may all the accents we have yet to consider—or have two or more words in its clause.

I. If the clause contain only *two* words, the first has generally a *servus*, e. g. שְׁאַל מִמֶּנִּי (Ps. ii. 8); but sometimes—when a slight pause or emphasis is to be marked—the pausal accent, L'garmeh, e. g. אַךְ־בְּצֶלֶם ׀ יִתְהַלֶּךְ־אִישׁ יִקְרָאֵנִי ׀ וְאֶעֱנֵהוּ (xci. 15); (xxxix. 7). Comp. the similar use of D'chî before Athnach (58. 7).

Such cases are not, however, numerous. I have noticed hardly more than a dozen in the whole of the Pss. And even where they occur, we are not bound by them. For Codd. often vary. And this is no more than we should have expected,—some punctators assigning an emphasis or pause to a particular word, which others drop[2].

II. When there are *three or more* words in the clause, the rules for the dichotomy are strictly carried out; and as there is no transformation before Great R'bhia, the division of the clause is always clear and distinct. The accents employed to mark it are L'garmeh and Pazer, the latter with a (relatively)

---

[1] The distinction between Great and Little R'bhia has been already alluded to, p. 12, note. We name them 'Great' and 'Little,' because, where they come together in the same verse (as in xx. 7, cxxxix. 14), we notice that the former has the *greater* pausal value,—the reason being that it marks the *main* dichotomy, whereas the latter marks only a *minor* dichotomy.

[2] In Ps. xv. 3 I would point with various Codd. וּלְשֹׁנוֹ ׀ עַל־לֹא רָגַל, and in xxxix. 4 חַם לִבִּי ׀ בְּקִרְבִּי. For the false accentuation יֹסֶר ׀ לֵץ (Prov. ix. 7) in common edd, point יֹסֵר לֵץ with Codd. and Baer.

greater disjunctive value than the former. The rules for their employment are as follows:

1. L'garmeh, when only *one* dichotomy is required, e. g. כִּי יְהוָֹה ׀ אֹהֵב מִשְׁפָּט (vii. 7); קוּמָה יְהוָה ׀ בְּאַפֶּךָ (xxxvii. 28); עָלֶיךָ ׀ נִסְמַכְתִּי מִבָּטֶן (lxxi. 6). And so, very often, for this is by far the most frequent division of R'bhia's clause[3].

EXCEPTIONS. (α) In a few instances, Pazer comes, with the second word, where we should have expected L'garmeh, as in יְפִיפִיתָ מִבְּנֵי אָדָם (xlv. 3); and in lxxix. 2; xcix. 5 (9); cvi. 23; Job x. 15; xxiv. 14. (The employment of Pazer here is parallel to that of Great R'bhia for D'chi, before Athnach, p. 58 below.)

(β) Again, Pazer *necessarily* takes the place of L'garmeh, when the melody introduces *two servi*[4] before the word on which the dichotomy rests, as in כִּי הִנֵּה הָרְשָׁעִים יִדְרְכוּן קֶשֶׁת (Ps. xi. 2); לוּ יֵשׁ נַפְשְׁכֶם תַּחַת נַפְשִׁי (Job xvi. 4); and in Ps. xliv. 4; lix. 4; lxxxix. 20; xc. 4; xcii. 10; cxxv. 3; Prov. vii. 23; xxx. 33; Job vi. 4. (Here L'garmeh could not have been used, because it admits of only *one* servus.)

2. When a minor dichotomy is required, either before or after the main dichotomy, Pazer marks the latter, and L'garmeh the former, e. g. מְמֻתִים יָדְךָ ׀ יְהוָה מְמֻתִים מֵחֶלֶד (Ps. xvii. 14); נַשְּׁקוּ־בַר פֶּן־יֶאֱנַף ׀ וְתֹאבְדוּ דֶרֶךְ (ii. 12); and so in iv. 2; vii. 6; cxxvii. 2; Prov. xxii. 29; xxiv. 31; &c.[5] The case is similar in Ps. xxxv. 13 and l. 1. Of course a minor dichotomy may *both* precede and follow, as in יִתַּמּוּ חַטָּאִים ׀ מִן־הָאָרֶץ וּרְשָׁעִים ׀ עוֹד אֵינָם (civ. 35), and so in xc. 10, cvi. 48, cxli. 4.

EXCEPTIONS. In xxxv. 13 (some texts), xlii. 9, and lxviii. 7, *two* L'garmehs are used, instead of Pazer and L'garmeh, on the principle that when an accent is *repeated*, it has the second time a less disjunctive value than the first[6].

---

[3] Cases like נְרַנְּנָה ׀ בִּישׁוּעָתֶךָ (xx. 6), בְּגִל ׀ עַל־יְהוָֹת (cxxxvii. 1), come under this head, because two accents in one word produce the same musical effect as if they stood in different words.

[4] For this use of two servi, see chapter on Pazer. It might always have been avoided (as the first word is small) by the employment of Maqqeph.

[5] In Prov. xxiv. 31 Pazer is wanting in common edd.

[6] Pazer itself is repeated, with L'garmeh preceding and following, in an unusually long sentence in Prov. xxx. 4, and I venture to think rightly (comp. the similar repetition of Sinnor, p. 56, note 6), although Ben-Bil. does not allude to it (1. 7). Some Codd., however, and Baer point with R'bhia.

Servus of Great R'bhia.

Great R'bhia has only *one* servus, which is Illuy or M'huppakh,—rarely Mer'kha,—according to the following rules:

1. When L'garmeh or Pazer precedes, the servus is,

α. In most cases, Illuy, e. g. יְפִיפִ֡יתָ יְהֹוָ֣ה ׀ נְחֵ֣נִי בְצִדְקָתֶ֑ךָ (Ps. v. 9); מִבְּנֵ֣י אָדָ֑ם (xlv. 3); and so in i. 3; ii. 12; x. 9; xi. 2; xviii. 16; xxii. 25; and often[7].

β. But M'huppakh with Ṣinnorith, if an open syllable directly[8] precedes the tone, e. g. עֲנֵ֣נִי ׀ אֱלֹהֵ֣י צִדְקִ֑י (iv. 2); לָא֣וֹר יָ֭קוּם רוֹצֵ֣חַ (Job xxiv. 14); comp. Ps. iii. 8; xi. 4; xv. 4; xvii. 3; xix. 5; xcix. 5. In two passages, בִּ֣ישׁוּעָתֶ֑ךָ (xx. 6) and נֶ֣חָמָתִ֑י (Job vi. 10), these accents appear in the *same word* with Great R'bhia, M'huppakh taking the place of Métheg.

2. When neither L'garmeh nor Pazer precedes, the servus is

α. Almost always M'huppakh, as שְׁאַ֣ל מִמֶּ֑נִּי (Ps. ii. 8); יְהֹוָ֣ה אֲדֹנֵ֑ינוּ (viii. 2); and so in x. 12; xx. 7; xl. 12; lii. 9; &c.[9]

Exceptions. אַ֣שְׁרֵי (i. 1; xxxii. 2; xl. 5); יַחְפְּשׂ֣וּ (lxiv. 7, see Norzi); לִפְנֵ֣י (xcviii. 9, see do.); and נִבְהָ֣ל (Prov. xxviii. 22). One loses patience at having to quote such trivialities, which are paraded—at least the first three—in the Masora[10], and supported by Codd. An anomalous accentuation is associated with an anomalous pronunciation! (That both are merely fanciful may be seen from comparing cxxvii. 5; Prov. ii. 4; Ps. xcvi. 13; xxx. 8; where the same forms are given, without any irregularity.)

β. Mer'kha, in the few instances in which another R'bhia precedes, e. g.

---

[7] Most of the mistakes in our texts have been already corrected by Baer. The following remain: בְּאָזְנֵ֑ינוּ (xliv. 2); קָמ֡וּ (liv. 5); שָׁכְבִ֑י (lxxxviii. 6); יָ֣ם (xciii. 4); שֶׁ֣בֶט (cxxv. 3); מֶ֣לֶךְ (cxxxv. 11); תַּ֣חַת (Job xvi. 4); שָׁמְרָ֣ה (xxiv. 15); יֵצֵ֣א (xxxi. 40). For all of these I have found Illuy in many Codd. For lxxvi. 8 and Job xxviii. 3, see pp. 36, 37. In xci. 4 the best texts have D'chi.

[8] I say 'directly,' because, if vocal Sh'va (simple or composite) comes between, as in אֹ֣יְבָי (xxvii. 6) and קָ֣מָתִים (xvii. 14), few Codd. point with Ṣinnorith. In וּמִ֣י (Job xxxiv. 29), the ו is too weak for Ṣinnorith. For lxxi. 3, see p. 36.

[9] The few mistakes in common edd. have been corrected by Baer; but he has himself wrongly introduced Mer'kha in lxxxv. 9; xcvii. 9 (see Norzi's note); and cxxv. 5. In xcv. 7 we must point כִּֽי־ה֤וּא אֱלֹהֵ֗ינוּ, with Ox. 1, 109; Cam. 12; Erf. 3; K. 599, 606.

[10] See Ginsburg's Masora, vol. i, p. 113, 'אשרי ד' רא' פסו' בטע' מארכין וסים וכו'. (The term מארכין applies both to Gaya and Mer'kha, see Frensdorff, *Die Masora magna*, p. 7. The fourth ex. is Prov. viii. 34.) The *Mas. fin.* 11ᵇ gives these exceptions in a form which has completely puzzled Rabbinical scholars, אשרי ד' בטעם ורקא! Has not a line fallen out, and may not the original reading have been ורקא [מארכין ר"פ ג' ברביע ודה] ד' בטעם, or something similar?

שְׁמָעָה יְהוָֹה ׀ צֶדֶק הַקְשִׁיבָה רִנָּתִי (xvii. 1); וַיֹּרֵנִי וַיֹּאמֶר לִי (Prov. iv. 4). I have noticed besides only Ps. lxxviii. 4; Prov. xxvii. 10; and Job xxxii. 5[11].

In Ps. lv. 24 and lxxxvi. 14 R'bhia appears in our texts with *two* servi. I correct the former תּוֹרִדֵם לִבְאֵר־שַׁחַת, with Erf. 1, 2; Fr.; K. 80, 155; De R. 350; and the latter זֵדִים קָמוּ־עָלַי, with Ox. 2323; Par. 30; Ber. 32; K. 80, 94; De R. 412.

CHAPTER X.

Ṣinnor.

The rules for the division of Ṣinnor's clause are the same as those we have just laid down for Great R'bhia.

I. If the clause consist of only *two* words, the first has generally a servus, e. g. חָנֵּנִי יְהוָֹה (Ps. vi. 3)[1]; but in a few instances,—where a slight emphasis is to be marked,—L'garmeh, e. g. הֵמָּה ׀ יֹאבֵדוּ (cii. 27). לָמָּה ׀ תְּרַצְּדוּן (lxviii. 17);

II. 1. When there are *three or more* words in the clause, and only one dichotomy is necessary, L'garmeh is employed to mark it, e. g. גַּם־אֲנִי ׀ אוֹדְךָ בִכְלִי־נֶבֶל (xviii. 7); בַּצַּר־לִי ׀ אֶקְרָא יְהוָֹה (lxxi. 22); אִם־יִשְׁמְרוּ ׀ בָנֶיךָ ׀ בְּרִיתִי (cxxxii. 12)[2].

---

[11] This accentuation seems to have been adopted for the sake of conformity with cases like לִמְשִׁיחוֹ לְדָוִד וּלְזַרְעוֹ (xviii. 51), which (as we have seen, p. 75) are so pointed in Codd. Of the exx. given above, the last is wrongly accented in all texts. Point פִּי־אָיִן with B. M. 7; Par. 6; K. 599; De R. 368, 1014, 1252.

[1] So Prov. xxiv. 24 is better pointed אֹמֵר לְרָשָׁע with B. M. 4; Ox. 17; Ber. 2; De R. 380, 518; and Jabl.

[2] This is the usual division of Ṣinnor's clause,—a single dichotomy, represented by L'garmeh. And here I would observe that this rule for the dichotomy is *most strictly carried out* in Codd., even where we should hardly expect it, as in אֲשֶׁר ׀ לֹא הָלַךְ (i. 1). Hence, the instances of laxity, which are found in the Heid.-Baer text, in i. 1, xxx. 6, xxxi. 21, xxxii. 7, liii. 6, lxii. 10, lxxxiv. 4, cix. 16, cxv. 1, must be all corrected. (In these cases common edd. are generally right.) In his last ed. of the Pss., Baer has introduced another exceptional case, xxvii. 4. But I cannot say that I have been convinced by the reasons adduced in his note.

But when the melody introduces *two servi* before the word, on which the dichotomy falls, as in כִּי כָלְךָ בְיָגוֹן חַיָּי (xxxi. 11), Pazer must be employed, as L'garmeh has never more than *one* servus. The other examples are v. 10; lvi. 14; cxxvi. 2.

2. When a minor dichotomy precedes or follows the main dichotomy, Pazer marks the latter, and L'garmeh the former, e. g. עַל־זֹאת יִתְפַּלֵּל (cxxxii. 11); נִשְׁבַּע יְהוָֹה ׀ לְדָוִד אֱמֶת כָּל־חָסִיד ׀ אֵלֶיךָ (xxxii. 6). The other examples are x. 14; xxxi. 12; xxxix. 13; lxxv. 9; lxxxiv. 4; Job vii. 20.

EXCEPTIONS. In one instance L'garmeh is *repeated :* רַבּוֹת עָשִׂיתָ ׀ אַתָּה ׀ יְהוָֹה אֱלֹהַי (xl. 6)[3]. Comp. the repetition of L'garmeh *after* Pazer in x. 14. The principle has been already explained.

SERVUS OF SINNOR.

Sinnor, like Great R'bhia, has only *one* servus, which is

1. Mer'kha, when the tone is on the *first* syllable, e. g. לֹא הָלַךְ (i. 1); הֲלֹא יֵדְעוּ (xiv. 4); מָלֵא מֶסֶךְ (lxxv. 9).

2. Munach, when on any other syllable, e. g. אָהַבְתָּ צֶּדֶק (xlv. 8); בְּחַסְדְּךָ בָטַחְתִּי (xiii. 6)[4].

EXCEPTIONS. (α) Munach is changed into Mer'kha, if the letter on which it is due is pointed with *Dagesh* (*forte* or *lene*), e. g. רַבִּים אֹמְרִים (iv. 7); מִי־יִתֵּן מִצִּיּוֹן (xiv. 7); יְרַפֵּי עַצְבוֹתָם (xvi. 4)[5]. (β) In two pas-

---

[3] So pointed in all the Codd. I have examined. In common edd. the second Paseq is out of its place, in the Heid.-Baer text omitted.

[4] *Mer'kha* has taken the place of Munach—according to Ben-Bil. (2. 20), the Erf. Mas. (MS.), and *textus receptus*—in חֶלְקָם בַּחַיִּים וּצְפוּנְךָ (xvii. 14), where we have the unique accentuation of *two consecutive Sinnors*. The irregularity is reflected in the servus preceding! [Since writing the above, I have found the same view expressed in a marginal note on the passage in Simson hanaqdan's חבור הקונים (Br. Mus. Or. 1016, p. 75[b]). ואני המניה כ"עם שנשתנה בציבור הב' זרקות רצופות.] Many Codd., however, point regularly with Munach. On a second exception, fixed by the Masora, אַשְׁרֵי אָדָם (Prov. viii. 34), see Great R'bhia (p. 79, note 10).

[5] According to Ben-Asher (Dikd. hat. 24. 22), Ben-Bil. (Arab. text), and *textus receptus*, the Munach is retained in three instances, לַמְנַצֵּחַ אַל־תַּשְׁחֵת (lix. 1); אָנָּה יְהוָֹה (cxvi. 16); and לֹא־תִשָּׂא שָׁוְא (Job vii. 21). One only wonders that it has not been oftener retained. For on what principle Dagesh is made to affect the servus, before Sinnor alone of all the accents, it is impossible to understand. There are between twenty and thirty such passages.

sages, where Paseq follows, Munach is changed into M'huppakh, הָאֵל ׀ לָנוּ (lxviii. 21); עַד־מָתַי ׀ פְּתָיִם (Prov. i. 22).

Ṣinnor is found with *two* servi in מַה רַב טוּבְךָ (Ps. xxiv. 10); מִי הוּא זֶה (xxxi. 20); and אֱלִיהוּא בֶן־בַּרַכְאֵל הַבּוּזִי (Job xxxii. 2)[7]. But in the two first instances, many Codd. have Maqqeph; and the last does not concern us, the irregularity being due to an attempt to force the poetic accentuation on a *prose* passage not at all suited to bear it. There is further the strange accentuation אֶת אֲרַם נַהֲרַיִם וְאֶת־אֲרַם צוֹבָה (Ps. lx. 2), where the first Mer'kha takes the place of Maqqeph[8].

CHAPTER XI.

D'CHÎ.

THE division of D'chî's clause would follow precisely the same rules as those given for Great R'bhîa and Ṣinnor, were it not that the law of transformation often interferes with their application. Those rules—to repeat them once more and apply them to D'chî's clause—are as follows:

I. When there are only *two* words in the clause, the first has always a *servus*, e. g. עַד־אָנָה יְהוָה לֹא־יִתְיַצְּבוּ הוֹלְלִים (v. 6); (xiii. 2). L'garmeh never appears, as in Great R'bhîa's and Ṣinnor's clauses, see next page.

II. 1. When there are *three or more* words in the clause and only *one* dichotomy is necessary, L'garmeh is employed to mark it, e. g. אֲשֶׁר אָמְרוּ ׀ לִלְשֹׁנֵנוּ נַגְבִּיר אֵלָה ׀ פִּידְהוּ מָלֵא (Ps. x. 7); (xii. 5). This is the most common division of D'chî's clause[1].

---

[6] Wrongly pointed in most Codd. and in common edd., thus הָאֵל ׀. But the *Masora parva* to B. M. 12, 16, expressly notes ד' ׀ to במ' ׀ הָאֵל in the text, (see also Baer, Accentuationssystem, p. 494, note 2.) A Concordance shews the three other passages to be Jer. xxxii. 18, Ps. lxxxv. 9, and Dan. ix. 4.

[7] In a treatise on the accents, assigned to Samuel the grammarian, in the Royal Library at Berlin (No. 118, p. 124), the above three instances are allowed, and no more. After quoting them, the writer adds ולא מצאתי יותר בשנים.

[8] It is fixed by the same Masora as the cases named, p. 63, note 24. Here we have *two* instances of את־ארם in the same clause. The one is by this fanciful accentuation *distinguished* from the other, as though the regular accents were not enough for that purpose!

[1] Some mistakes in our texts—Ps. v. 3, xxxii. 5, xcv. 7, Prov. xxviii. 23—I have

EXCEPTIONS. (α) In three passages Pazer appears, with the second word, where we should have expected L'garmeh, יִגְאָלֻהוּ חֹשֶׁךְ וְצַלְמָוֶת (Job iii. 5), and Ps. lxviii. 5, and cix. 16.

(β) In two passages Pazer *necessarily* appears, because *two servi* precede the word on which the dichotomy falls, כִּי לֹא יָבִינוּ אֶל־פְּעֻלֹּת יְהוָה (xxviii. 5) and כִּי פִּי רָשָׁע וּפִי מִרְמָה (cix. 2).

2. When a *second* dichotomy is necessary, both Pazer and L'garmeh appear, כִּי שָׁם ׀ שְׁאֵלוּנוּ שׁוֹבֵינוּ דִּבְרֵי־שִׁיר (cxxxvii. 3); אִם־תִּכְתּוֹשׁ אֶת־הָאֱוִיל ׀ בַּמַּכְתֵּשׁ בְּתוֹךְ הָרִיפוֹת (Prov. xxvii. 22). The other exx. are Ps. v. 12 (corrected p. 89) and cxxii. 4 (ditto). xliv. 3 and xlv. 8 are similar. D'chî's clause is seldom of sufficient length to require more than *one* dichotomy.

The cases in which the above rules are affected by the law of transformation are the following:

First, L'garmeh when due by emphasis or the dichotomy *in the word immediately preceding D'chî*, cannot stand there[2]. It must have been contrary to the laws of melody to bring these two accents together. A servus therefore takes the place of L'garmeh. Thus the emphasis is not marked in עַד־אָנָה ׀ יְהוָה (xiii. 2); and instead of תּוֹרַת יְהוָה ׀ תְּמִימָה (xix. 8),—as the dichotomy requires, comp. יִרְאַת יְהוָה ׀ טְהוֹרָה, ib. 10,—we have תּוֹרַת יְהוָה תְּמִימָה. So also instead of בְּנֵי־אִישׁ עַד־מֶה כְבוֹדִי ׀ לִכְלִמָּה (iv. 3) we find עַד־מֶה כְבוֹדִי לִכְלִמָּה. This rule of transformation is strictly carried out[3]. For other exx. see xiv. 1, xxxv. 15, lv. 19, lvii. 8, lxiii. 2. In xxiii. 6 and lvi. 1, 10, L'garmeh

---

already corrected pp. 51–53, 64. ׀ הִנֵּה must have L'garmeh in Ps. xxxiii. 18, Job iii. 7, v. 17, with various Codd. The Heid.-Baer text has wrongly dropped the dichotomy in Ps. lxix. 3, cxxi. 4, cxxxiv. 1, and cxlv. 12.

Observe that in xxxv. 1, ciii. 1, cxi. 1, cxii. 1, cxlviii. 1, and cxlix. 1, the L'garmeh *does not mark the dichotomy* in D'chî's clause, but is the representative of Olév'yored (34. 13). The same remark applies to the first L'garmeh in xxvii. 1.

[2] This peculiarity has been observed by Christian writers on the accents, as Wasmuth (p. 183) and Spitzner (p. 227). I believe that we have a parallel in the transformation of L'garmeh before Silluq, when Great Shalshéleth precedes (67. 13).

[3] Norzi, Baer, and perhaps Ben-Asher are therefore wrong in xxxi. 3. Other texts are right; comp. lxxi. 3.

would have been *repeated* (comp. 78. 26 and 81. 10), if there had been no transformation[4].

That transformation has really taken place is clear not only from the requirements of the dichotomy, but from the circumstance that the servus preceding is always that which would have come, *had L'garmeh remained in its place.* (See the exx. given above.)

Secondly, although the dichotomy is generally marked, when it falls on the *second* word before D'chî (comp. the exx. under § II), *small words*, standing at the beginning of the clause and accented on the *first* syllable, reject it and take a *servus* (or Maqqeph) instead, thus: שְׁמַע קוֹל תַּחֲנוּנָי (xxviii. 2); טוֹב אִישׁ־אֹהֵב אֲרֻחַת יָרָק (Prov. xv. 17); כָּל פָּעַל יְהוָה (xvi. 4); חָכְמָה (xxix. 3). (It is only when an *emphasis* is made to rest on them that the sign of the dichotomy remains. The few instances are: סֹלּוּ (Ps. lxviii. 5); זֹאת (cix. 20); and זֶה (Job xx. 29).) This peculiarity is shared with D'chî by Pazer and Little R'bhia—minor pausal accents like itself—but not by Great R'bhia and Sinnor. The comparative slightness of the musical pause following was doubtless the cause that the melody did not *dwell* on the small words in question.

It is important to notice that, even in the cases where D'chî undergoes transformation (60. 11), the above rules remain unchanged. L'garmeh appears in the *second* word, when due there, just as if D'chî were present (see 60. 24; 75. 6)[5]. On the other

---

[4] Again, we must be careful to distinguish the cases, in which L'garmeh precedes D'chî, *as the representative of Olév'yored*, for instance, cxiii. 1, cxxxv. 1, cxlvii. 1. To this class belongs also וּבַת־צֹר ׀ בְּמִנְחָה (xlv. 13). L'garmeh proper, even if it were admissible, would give no sense here, and must have been marked with M'huppakh, not Azla, as וּבְרָכֶיךָ ׀ (lxxii. 19). The translation usually adopted would require the accentuation וּבַת־צֹר בְּמִנְחָה. With the accents of the text, וּבַת־צֹר can only be taken as the *vocative* (with Jerome, Hupf., and Hitz.)—comp. Olév'yored with the voc., cxxxvii. 8;—or, which is far less natural, as *nom. absol.* (with Delitzsch). Whether the punctators were right is another question. (No doubt, the L'garmeh in these cases was chanted with a special pause, and the melody began anew with D'chî.)

[5] My readers must not imagine that these are trifling matters, which might be passed over without notice; for, unless we observe them, we shall be in danger of

hand, it is always absent from the *first* word, e. g. לַעֲשׂוֹת רְצוֹנְךָ
[6].(לַעֲשׂוֹת רְצוֹנְךָ ׀ אֱלֹהַי חָפָצְתִּי) (xl. 9; properly אֱלֹהַי חָפַצְתִּי
And small words, like those named above, are not marked by the
dichotomy, unless, as before, an *emphasis* is laid upon them, e. g.
עוּרָה ׀ לָמָּה תִישַׁן ׀ אֲדֹנָי (cxix. 66), but (טוּב טַעַם וָדַעַת לַמְּדֵנִי
(xliv. 24)[7]. It is but rarely that even ordinary edd. exhibit any
deviation[8].

---

falling into such mistakes as Delitzsch has made, in his explanation of the passage:
עַד־אָנָה ׀ תְּשִׂימוּן ׀ קִנְצֵי לְמִלִּין (Job xviii. 2): 'Die Accentuation nimmt עַד־אָנָה (mit
Legarmeh) für sich: Wie lange noch? Macht ein Ende den Worten!' But had
this been the meaning designed by the accentuation, עַד־אָנָה must have been marked
with *R'bhia*. As it is, it is just like ׀ צַל־מָוֶת (xiii. 14).

[6] The double transformation thus introduced completely obscures the division
(logical and syntactical) of Athnach's clause. Still, from the rules laid down, we
need never be at a loss to know what the true division is, and what the sense
designed by the accentuation. Thus in the difficult passage הֲפַכְפַּךְ דֶּרֶךְ אִישׁ וָזָר
(Prov. xxi. 8) we may be sure, from the pointing of the first word, that L'garmeh
has fallen out, and that, if there had been no transformation, the accentuation would
have been הֲפַכְפַּךְ ׀ דֶּרֶךְ אִישׁ וָזָר,—the meaning of which can only be: *Perversus
viæ est vir, et deflectens* (scil. *a recta via*), 'a man' (i. e. one man and another) 'is
perverse in his way, and goes wrong.' My friend Professor Delitzsch will, I am sure,
excuse my again pointing out that his explanation of the accents cannot stand. If,
as he supposes, דֶּרֶךְ אִישׁ was meant to be taken as *subject*, and הֲפַכְפַּךְ as *predicate*,
the pointing must have been הֲפַכְפַּךְ ׀ דֶּרֶךְ אִישׁ וָזָר.

[7] The other similar exx. are ׀ פֶּן (lxi. 9); ׀ שָׁוְא (cxxvii. 1, ïn some Codd.); ׀ שָׁם
(cxxxii.17); and ׀ זֶה (Job xxvii. 13). We have also a slight (emphatic) pause after
כִּי in a few passages, as Ps. xvi. 10, 'For—Thou wilt not leave my soul to Hades;'
and in li. 18; xciv. 14; xcvi. 5; Prov. xxiv. 20; Job v. 6; xx. 20. The ׀ כִּי in these
cases is fixed by the Masora (see Ginsburg, vol. ii, p. 29). In trifling matters of
this kind we may or may not agree with the Masoretes.

[8] There is, however, one passage, Ps. v. 5, in which both printed texts and
Codd. exhibit an extraordinary confusion. The regular pointing would have been
כִּי לֹא־אֵל ׀ חָפֵץ רֶשַׁע ׀ אָתָּה, but we may be satisfied that the original accentuators
shrank from such an accentuation, as suggesting an idea which was nothing short of
blasphemy (comp. Deut. xxxii. 21). To avoid the possibility of such a rendering,
they joined אֵל by Maqqeph to the word following. (Here common edd. are right.)
כִּי לֹא ׀ was then left for the dichotomy. But לֹא is never so separated from its
clause. The dichotomy was therefore moved back (a case certainly without parallel)
to the *third* word from D'chî (transformed), and the accentuation fixed in the form
כִּי ׀ לֹא אֵל־חָפֵץ רֶשַׁע ׀ אָתָּה. If any one wishes for authority for the Tarcha and
Mer'kha, according to rule (62. 10), it is found in B. M. 1; Ox. 15, 17, 71, 96; Par. 3.
׀ כִּי is fixed by the Masora quoted in note 7.

Servi of D'chî.

D'chî may have one or two servi.

1. One servus. This is always Munach, e. g. וּבְדַרְכּ֧וֹ חַטָּאִים (i. 1); בְּרֹ֧ב חַסְדֶּ֑ךָ (v. 8).

This servus may appear, instead of Métheg, in the *same word* with D'chî, e. g. וְהַנֶּ֧פֶשׁ (xxiv. 7); וַיֹּ֧אמְר֛וּ (xciv. 7)[9]. The substitution is, however, subject to certain conditions. Ben-Bil. (4. 14) restricts it to such cases, as those just given, in which Qámeṣ or Chôlem, followed by vocal Sh'va, immediately precedes the tone-syllable. And Codd. agree with him[10]. Other exx. may be seen, in Baer's text, in xxxvii. 38; lxxvi. 7; xcviii. 6; cvi. 28; cvii. 32. (Common edd. generally retain the Métheg.)

2. Two servi. The servus adjoining D'chî remains Munach; the first servus is M'huppakh or Illuy, according to the rules already laid down (pp. 62, 63) for the first of three servi before Athnach.

The presence of *two* servi is—as in the cases of Athnach and Silluq—entirely due to *transformation*. The difference in the case of D'chî is, that the transformation may take place not only in the *first* but in the *second* word: (*a*) in the *first* word (83. 16), in which case L'garmeh leaves its servus behind it, which becomes the first servus of D'chî[11]; (*b*) in the *second* word, if that word has the tone on the *first* syllable (84. 8). The first servus is then

α. M'huppakh, when the tone is on the *first* syllable, e. g. זֶ֣ה עָנִ֧י קָרָ֛א (xxxiv. 7); שְׁמַ֣ע ק֧וֹל תַּחֲנוּנַ֛י (xxviii. 2); and often.

β. M'huppakh, when the tone is on the *second* syllable, and vocal Sh'va does not precede, e. g. עַד־מֶ֣ה כְבוֹדִ֧י לִכְלִמָּ֛ה (iv. 3). The other exx. are [12]אַנְשֵׁ֣י (lv. 24); [13]עַל־יוֹנַ֧ת (lvi. 1); יִשְׂמַ֧ח (lxiv. 11); and יָרֵ֧עַ (Job xxxvii. 5).

---

[9] Of course, in the chanting, the Munach was first given, and then the D'chî on the tone-syllable of the word.

[10] Many Codd. and common edd. have, however, two instances with Chîreq, לְהַצִּ֧ילְךָ (Prov. ii. 12, 16) and מֵהַשְׁפִּ֧ילְךָ (xxv. 7). Comp. the exceptional case, בְּגִירְתָ֧א, under a similar rule in the prose accentuation (משפטי הטעמים, 26ᵇ).

Three manifest blunders (query, in some model Cod.?), הַלְעֹזְבִ֧ים (Prov. ii. 13), הֲמִירְאָ֧תְךָ (Job xxii. 4), and תַּסְמִּינָ֧תְךָ (xxxix. 26), have been magnified by Ben-Asher (Dikd. hat. 26. 20) into *exceptions!* But Ben-Bil. does not accept these exceptions, for he makes the second ex. a case of *regular pointing*, הֲמִירְאָ֧תְךָ.

[11] And as Athnach takes over all D'chî's accents, without any change, when D'chî is transformed, we now understand how it is that the servus of L'garmeh, the first of two servi of D'chî, and the first of three servi of Athnach, *are all fixed by precisely the same rules* (the transformation under (*b*) not making any difference in those rules).

[12] The vocal Sh'va is here so slight, that it is not taken into account.

[13] So I point with Ox. 15, 72, 98; K. 538; De R. 331, 1261.

γ. Illuy, when the tone is on the second syllable, *vocal Sh'va preceding*,— or when it is on the *third* syllable, e. g. יְשַׁלַּח בָּהֶם עָרֹב (Ps. lxxviii. 45); נֶאֶסְפוּ עָלַי נֵכִים (xxxv. 15); הָיְתָה־לִּי דִמְעָתִי לֶחֶם (xlii. 4). There are only two other examples[14], שִׂמְחֹה (xxxii. 11); מַלְכִּי (lxxii. 10).

δ. M'huppakh with Ṣinnorith, when an open syllable comes directly before the tone, e. g. אָמַר נָבָל בְּלִבּוֹ (xiv. 1; liii. 2). The other exx. are, יָבֵשׁ (vi. 11); תּוֹרַת (xix. 8); פִּקּוּדֵי (xix. 9); וְהָרֵק (xxxv. 3); פָּדָה (lv. 19); יָשׁוּבוּ (lvi. 10); נָכוֹן (lvii. 8); נָתַתָּה (lx. 6); עֲלוֹת (lxvi. 15); וְהָשֵׁב (lxxix. 12); יְהֹוָה (lxxxiv. 9); וַיְשִׂימוּ (cix. 5); זָרַח (cxii. 4); טָמַן (Prov. xix. 24; xxvi. 15); לָבֵשׁ (Job vii. 5); גֵּרִי (xix. 15); and צָעִיר (xxxii. 6).

3. Of three servi there is only one example[15], כִּי יֹסִיף עַל־חַטָּאתוֹ פֶשַׁע (Job xxxiv. 37), where כִּי (Mer'kha instead of Maqqeph) is fixed by the Masora; see Athnach, p. 63, note 23.

CHAPTER XII.

Pazer.

Pazer's proper office is (as we have seen) to mark the major dichotomy in the clauses of Great R'bhîa, Ṣinnor, and D'chî. It is particularly common before Great R'bhîa.

Its own clause is always short, never exceeding four words. One disjunctive therefore—L'garmeh—generally suffices.

I. This disjunctive may appear, when there is a slight emphasis, in a clause consisting of only *two* words, as in עַל־כֵּן ׀ מְשָׁחֲךָ (Ps. xlv. 8); [1]אֵל ׀ אֱלֹהִים (l. 1); and xxxv. 13 (some Texts) and xliv. 3 (ditto). These are the only examples.

II. Instances of the dichotomy with *three* or *four* words are: יִתַּמּוּ חַטָּאִים ׀ מִן־הָאָרֶץ (lxxxiv. 4); גַּם־צִפּוֹר ׀ מָצְאָה בַיִת

---

[14] And these some Codd. point with M'huppakh, שִׂמְחֹה, מַלְכִּי,—owing to the slightness of the vocal Sh'va.

[15] The Heid.-Baer text has indeed two other exx. in Ps. xxiii. 6 and lvi. 1; but common edd. have there rightly L'garmeh.

[1] Most edd. have here a stupid mistake, אֱלֹהִים (like וְהִנֵּה Prov. xxiv. 31). But Pazer appears in the more correct texts of Opit., Jabl., Mich., and Heid.-Baer.

(civ. 35); בָּרוּךְ יְהֹוָה ׀ אֱלֹהֵי יִשְׂרָאֵל (cvi. 48). If we make the corrections, suggested at the end of this chapter, the rules for the dichotomy will be found carefully carried out[2].

The only exceptions will then be,—as in the cases of D'chî and Little R'bhîa,—when the word on which it should fall (at the beginning of the clause) is a *monosyllable*, viz. כִּי (v. 10, and often); גְּעָר (lxviii. 31); אָז (cxxvi. 2); עַד (Prov. vii. 23); and לוֹ (Job xvi. 4).

Servi of Pazer.

1. When there is *one*, it is Galgal, e. g. מָצְאָה בַיִת (Ps. lxxxiv. 4); אֱלֹהֵי יִשְׂרָאֵל (cvi. 48). In אוֹרִיעֲךָ (xxxii. 5) and וַתִּשְׁקְקָה (lxv. 10) Galgal appears, instead of Métheg, in the same word with Pazer.

Exceptions. Galgal is changed into M'huppakh, in the two passages לִדְבַר ׀ רָע (cxli. 4) and אֵפוֹא ׀ בְּנִי (Prov. vi. 3, see below), because of Paseq following.

2. When there are *two* servi, the second remains Galgal; the first is (a) M'huppakh, when it falls on the *first letter* of the word, as כִּי אֵין־בְּפִיהוּ (Ps. v. 10); (β) Azla on the *second letter* and further. Most of the passages, in which Azla occurs in our texts, I have ventured to correct (see *Corrigenda*, next page). But we may retain it, with Ben-Asher, in עֲשֵׂה־זֹאת ׀ גְּעָר[3] חַיַּת קָנֶה (lxviii. 31), and in בְּנִי ׀ אֵפוֹא (Prov. vi. 3), where the slight pause made by Paseq may be taken to mark the dichotomy[5].

---

[2] Ordinary texts must be further corrected in lxv. 10; cxxvii. 2; Prov. xxiii. 29; and the Heid.-Baer text in xl. 13 and cxxvii. 3, where the former are right.

[3] This is the only instance—even if we retain all Ben-Asher's examples—of Azla on the second *letter* (as opposed to the second *syllable*); but the rule is found in the prose accentuation for the corresponding servus of Pashta and T'bhîr (see משטמ׳ הטעמים, 25ᵃ and 29ᵃ), and may be accepted here.

[4] So I point with B. M. 9, Ox. 96, Cam. 25, Par. 10, De R. 413, 941, &c. See also chapter on Paseq, § IV.

[5] Galgal is strangely interchanged in ordinary texts with M'huppakh (comp. v. 12 with xiii. 3; xxviii. 5 with xliv. 4; lvi. 14 with lix. 4),—a source of great perplexity to Christian writers on the accents. I have already drawn attention (p. 57, note 9) to the confusion between these accents before Olév'yored. The explanation is the same here. Ben-Naphtali's pointing (M'huppakh) has found its way (more or less) into some Codd. and printed texts. But Bomb. 1, and of course Heid. and Baer,—to say nothing of Codd., as B. M. 4, 5, 7; Ox. 1; Cam. 13, &c.,—have regularly Ben-Asher's accentuation, Galgal.

Corrigenda.

Most texts, following Ben-Asher[6], have excluded the dichotomy from the following passages. But as no reason can be assigned for its omission, and it is actually found in many Codd., I do not hesitate to propose its insertion:

Ps. v. 12.   וְיִשְׂמְח֣וּ ׀ כָּל־ח֣וֹסֵי בָ֑ךְ (Vat. 468, K. 155, De R. 2, &c.);

Ps. xiii. 3.   עַד־אָ֗נָה ׀ אָשִׁ֥ית עֵצ֡וֹת (Vat. 468, K. 155, De R. 2, &c.);

Ps. xxii. 25.   כִּ֤י לֹֽא־בָזָ֨ה ׀ וְלֹ֪א שִׁקַּ֡ץ (Ox. 98, Par. 4, Fr., &c.);

Ps. xxiii. 4.   גַּ֤ם כִּֽי־אֵלֵ֨ךְ ׀ בְּגֵ֪יא צַלְמָ֡וֶת (Ox. 98, Par. 4, Fr., &c.);

Ps. xxvii. 6.   וְעַתָּ֨ה ׀ יָר֪וּם רֹאשִׁ֡י (Ox. 79, 111; Bomb. 1, &c.);

Ps. xxxi. 12.   מִכָּל־צֹרְרַ֨י ׀ הָיִ֪יתִי חֶרְפָּ֡ה (B. M. 1, 8, K. 525, &c.);

Ps. xxxii. 5.   חַטָּאתִ֨י ׀ אוֹדִ֪יעֲךָ֡ (Ox. 98, De R. 2, K. 525, &c.);

Ps. cvi. 38.   וַיִּשְׁפְּכ֨וּ ׀ דָּ֪ם נָקִ֡י (Par. 4, Erf. 2, K. 246, &c.);

Ps. cxxii. 4.   שֶׁשָּׁ֨ם ׀ עָל֪וּ שְׁבָטִ֡ים (Ox. 93, 111, K. 246, &c.);

Ps. cxxiii. 2.   הִנֵּ֨ה ׀ כְּעֵינֵ֪י עֲבָדִ֡ים (B. M. 8, Par. 4, K. 246, &c.);

Ps. cxxxviii. 2.   אֶשְׁתַּחֲוֶ֨ה ׀ אֶל־הֵיכַ֪ל קָדְשְׁךָ֡ (B. M. 13, Ox. 13, 93, &c.);

Prov. xxvii. 10.   רֵ֭עֲךָ ׀ וְרֵ֣עַ אָבִ֡יךָ (B. M. 8, Erf. 2, Bomb. 1, &c.)

N. B. Writers on the accents have quietly adopted the above corrections as necessary, see Ouseel, p. 94, and Spitzner, p. 231. The former simply remarks *Psiq nonnunquam excidit!*

Beside the above, I propose to correct:

Ps. lix. 6.   וְאַתָּ֤ה יְהֹוָֽה־אֱלֹהִ֨ים ׀ צְבָא֡וֹת. (The first dichotomy at וְאַתָּ֤ה[7] with B. M. 7, Ox. 12, Par. 30, Fr., De R. 350, &c.; for the second, see p. 96. 18.)

And Ps. xc. 10.   יְמֵֽי־שְׁנוֹתֵ֨ינוּ ׀ בָּהֶ֡ם ׀ שִׁבְעִ֨ים שָׁנָ֜ה. Here a second dichotomy is needed at בָּהֶם, and is indicated by Codd.,—as Vi. 3, De R. 2,

---

[6] We have already seen that Ben-Asher is no infallible authority. Such variations, as those here pointed out—which he of course merely copied from texts before him—may have originated in the desire to make the *melody* more easy and flowing, a result which was perhaps attained by the substitution of Azla for L'garmeh. But at least consistency should have been observed. If the change was made in xxxi. 12, why not in lxxxiv. 4? If in xxii. 25 and xxiii. 4, why not also in lxxi. 3 and cxxvii. 2? Such irregularity of itself points to mistakes made. The original accentuators could hardly have been so inconsistent.

[7] Not as in the Heid.-Baer text at יְהֹוָֽה ׀. The two words יְהֹוָה אֱלֹהִים must be kept together,—either by Maqqeph or by a conjunctive accent,—as in lxxx. 5, 20; lxxxiv. 9.

K. 246,—which point שָׁנָה שִׁבְעִים בָּהֶם; but no Cod. has a second L'garmeh. Some Codd. have L'garmeh after בָּהֶם, but then it fails before. We need it *both* before and after. Comp. the division in Job xxviii. 5, אֶרֶץ מִמֶּנָּה יֵצֵא לָחֶם (Baer's text). For the two L'garmehs, comp. Ps. xl. 6 (81. 10).

CHAPTER XIII.

LITTLE R'BHÎA.

THE division of Little R'bhîa's clause is of the simplest character. We have never more than a single dichotomy, represented by L'garmeh[1]: אֱלֹהִים ׀ אֵלִי אָתָּה (lxiii. 2); שֵׁם כְּבוֹדוֹ וּבָרוּךְ (lxxii. 19); הֲתָעִיף עֵינֶיךָ בּוֹ (Prov. xxiii. 5); מִי זֶה ׀ מַעְלִים עֵצָה (Job xlii. 3); לֹא לָנוּ ׀ יְהוָה (Ps. cxv. 1 with Codd.)[2]

The dichotomy fails—as with D'chî and Pazer—in the case of small words, standing at the beginning of the clause[3] and accented on the first syllable, as כִּי in כִּי אִם־בְּתוֹרַת יְהוָה (i. 2); לֹא (lii. 9); אֲשֶׁר (cxxvii. 5); כָּל (cxxxv. 6); עַל (cxxxix. 14); מִי (Job xxxviii. 41). Still, if the punctators wished to lay an emphasis on these small words, they were at liberty to retain the dichotomy, as in לְמַעַן (Ps. lxviii. 24); כִּי (Prov. xxiii. 7); and בֵּן (xxiv. 14; xxx. 20).

Twice L'garmeh comes, with a certain emphasis, in a clause of only *two* words: אָוֶן ׀ יַחְשֹׁב (Ps. xxxvi. 5, comp. xii. 3) and נַעַר ׀ הָיִיתִי (xxxvii. 25).

---

[1] Little R'bhîa's clause rarely contains more than *three* words. Only in lxxi. 20, xc. 17, Job xxxii. 6 (prose), and xlii. 3 are there *four*. The clause being small, one disjunctive is all that is required.

[2] The rules for the dichotomy are strictly observed. I have no corrections to propose, except that in Ps. lv. 13 I would introduce it for the sake of emphasis, כִּי לֹא־אוֹיֵב ׀ יְחָרְפֵנִי, with Ox. 71, 118; Hm. 7; Cop. 2; Vi. 2. It must be replaced in Baer's text, in cxxxviii. 7 and Prov. xxiii. 5.

[3] In one case, וַיְהִי ׀ נָעֵם אֲדֹנָי אֱלֹהֵינוּ (xc. 17), it is the *second* dichotomy that fails.

Servi of Little R'bhia.

Little R'bhia may have one or two servi.

α. If there is one servus, it is Mer'kha, as אֲנִי שְׁכַבְתִּי (iii. 6); אֱלֹהִים ׀ דִּבֶּר בְּקָדְשׁוֹ (lx. 8); and often.

β. If there are two servi, the first is M'huppakh, the second as before Mer'kha, e. g. אִם־בְּתוּרַת יְהֹוָה חֶפְצוֹ כִּי (i. 2). This additional servus occurs properly only in the case of the small words named above, כִּי, אֲשֶׁר, כָּל, &c.[4]

The two servi appear, however, occasionally in the *same word*, when the syllable immediately preceding the tone is an open one, e. g. יָגֵל לִבִּי (xiii. 6); וַיֵּשֶׁב קֶדֶם (lv. 20). And so in xxvii. 11; l. 3, 23; lxviii. 36; lxxix. 13; Prov. vii. 22. This rule—which reminds one of the introduction of Ṣinnorith before the servus (Mer'kha) of R'bhia mugrash (76. 14)—was perhaps observed by Ben-Asher[5], but is only very partially regarded by the punctators; nor does Ben-Bil. or any other early authority on the accents allude to it. Even Baer, who recognises it, seems to count it more honoured in the breach than the observance. But a rule that is only half observed, is no rule at all. We may then dispense with it (as some Codd. do), even in the case of the few words (not more than nine or ten) to which it has been applied.

CHAPTER XIV.

L'garmeh

marks, where it occurs, the last division (sometimes the last *two* divisions) in a clause. With it the continuous dichotomy comes to an end. L'garmeh has, in consequence, no disjunctive accent in its own clause[1].

---

[4] Exceptions in our texts are the two prose passages, Ps. xviii. 1 and Job xxxii. 6. In the former, however, we must, no doubt, point לְעֶבֶד ׀ יְהֹוָה לַמְנַצֵּחַ, with Ox. 9; K. 164, 224; De R. 940. (Many other Codd. have *M'huppakh* L'garmeh.) The latter ought properly to be divided (as many Codd. do divide it) into *two* verses. Little R'bhia would then be changed into R'bhia mugrash.

[5] See the הלופי נקוד to Ps. l. 23 and Job xviii. 4.

[1] One is sometimes in doubt—as in דּוֹם ׀ לַיהֹוָה (xxxvii. 7); אֵל ׀ אֱלֹהִים (l. 1)—whether Paseq or L'garmeh is intended by the accentuation. A correct list of the Paseqs would therefore be of service. This some Codd. (as B. M. 1, 15; Pet.; K. 542) undertake to furnish. Many more (as B. M. 1; Ox. 15, 71; Par. 107; Erf. 3; Vat.

The two forms of this accent are one and the same in disjunctive value. They differ only musically. The laws for the selection of the one or the other are as follows:

1. When a servus precedes, Azla L'garmeh is always used, e. g. ׀ יְהֹוָה יְצַוֶּה (Ps. xlii. 9); ׀ כֵן עָשָׂה לֹא (cxlvii. 20).

2. When there is no servus,—if the tone fall on the *first* or *second* syllable, M'huppakh L'garmeh is employed; if on the *third or further*, Azla L'garmeh.

  a. On the *first* syllable, e. g. ׀ כִּי (v. 5); ׀ עֲנֵנִי (iv. 2); ׀ חֶרֶב (xxxvii. 14)[2].

  β. On the *second* syllable, as: ׀ יֵשֵׁב (x. 8); ׀ יְהֹוָה[3] (v. 9); ׀ אוֹדְךָ (lxxi. 22); ׀ גַּם־אֲנִי (xx. 6); ׀ גְּרֹנָהּ (xliv. 2); ׀ אֱלֹהִים[3] (lxxxvi. 12); ׀ לַמְדֵנִי (cxliii. 10)[4].

  γ. On the *third* syllable and further, as: ׀ יִתְיַצְּבוּ (ii. 2); ׀ בְּהִתְהַלֶּכְךָ (Prov. vi. 22); ׀ מִן־הָעוֹלָם (cvi. 48).

EXCEPTIONS. The L'garmeh between R'bhia mugrash and Silluq (p. 67) is always M'huppakh L'garmeh. Hence we have ׀ מִשָּׁמַיִם (Ps. cii. 20) and ׀ וְהִתְבּוֹנֵן (Job xxxvii. 14).

SERVUS OF L'GARMEH.

L'garmeh has only *one* servus, which is M'huppakh or Illuy, according to rules, which we are already familiar with (see pp. 62 and 86):

  a. M'huppakh, when the tone is on the *first* syllable, e. g. אֲשֶׁר יַחֵן ׀ פִּרְיוֹ (Ps. i. 3); סִתְרוֹ ׀ חֹשֶׁךְ יָשֶׁת (xviii. 12); and very often.

EXCEPTIONS. The two parallel passages, תֹּאמַרְנָה ׀ עַצְמֹתַי כָּל (xxxv.

6; K. 94, 446; De R. 2, 319, 331, 775, 1261) seek to smooth matters for the Reader by marking in the margin לג for L'garmeh, and פס for Paseq. But as ἀκρίβεια is not the forte of Jewish punctators, neither this notation nor the lists they give us are by any means trustworthy. The most correct Paseq-list I have seen is in Bomb. 2 (see p. 96).

[2] ׀ אָז (lvi. 10) furnishes a curious instance of the way in which a trifling error perpetuates itself. It is found so pointed in almost all Codd. But B. M. 8, Ox. 96, Cam. 25, K. 434, 525, De R. 350 are right, ׀ אָז.

[3] So Texts and Codd., almost without exception. Yet Baer points always with Azla L'garmeh.

[4] Recognised exceptions are ׀ לְדָוִד, the first word in certain Pss.,—where Azla L'garmeh stands for Olév'yored, see p. 34 a.

10) and כָּל־אֲחֵי־רָשׁ ׀ שְׂנֵאֻהוּ (Prov. xix. 7), in which Mer'kha has taken the place of Maqqeph[5].

β. M'huppakh also, when the tone is on the *second* syllable and vocal Sh'va does not precede, e. g. מִפִּי עוֹלְלִים ׀ (Ps. viii. 3); יֵשְׁלַח מִשָּׁמַיִם ׀ (lvii. 4); and often[6].

In the following cases the punctators found the vocal Sh'va so slight, that they took no account of it: שִׂמְעָה (xvii. 1; l. 7); מִקְצֵה (xix. 7); יִרְאַת (ib. 10); יְרָאֵי (xxii. 24); שְׁפָטֵנִי (xliii. 1); וַיְגָרֶשׁ (lxxviii. 55); בְּפָרֹחַ (xcii. 8); אִמְרֵי (xcvi. 10); לִפְנֵי (ib. 13); שְׁמֹרֵנִי (cxl. 5). It is not necessary to add any of these cases to the mistakes enumerated in note 7 below.

γ. Illuy, when the tone is on the second syllable, *vocal Sh'va preceding*,— or when it is on the *third* syllable, e. g. יֶאֱרֹב בַּמִּסְתָּר ׀ (x. 9); נִכְסְפָה וְגַם־כָּלְתָה ׀ (lxxxiv. 3); יְצַוֶּה יְהוָֹה ׀ (ib. 9); צָמְאָה נַפְשִׁי ׀ (xlii. 3); וַיִּרְעֵם בַּשָּׁמַיִם ׀ (xviii. 14). and יֹגְמָר־נָא רַע ׀ (vii. 10); The exx. are far too numerous to quote in full[7].

EXCEPTIONS. יִרְדֹּף (vii. 6) and שִׁמְעָה (xxxix. 13),—an anomalous *accentuation* joined to an anomalous *vocalization!* (comp. similar cases before R'bhia, p. 79. 17.) No doubt מְמֹתִים (xvii. 14) would have been accented regularly, but that another מְמֹתִים immediately follows, and the fancy was to *distinguish* one from the other by their accents! We have had a parallel instance, p. 82, note 8[8].

δ. M'huppakh with Ṣinnorith, when an open syllable directly pre-

---

[5] Fixed by the *Masora magna* to Ps. xxxv. 10. L'garmeh is often followed immediately by another pausal accent, but these are the only instances, in which כֹּל precedes. And it really seems as if, on this account, they were made to pair off, attention being drawn to them by an anomalous accentuation! It is impossible to hold the original accentuators responsible for such trifling.

[6] So Codd. point rightly יִהְיוּ לְרָצוֹן ׀ (xix. 15), the Sh'va not being pronounced. (See Baer, *Die Metheg-setzung*, in Merx's Archiv, vol. i, p. 65.)

[7] The mistakes of common edd.—in xxxii. 6; lv. 24; lxv. 14; lxxix. 13; xciii. 3; cvi. 1 (and elsewhere); cxli. 5; cxlvii. 8; Prov. xxvii. 22; Job x. 17—have been corrected by Heid. and Baer, with more or less support from Codd. וְאִם־בָּא (Ps. xli. 7) must be also corrected with Erf. 3 (other Codd. have *Munach inf.*) But for בְּקֹל (xxvii. 2); כַּאֲשֶׁר (xlviii. 9); וַאֲנִי (lxix. 14); בְּרָבוּ (ciii. 22, comp. קָרְאוּ Job xvi. 10); and לְרַשֹּׁוֹת (cxlix. 9), the testimony of Codd. fails altogether. In fact, the punctators never rightly apprehended the rules for the servus of L'garmeh. Ben-Bil. does not venture to give them. Simson (Br. Mus. Or. 1016, p. 76ᵇ) confesses the general ignorance: ולא נתברר לנו טעם משרתיו למה זה ככה ולמה זה ככה. Only Samuel the grammarian (Berl. 118, p. 126) makes a feeble attempt to supply the deficiency. No wonder then that Codd. are full of blunders.

[8] On the still more extraordinary pointing with Ṭarcha, cxxv. 3, see p. 73.

cedes the tone, c. g. בְּתוֹבָחוֹת עַל־עָוֹן ׀ קוּמָה יְהוָה (iii. 8); ׀ (xxxix. 12);
וַיִּרְדּוּ בָם יְשָׁרִים ׀ (xlix. 15); and very often[9].

The servus may appear in the *same word* with L'garmeh, instead of Métheg, c. g. וְלָרָשָׁע ׀ (l. 16); וַיִּירְאוּ ׀ (lxv. 9); מַה־תִּשְׁתּוֹחֲחִי ׀ (xlii. 6). The cases are not, however, numerous in which the change can take place; and in several of these it is lacking in Codd. The one pointing was simply more musical than the other.

In only two passages has L'garmeh more than *one* servus: כִּי נָבָר
עָלֵינוּ ׀ חַסְדּוֹ (cxvii. 2); כִּי רָדַף אוֹיֵב ׀ נַפְשִׁי (cxliii. 3); where Mer'kha has taken the place of Maqqeph (comp. כָּל above). These passages are fixed by the Masora to cxliii. 3; see p. 63, note 23.

CHAPTER XV.

SHALSHÉLETH.

I. ALL that it is necessary to say about Great Shalshéleth has been already given, pp. 67, 68. Its presence in the latter half of the verse was there accounted for. It is distinguished from Little Shalshéleth by the Paseq-sign attached to it, which constitutes it a disjunctive accent[1].

II. But what reason led to the introduction of Little Shalshéleth, as a conjunctive accent, we can only conjecture. It occurs eight times[2]; once before Silluq—virtually before Athnach (transformed) —(p. 72); four times before Athnach (p. 63); and three times

---

[9] It is only very rarely that this accentuation is adopted, when vocal Sh'va intervenes, as אֱרָב (Ps. x. 9) in B. M. 1, Ox. 6, Par. 3; בְּצָרָה (xxiii. 5) in B. M. 1, Par. 3, De R. 1261; צָרָי (Job xvi. 10) in B. M. 1, K. 446, De R. 1261.
One strange mistake occurs in common edd. הַתָּצִיץ for הֲתָעִיף (Prov. xxiii. 5).

[1] Common edd. are, however, quite indifferent to this distinction, see Ps. x. 2; xiii. 2, 3; lxv. 2; lxviii. 15; &c.

[2] These eight passages are fixed by Ben-Bil. (3. 2), the Erf. Mas. (MS.), and the *Masora parva* to Ox. 96 (ח׳ שלשלן דלא פסק). Seven of them are found in the *first half* of the verse; and it has sometimes seemed to me that they were intended as a kind of counterpart to the seven Shalshéleths that appear in the *first half* of the verse in the prose Books. The 8th ex., which comes in the *latter half* of the verse (Ps. iii. 3), would then stand *per se*.

before R'bhia mugrash—where again Athnach has been transformed—(p. 77)³. In Ps. xxxiv. 8 and cxxxvii. 9 it interferes with the introduction of the dichotomy, and perhaps this circumstance marks it as of *later date* than the other accents. The later date is, as it seems to me, further indicated by the absence of a list of the passages in which it occurs from the *Masora magna*.

It is unnecessary to say anything about its servi, as it occurs so seldom. The servi of Great Shalshéleth, in the few instances in which it has them,—Ps. xlii. 2 (see p. 72), lxxxix. 2; Job xxxii. 6, xxxvii. 12,—are the same as those of R'bhia mugrash, for which it stands.

CHAPTER XVI.

Paseq.

THE form of Paseq is a short perpendicular line between two words. (In Codd. it is just like Métheg and Silluq.) The name פָּסֵק, 'cutting off,' i.e. separating, the one word from the other,—used e.g. by Ben-Asher and Ben-Bil'am,—is more suitable than that commonly employed, פָּסִיק, 'cut off,' separated.

Placed after Shalshéleth, Azla, and M'huppakh, it transforms them into disjunctive accents, with new and distinctive melodies.

It might have been well perhaps (I speak, of course, only of the three Books) if it had been confined to this use. There was no necessity for employing it elsewhere; and much confusion would have been avoided.

But the accentuators thought otherwise, and they have introduced it into some 57 other passages, for reasons that are not always clear and have not, as yet, been satisfactorily explained[1]. In these passages Paseq marks a slight pause between two words

---

[3] Little Shalshéleth then *precedes* Athnach (proper or transformed), whereas Great Shalshéleth always *follows* it.

[1] Ben-Asher's rules (Dikd. hat. § 28) do not meet all the cases that occur; and Norzi, who explains where all is clear, passes over, *sicco pede*, most of the passages in which there is any difficulty.

that would, without it, be joined by the accents[2]. Properly speaking, therefore, it changes every conjunctive accent, with which it is associated, into a disjunctive. But as it has no modulation of its own, it is not counted among the accents.

The most correct (printed) list of the Paseqs is that given in the 2nd ed. of Bomberg's Rabbinical Bible (*Mas. fin.* letter ס), and copied thence into Buxtorf's Rabbinical Bible (ditto, p. 61).

This list I have been able to compare with four MS. lists, found in the following Codd., B. M. 1, 15; Pet.; and K. 542. B. M. 1 and Pet. are two of the *oldest*, B. M. 15 and K. 542 two of the *youngest*, MSS. Together, therefore, they may be taken to cover the whole ground. And as they nearly agree, it is possible to ascertain with approximate accuracy what the Paseqs were, which the early Masoretes appointed. After careful comparison, the only change I find it necessary to propose in the Bomb. list (which is identical with B. M. 15[3]) is the omission of Ps. lix. 6, lxviii. 36,—which do not appear in the two older Codd.,—and lxxxiv. 4, which appears only in B. M. 15. (Ps. lix. 6 is pointed with L'garmeh in many Codd., as B. M. 2, 11, 13, Ox. 6, 15, 71; lxviii. 36 is evidently false; and for lxxxiv. 4 Paseq fails in Codd. generally.)[4] Having deducted these three, I give the other examples under the heads that follow.

Various reasons led to the introduction of Paseq.

I. Most frequent in the three Books, is the use of what we may call *Paseq euphemisticum*, which occurs before or after the Divine Name, to prevent its being joined, in the reading, to a

---

[2] Of course, it is not needed after a *pausal* accent (comp. e. g. Ps. xviii. 50 with 2 Sam. xxii. 50, or Job xx. 29 with xxvii. 13), although common edd. often place it there, as in Ps. v. 13; x. 14; lv. 20; lxxxvi. 1; ciii. 20; &c. Even Olshausen, § 43, has been misled by this false pointing. But common edd., like many Codd., go all wrong in the matter of Paseq, placing it where it should not occur, and omitting it— e. g. in v. 2, 5; xviii. 50; lxvi. 18; lxxxv. 9—where it should occur.

As Paseq marks a pause, it is followed by *Dagesh lene*, in אִם ׀ בְּנִי (Prov. vi. 3).

[3] This identity led me to suspect that the Bomb. list was derived from this very Cod. And on examination I found that the Cod. *came from Venice*, where the Bomberg press was established. It is the one briefly described by Kennicott, No. 572. When one takes into account the rarity of the Paseq-lists in MSS., the circumstantial evidence may suffice, I think, to establish my point.

[4] Baer's additions of xxii. 2, xxxvi. 7, xxxvii. 7, l. 1, lv. 20, lxix. 34, lxxxvi. 1, cxviii. 27, Job vii. 20 are not found in any of the lists, and must therefore be rejected. Unfortunately, the list printed in Ginsburg's Masora, vol. i, p. 650, is of no value.

word, which—in the opinion of the accentuators—it was not seemly, משום כבוד השם, to bring into contact with it, e. g. מְשַׂנְאֶיךָ ׀ יְהוָה (cxxxix. 21), נֵאֲצוּ ׀ אֹיְבֵי ׀ יְהוָה (x. 13); גֵּאֶה ׀ רָשָׁע ׀ אֱלֹהִים

Thus it was counted unbecoming to speak of 'the heathen' (xviii. 50; lvii. 10; lxvi. 8; lxvii. 4, 6; cviii. 4; cxiii. 4); of 'the wicked' (xciv. 3; cxxxix. 19; Job xxvii. 13); of 'God's enemies' (Ps. lxxxix. 52) or 'the Psalmist's enemies' (lix. 2; cxliii. 9), who were one and the same; of 'other gods' (lxxxvi. 8), or 'a plurality,' רַבִּים (cxix. 156),—in the same breath with the Divine Name. (In one instance, v. 5, the personal pronoun takes the place of the Divine Name.) So also verbs signifying 'to abominate' (v. 7), 'to despise' (x. 3), 'to destroy, overthrow' (lviii. 7, Prov. xv. 25), 'to abuse' (Ps. lxxiv. 18), 'to reject' (lxxvii. 8),—even when the Divine Being Himself is the subject,—are separated by a pause from the Divine Name following. The verb 'to sleep' (xliv. 24) and the adj. 'sleeping' (lxxviii. 65),—as conveying a strongly anthropomorphic idea,—are treated in the same way. For the fanciful reasons that commended themselves to the punctators for the employment of Paseq in lxxxix. 9, 50, cxix. 52, I must refer to Norzi's notes.

Paseq is otherwise very loosely employed. Thus we have,

II. *Paseq euphonicum*, introduced in a few cases, to insure distinct pronunciation, when one word ends, and the next begins, with the *same letter*, הָאֵל ׀ לָנוּ (lxviii. 21); כְּאֵל ׀ לְךָ (Job xl. 9); לְדַבֵּר ׀ רַע (Ps. cxli. 4); אֹהֲבַי ׀ יֵשׁ (Prov. viii. 21). But this rule is more frequently neglected than observed, see cxx. in Ps. xxx. 12; xxxvii. 7, 24; xlix. 15; lxiv. 6; cvii. 35; Job xxi. 17; &c.[5]

III. *Paseq emphaticum*. Such, in my opinion, is the explanation of its use in יְהוָה ׀ יְהוָה (Ps. v. 2); אִמְרַי ׀ הַאֲזִינָה הוֹשִׁיעַ ׀ יְהוָה מְשִׁיחוֹ (xx. 7);[6] לֹא ׀ יִשְׁמַע ׀ אֲדֹנָי (lxvi. 18; cxvi. 1; comp. Job xxvii. 9; xxxv. 13); הָאֵל ׀ יְהוָה (lxxxv. 9); עַד־מָתַי ׀ פְּתָיִם (Prov. i. 22); עַד־מָתַי ׀ עָצֵל ׀ תִּשְׁכָּב (vi. 9). We have seen, again

---

[5] In Job xxxviii. 1, xl. 6, Paseq comes, for distinctness of reading, to mark the Q'rî. Comp. Neh. ii. 13.

[6] Delitzsch (see his note on cxvi. 1) explains these two cases thus: 'Das Paseq hinter יִשְׁמַע will die Verflösung des Auslauts *a'* mit dem Anlaut *'a* von אדני verhüten;' but he says nothing of the numberless instances in which his rule fails, e. g. i. 6; vi. 9, 10; xxvii. 7; lxxviii. 21; cx. 4; &c.

and again, that the punctators claim the liberty of marking the emphasis wherever they please. And in most of the above cases they could only do so by the employment of Paseq. In the others, they had the choice of Paseq or L'garmeh.

Perhaps under this head we may place the instances in which Paseq marks the *repetition* of a word, viz. יוֹם ׀ יוֹם (Ps. lxi. 9; lxviii. 20; Prov. viii. 30, 34); עָרוּ ׀ עָרוּ (Ps. cxxxvii. 7); הֵב ׀ הַב (Prov. xxx. 15); הָאָח ׀ הָאָח (Ps. xxxv. 21; xl. 16; lxx. 4); אָמֵן ׀ וְאָמֵן (xli. 14; lxxii. 19; lxxxix. 53). But this rule is not carried out in xxii. 2; lxviii. 13; Prov. xx. 14.

IV. I believe that in only one passage, Prov. vi. 3, is Paseq used simply to mark the *dichotomy*, see p. 88. In the prose accentuation it seems not unfrequently so employed. Comp., for instance, Gen. i. 27; ii. 21; xviii. 15; xxi. 14; xxvi. 28.

CHAPTER XVII.

Transformation.

I BRING together in this chapter the various instances of transformation to which I have already drawn attention in the chapters preceding, as some additional remarks are necessary.

Transformation is, as we have seen, of two kinds, that of a disjunctive into a conjunctive accent; and that of one disjunctive into another. It is always due to *musical* considerations alone. Its advantage, in the most important instances of its occurrence, was, that it gave *variety to the melody*, and did away with much of the stiffness and sameness, that characterises the prose accentuation.

I. Of the class first named above are—

1. The transformation of R'bhîa mugrash, when it falls on the word immediately preceding Silluq. For, that R'bhîa mugrash may occupy this position, Silluq's word must have *two or more* syllables before the tone, e. g. וְגִ֥ילוּ בִּרְעָדָֽה׃ (Ps. ii. 11),

הוֹרִדְךָ עַל־הַשָּׁמָיִם (viii. 2); or, if but *one* syllable, that syllable must have a long vowel[1], followed by vocal Sh'va, e. g. בַּל־תַּנִּיחֵנִי לְעָשְׁקִי (cxix. 121); הוּא יְשָׁרְתֵנִי (ci. 6); If these conditions are not fulfilled, a servus takes the place of R'bhîa mugrash. Comp. וּמַלְאַךְ יְהוָֹה רֹדְפָם (xxxv. 6) with וּמַלְאַךְ וְתוֹרָתְךָ שַׁעֲשֻׁעָי (cxix. 174) with וְתוֹרָתְךָ יְהוָה דָּחָה (ib. 5); וּבְפִי רְשָׁעִים תֵּהָרֵס (Prov. xi. 11) with אֱמֶת (ib. 142); and וּבַאֲבֹד רְשָׁעִים רִנָּה (ib. 10). The *sense* may very clearly require a disjunctive accent, as in שֶׁקֶר רְדָפוּנִי עָזְרֵנִי (Ps. cxix. 86), but the melody does not allow it.

Exceptions to the rule are the verses in Job, which introduce the speeches, e. g. וַיַּעַן אֱלִיפַז הַתֵּימָנִי וַיֹּאמַר (iv. 1); וַיַּעַן אִיּוֹב וַיֹּאמַר (iii. 2); and וַיֹּסֶף אִיּוֹב שְׂאֵת מְשָׁלוֹ וַיֹּאמַר (xxvii. 1). But these are prose passages, which do not concern us.

In ordinary texts the rule is not always carried out,—see Ps. xix. 10; xxxiv. 3; xxxv. 15,—but such cases, not many in number, are corrected in Codd. and better edd.[2]

2. The transformation of D'chî in the word immediately before Athnach, which is subject to precisely the same conditions as that of R'bhîa mugrash before Silluq. Thus it is required in יַשִּׂגוּ אָחוֹר וְיִכָּלְמוּ (Ps. xxxv. 4), but not in יִסֹּגוּ אָחוֹר וְיַחְפְּרוּ (xl. 15); in יִרְאוּ אֶת־יְהוָה קְדֹשָׁיו (xxxiv. 10), but not in יְהַלְלוּ (xxii. 27); in חֵלֶק־אָדָם רָשָׁע עִם־אֵל (Job xxvii. 13), but not in חֵלֶק־אָדָם רָשָׁע מֵאֱלֹהִים (xx. 29). As before, the transformation often interferes with the *logical* division of the clause, e. g. in הֲלֹא־מְעַט יָמַי יַחְדָּל (Job x. 20)[3].

---

[1] In practice this long vowel is Qámeṣ or Chôlem. Of Ṣere (for this rule and those following) I have found only two exx., Ps. lxix. 24ᵃ and Job xxxiii. 12ᵇ; of Shûreq and long Chîreq I have not noticed a single example.

[2] On the other hand, transformation is sometimes introduced, where it is not required, e. g. עַם לֹא־יָדַעְתִּי יַעַבְדוּנִי (xviii. 44), as though the last word had been pointed יַעַבְדוּנִי. Similar instances occur in xxvii. 10; cxix. 175; Prov. xxix. 4; Job vi. 4; xxx. 18.

[3] It is interesting to compare (as far as they admit of comparison) the passages in Ps. xviii, in which transformation has taken place according to rules 1 and 2, with the prose accentuation of 2 Sam. xxii. Here we find, *in every instance, the*

The few mistakes in common edd. have been mostly corrected by Baer, but in Prov. xxvii. 22, if we retain D'chî, we must point בְּתוֹךְ הָרִפוֹת בַּעֲלִי, with Erf. 1, 2; K. 198, 599, 606; Sonc.—Erf. 1 has in margin to בַּעֲלִי, נקוד וכן ל.

3. The *transformatio perpetua* in the word before Silluq, when Great Shalshéleth precedes, see p. 67.

4. The *transformatio perpetua*, when L'garmeh is due in the word immediately preceding D'chî, see p. 83.

5. The *transformatio perpetua*, when R'bhîa mugrash's clause consists of three words, Athnach preceding, see p. 74.

6. The transformation in monosyllables, and other small words with the tone on the first syllable, coming in the second place before D'chî, Pazer, and Little R'bhîa. See the chapters on those accents.

II. To the second kind of transformation belongs—

1. That of Athnach into R'bhîa mugrash, which must always take place, when Athnach would come on the word *immediately preceding* Silluq, see p. 66[4].

2. The same change in the *second* word before Silluq, when R'bhîa mugrash has been transformed in the first word, and that word—like Silluq's word—has not two syllables before the tone, nor one syllable with a long vowel and vocal Sh'va. Thus Athnach will stand in such cases as : יוֹשֵׁב בַּשָּׁמַיִם יִשְׂחָק אֲדֹנָי יִלְעַג־לָמוֹ (ii. 4); דֶּרֶךְ־אֱמוּנָה בָחָרְתִּי מִשְׁפָּטֶיךָ שִׁוִּיתִי : (cxix. 30); יְהוָה בְּאַפּוֹ : מִשְׁפְּטֵי־יְהוָה אֱמֶת צָדְקוּ יַחְדָּו (xix. 10); יְבַלְּעֵם וְתֹאכְלֵם אֵשׁ : (xxi. 10). But it must be transformed in עִירָה הַגֶּבֶל (lv. 22); רַכּוּ דְבָרָיו מִשֶּׁמֶן וְהֵמָּה פְתִחוֹת : וּכְבוֹר אֲעִירָה שָׁחַר : (lvii. 9)[5].

---

disjunctive accent (Tiphcha) introduced,—a further proof of the reality of our rules. See vv. 5[b], 6[a], 23[a], 33[b], 36[b], 41[a], &c.

[4] Here a double transformation may take place,—but is very rare,—that of Athnach into R'bhîa mugrash, and then of R'bhîa mugrash into a servus. See p. 69, note 8, and p. 33 (3).

[5] The short *vv.* of Ps. cxix furnish many exx. of this transformation, e. g. 2, 4, 5, 12, 14, 17, 24. In *vv.* 3, 6, 8, 9, 10, 13, &c., on the other hand, Athnach remains unchanged.

Common edd. have, of course, their mistakes, which however all yield to the collation of Codd., save Prov. iv. 6 (where I have found De R. 874 alone right) and Job xxxix. 12 (where all Codd. are wrong). These may be regarded as the exceptions that prove the rule. Even Baer's text is wrong in Ps. v. 2 (where we must point יְהֹוָה בִּינָה הֲגִיגִי׃, with Codd., see Norzi's note בס״ס בטעם מיושב בשם) and cxix. 165 (where common edd. are right).

3. The transformation of R'bhîa mugrash into Great Shalshéleth, as explained p. 67.

4. The transformation of Great R'bhîa—when it would come in close proximity to Little R'bhîa—into Ṣinnor, see p. 56 below.

Such are the laws of transformation. Perhaps some of my readers may think that no little confusion must be the result of their application, and that it will be often difficult to trace the true logical (or syntactical) division, underlying this purely musical accentuation. But, in reality, there need be no confusion or difficulty at all. The main point to bear in mind is that, wherever two or more servi precede Athnach or Silluq, a pause is due from the dichotomy, and *should be made in the reading, on the last servus.* Cases I. 1–3 are thus disposed of.—In a few instances under I. 4, it will be necessary to allow for the transformation which has taken place in the word immediately preceding D'chî (proper or transformed). Prov. xxi. 8, as explained p. 85, note 6, is an example in point.—Under I. 5 and 6, I have not noticed a single instance in which the sense is in the slightest degree obscured by the transformation. And as for II. 1–4, no confusion or difficulty is possible, for we have merely a *change* in the disjunctive accent. The logical (or syntactical) division remains as clearly marked as if no transformation had taken place.

For the discovery of these remarkable laws of transformation we are mainly indebted to Christian accentuologists of the seventeenth century. They are almost all found in Wasmuth's *Institutio methodica accentuationis Hebrææ* (Rostock, 1664). Rabbinical writers on the accents had not the slightest idea of them.

APPENDIX

CONTAINING THE ORIGINAL ARABIC OF THE TREATISE, ASSIGNED TO
R. JEHUDA BEN-BIL'AM, ON THE ACCENTS OF THE THREE BOOKS.

Two years ago, Dr. Bytschkow, Vice-director of the Imperial Library at St. Petersburg, was good enough to send me a MS., containing a portion of the following text[1]. And last year, when I visited St. Petersburg, Dr. Harkavy, Sub-librarian of the Imperial Library, handed me a bundle of fragments of MSS. (on Hebrew grammar, &c.), —which had been collected by Firkowitsch in various parts of the East,—and left me to see if I could find anything for my purpose among them. After no little trouble, I succeeded in arranging the *disjecta membra*, so as to produce portions of three several copies of the text. Fortunately, the fragments supplement one another, so that the Treatise is now submitted *complete* to scholars. The four MSS. I name A, B, C, and D. The first is decidedly the oldest, and D perhaps older than B and C, which have epigraphs assigning them to the years 1337 and 1339 respectively. All four are written on paper (small size) and in Rabbinical characters[2].

That the Hebrew text, often quoted in the previous pages, is a translation from the Arabic, has been long known to scholars from the superscriptions to the Ox. and Vat. MSS.[3] But up to the present time the original Arabic was not known to be in existence. That the following text supplies it will be clear to any one who will take the

---

[1] I am indebted to Dr. Neubauer for having drawn my attention to this MS., and to the Marquis of Salisbury, then Secretary of State for Foreign Affairs, for having condescended to use his influence to procure me the loan of it.

[2] They all come under the same No. 634 of the second Firkowitsch Collection. I noticed only one MS., B, to contain a part of the treatise on the accentuation of the twenty-one Books.

[3] The Ox. MS. is No. 1465 in the Bodleian Catal., and belonged formerly to Oppenheim. The Vat. MS. is No. 402 in Assemani's Catal. The superscription in these MSS. is as follows: זה ספר הורית [.Vat הוריית] הקורא אשר הובא מירושלים לבאר [.Vat נבאר] בדרך קצרה והביאו יוסף בן חייא הסופר משם מתורגם בלשון ערבי כאשר העתיקו לשם וו' נחנאל בו' משלם [.Vat ר' משלם בן נחנאל] הפכו מלשון ערבי ללשון הקורש בעיר מיינצא. (Having collated the Vat. MS. I am able to state that Assemani's transcript of these words is far from correct.) For בדרך קצרה לבאר I propose to read נשלם בדרך קצרה (the mistakes in the Heb. text are often perfectly astounding, see p. 103, note 1), 'complete in a compendious form,' answering to the words at the close of the Vat. MS.: חם ספר הוריית הקורא ונשלם בדרך קצרה. The statement ערבי בלשון מתורגם, '*translated* in the Arabic tongue,' may be set down as a *conjecture* on the part of the writer, like many other unfounded conjectures, that have been since made, on the subject of the Work. The city מיינצא is no doubt Mainz. It may be mentioned that our treatise forms the last part of this compendium of הוריית הקורא. It is preceded by rules for the נקודים (Dagesh, the vowels, and Sh'va), and for the accentuation of the twenty-one Books.

trouble of comparing it with the Hebrew. Its publication is not without importance, as it enables us to correct the serious mistakes which so often interfere with the sense in the Hebrew translation[4].

That this treatise is abridged from a larger Work is stated in the epigraphs to B and C, which both begin חם אלמכתצר, 'the *Compendium* is finished.' The name also of this larger Work is given (see p. 110, l. 19)[5], הדאיה אלקארי, i. e. هِدَايَةُ ٱلْقَارِ, 'Direction for the Reader.' We thus recover the long-lost original title, of which הוֹרָיַת הַקּוֹרֵא (see note 3) is the translation. But I have a still more interesting announcement to make, and that is that a portion of the larger Work itself has been at length discovered. M. Shapira of Jerusalem acquired, during a recent visit to Yemen, a MS. on the טעמי אמ״ת, from which he kindly sent me some extracts, and which he has just brought to England and disposed of to the British Museum. I have delayed putting the finishing stroke to my Work, that I might examine this MS. The result of my examination has been to satisfy me that it contains a part of הדאיה אלקאר, in the original Arabic. The reasons for my conclusion are the following: First, the general plan and arrangement is the same as in the Compendium. Secondly, as was bound to be the case, the subject is treated more fully and completely. Thirdly, the examples, even the false ones (e. g. p. 110, note 30), given in the Compendium are almost all (100 out of 105) found in the larger Work. Fourthly, in p. 110, l. 19, we read: 'Thou wilt find in הדאיה אלקאר a *sixth* reason,' i. e. for Mer'kha before Athnach; and on turning to the larger Work we find this additional reason given[6]. Against these grounds for the identification, there is only one point to be mentioned, that two of the *servi* (כדאם) have different names; נלגל is called שופר מקלוב,—תלשה צנירה (M'huppakh) שופר מקלוב and תלשה כבירה being the name given to the upper sign of Olév'yored[7]. We may suppose that the author himself, when he prepared the Compendium[8] (perhaps after an interval of some years), changed these names into others, which he found more generally in use.

---

[4] I have before me a long list of these mistakes. The following may serve, by way of specimen : p. 3, l. 18, סוף for ראש; p. 4, l. 12, שבסוף for שבפסוק; p. 6, l. 18, עלוי for עליו, או for או, and מניע for מנוע; ib., l. 29, דלה for ריש; p. 7, l. 15, ימצא for ויצא; ib., l. 26, דיבור for מאיילא; p. 8, l. 24, הם for ח'; p. 9, l. 22, שלא omitted.

[5] This form is used all through the text for קארי, قَارِئ.

[6] It refers to cases that do not come under the previous heads, and is thus expressed: אלא ליס בין אלאתנ׳חה ובין מרקבהא לא נג׳מה ולא שוא פאנהא איצ׳א במארנה כקו' ומפני רב (Ps. xix. 11) אף־ילך לילה (lxxiv. 16) לעשות רע (Prov. ii. 14). ואמתאל ד׳אלך.

[7] We now understand Chayyug's list (Nutt's ed., p. 129, l. 3), which has hitherto baffled all attempts at explanation. The list at the end of Ox. 125 (Hunt 511) is similar. My own note p. 20 must be cancelled.

[8] That both Works were written by the same author, we learn from a statement in the first section of the prose accents : וכבר זכרהי בס׳ הורית הקורא וכו.

The MS. is not complete. The part of the Compendium to which it corresponds is from p. 108, l. 9 to p. 115, l. 3, and again p. 117, ll. 6–15. It is clearly written in Yemenite characters, on paper (? fifteenth century). The following pages were already in type when I examined it. But, had I seen it earlier, I should not have decided to print it in preference. The author's later Work is the better of the two. It is better arranged and more clearly expressed; and, as it is complete, is in every way more fitted to give the student an idea of the rules that commended themselves to Rabbinical scholars in the Middle Ages. I have given one extract from the larger Work, and that may suffice. Indeed, I have found nothing else of sufficient importance to copy[9].

As to the *authorship* of our treatise, it is assigned in A (see p. 108, note 15) to Sa'íd 'Ali,—a name otherwise (I believe) unknown. An isolated notice of this kind—although occurring in what is probably the oldest MS.—cannot, however, be taken to settle the question. On the other hand, modern authorities agree in regarding Ben-Bil'am as the author; but, as it seems to me, on quite insufficient grounds.

The *only* authority for attributing the Work to him has been the title prefixed to the Paris MS. (1221), ספר טעמי המקרא המתייחס לר׳ יהודה [10]בן בלעם ספרדי נע׳. On the ground of this title, Mercerus, when he published the text from the Paris MS., announced Ben-Bil'am as the author, and scholars since have, one and all, accepted his statement. Yet what is the value of this title? The very name, ס׳ טעמי המקרא, with which it begins, betrays its later origin[11]. There is nothing answering to this name in the original Arabic, or in the superscription to the translation made from the Arabic (see note 3). The 'assignment' of the Work to Ben-Bil'am has, in the same way, no support from the earlier texts. Nor can testimony be cited in its favour from any other source. Not a single one of those who borrow from the Work or quote it,—as Hadassi, Simson, Jequtiel,—associates Ben-Bil'am's name with it. And no other Rabbinical author can be named who makes mention of it, as written by him[12]. Indeed, so far from a

---

[9] Should any of my readers be curious to see what is preserved of the הדאיה אלקאר proper, their curiosity will soon be gratified, for Dr. Ginsburg purposes printing it in the Appendix to the 2nd volume of his ed. of the Masora, which will appear shortly.
[10] 'The De R. MS. (488) has the same title; but these two MSS. agree so exactly, *verbatim et literatim*, that their testimony can only be counted as that of one MS. Either the one was copied from the other, or both must have been copied from the same MS.
[11] The name is also a *misnomer*, for the greater part of the Work is *not* taken up with the טעמים, but with the נקודים.
[12] Dr. Steinschneider has suggested (*Catal. libr. hebr. bibl. Bodl.* col. 1295) that our Work, הוריה הקורא, '*Direction* for the Reader,' is identical with Ben-Bil'am's כתאב אלארשאד, 'Book of *Direction*,' described by Moses ben-Ezra. (Perhaps the same idea may have led, in the Middle Ages, to the 'assigning' of it to him.) But now that we have the Arabic title of our Work we know that there is nothing in the suggestion. Were it necessary, it might be shewn that the two Works differed in *contents* as well.

APPENDIX. 105

Western writer, like Ben-Bil'am (who belonged to Toledo, in Spain), having been the author, the evidence, both external and internal, points to an *Eastern origin* of the Work. (α) The known MSS. can be traced directly or indirectly to the East[13]; and now too a part of the original הדאיה אלקאר has been brought from a remote corner of the East. (β) The Work was known and used in the East—as by Hadassi in אשכל 'ס, p. 61 (A.D. 1148)—long before any Western writer made use of it[14]. (γ) The acquaintance the author shews with the *melody* of the three Books may suit an Eastern (see p. 2, note 7), but is irreconcilable with a Western, origin. Lastly, the rules about המזה (p. 112) could not have been drawn up from Western MSS., for Western punctators do not employ this sign. (The old Cod. Erf. 3 which has this sign is doubtless of Eastern origin[15].)

If, on these grounds, we reject the authorship of Ben-Bil'am[16], we have no *data* for fixing the age of our treatise. We know only that it is older than Hadassi (early part of twelfth century).

In the following text, the words in brackets have been added and a few obvious faults have been corrected. I am also responsible for the interpunction, and for the vocalization and accentuation of the examples cited. Otherwise I have printed the text as I found it. The few grammatical irregularities and orthographical inconsistencies will not cause the reader any trouble. Of course he will be prepared to meet with modern Arabic forms.

---

[13] Eight MSS. are known. Four of these were brought by Firkowitsch from the East. Two, Ox. 1465 and Vat. 402, carry on their forefront (see note 3) that they are derived from an Eastern MS. The remaining two, Par. 1221 and De R. 488, are undoubtedly copies of this same translation. I have collated them carefully (as far as our treatise is concerned), and find that they have *common mistakes with Ox. and Vat., not found in the Arabic*, whilst the variations admit of ready explanation.

[14] The first Western writers (as far as it is at present known) to make use of it were the Naqdanim, Simson, Moses, and Jequtiel, all of whom belong to the following century, and are a hundred years (more or less) later than Hadassi.

[15] Comp. Baer's statement, made on other grounds, in the pref. to his ed. of the Minor Prophets, p. vii: *Cod. Erf. 3 sine dubitatione ab homine Orientali scriptus est.*

[16] That I have always cited the treatise as by Ben-Bil'am was unavoidable. I had to adopt a name, and could of course only employ that by which it is generally known.

P

אלכלאם פי אלחאן אלתלתה אספאר
תהלות ואיוב ומשלי.

אעלם אן הדה אלתלתה אספאר מתניירה מן אלואחד ועשרין ספר בתלתה
וגוה. אלואחד נפס כתאבתהא ונטר תסטירהא פי תוריק אלצחף פאן דלך
תשריג אלכתאב בתרך בעץ אלאסטר כאליה עלי בניה אלשירה פי אלכתאבה·
ואלתאני אן פואסיקהא צגאר· ואלתאלת נייר אלאלחאנהא¹:

פצל. אלחאן הדה אלתלתה אספאר תמאניה והי פזר וזרקה ורביע ולגרמיה ו
ויתיב וטפחה ואתנחה וסלוק. וכדאמהא שופר רפע וגלגל ושופר מקלוב ושופר
תכסיר ומאילה ומארכה וסלסלה ומקל וצנורית ושוכב ודחויה:

פצל. אעלם אן אלחאן הדה אלתלתה אספאר פיהא מא יגוז תראדפה
ואחד בעד אלאכר ופיהא מא ימתנע פיה אלתראדף· פאלדי ימכן פיה
אלתראדף רביע וזרקה ולגרמיה ומא סואהם פממתנע אלתראדף:

פצל פי מואצע אלכראם. אעלם אן הדה אלתמאניה אלחאן תנקסם פי
תרתיב אלכראם ארבעה אקסאם. אלאול מא אמכן אן יכון לה באדמין ולא
אכתר והמא אלזרקה ואלטפחה נחו הָאֵל ׀ לָנוּ² ואמתאלה ונחו עֵדוּת יְהֹוָה
נֶאֱמָנָה³ גיר אן תם ואחד ליס מתלה לה ארבעה כראם והו בְּיוֹם הִצִּיל־יְהֹוָה
אוֹתוֹ מִכַּף כָּל־אֹיְבָיו⁴. ואלתאני הו מא יכון לה תלתה כראם ולא אזיד והמא

---

¹ Three points are mentioned in which the three Books differ from the others: 1st, their writing; 2nd, the shortness of their verses; and 3rd, their accents. The first point of difference is expressed thus: 'Their writing itself, with the observing of their lineation in the copying (see Dozy) of the pages, and that arrangement of the writing consists in leaving a part of the lines blank (خَالِيَة), according to the build of the שירה in the writing.' The 'lineation' or ruling named may be seen in any Cod. (It is the same for the three, as for the twenty-one, Books; hence in the Heb. we have ספר כתיקון שירטוטם תיקון.) The other directions are taken from Sopherim, xiii. 1, where פתיחות באתנחייתא ובסוף פסוק (open spaces at Athnach and at Sôph Pasûq) are enjoined for the three Books, together with the form of the שירה (as in Ex. xv and Judg. v). But in practice, this calligraphical arrangement is confined to Ps. xviii, and even for that is rare in Codd.

² Ps. lxviii. 21.   ³ xix. 8.   ⁴ xviii. 1.

APPENDIX. 107

אתנאן לנרמיה ופזר נחו פִּי נָבָר עָלֵינוּ ¹ חַסְדּוֹ ¹ גַּם כִּי־אֵלֵךְ בְּגֵיא צַלְמָוֶת ².
ואלתאלת מא אמכן אן יכון לה ארבעה כדאם ולא אזיד והמא אתנאן רביע
ויתיב נחו זָבַרְתִּי מִשְׁפָּטֶיךָ מֵעוֹלָם ¹ יְהוָה ³ כִּי יוֹסִיף עַל־חַטָּאתִי פֶשַׁע ⁴. ואלראבע
מא אמכן אן יכון לה כמסה ולא אזיד והמא אתנאן אתנחה וסוף פסוק
נחו כִּי אֶת אֲשֶׁר יֶאֱהַב יְהוָה יוֹכִיחַ ⁵ וְאַתָּה נָשָׂאתָ עֲוֺן חַטָּאתִי סֶלָה: ⁶

פצל פי שרח עלל אלאלחאן.

אלפזר קד יכון שכלין צורה טית[ע] וצורה צדי[ע] ואלדי אונב לה צורה
אלטית אלגלגל ⁷ ומא ערפת פרק בין תנגים אלצורתין פי הדה אלתלתה
אספאר. אלפזר אדא כדמה כאדמין קד יכון אלאול מארכה וקד יכון
שופר מקלוב ואלתאני קד יכון שופר מקלוב וקד יכון גלגל· ואלשרט פי דלך
אנה אן כאן אלאול מע אול חרף מן כלמתה כאן שופר מקלוב ואדא כאן
איצא אלתאני מע אול כלמתה כאן גלגל מתל כִּי בָם בְּיַד־יְהוָֹה ⁸ כִּי לָא
בְחָרְבָּם ⁹. פאן זאל אלכאדם אלאול ען אול חרף צאר במארכה או מקל לאנה
כלף מתל וְיִשְׂמְחוּ כָל־חֹסֵי בָךְ ¹⁰ ואדא זאל איצא אלכאדם אלתאני ען אול
אלכלמה צאר בשופר מקלוב· ואכלאף אלקרא פי הדא אלמוצע כתיר ודאך
אן פיהם מן אדא זאל אלכאדם אלתאני ען אול אלחרף געלה גלגל מתל
וְעַתָּה יָרוּם רֹאשִׁי ¹¹ ופיהם מן יקרא וְעַתָּה יָרוּם רֹאשִׁי ופיהם מן לא ידכל פי
כדמה אלפזר גלגל פי אלתלתה אספאר בתה· פמתי ראית פי אלמצאחף הדה
אלתנייראת לא תטן אנהא אגלאט:

אלורקה אדא כדמהא כאדם ואחד אן כאן מע אול חרף כאן מארכה
מתל אַתָּה· סֵתֶר לִי ¹² לָא הָלַךְ ¹³ ואן כאן אלכאדם עלי אלחרף אלתאני מן
כלמתה וכאן תחת אלחרף אלאול שוא כאן אלכאדם מארכה איצא מתל

---

¹ Ps. cxvii. 2. ² xxiii. 4. ³ cxix. 52. ⁴ Job xxxiv. 37.
⁵ Prov. iii. 12. ⁶ Ps. xxxii. 5.
⁷ In the twenty-one Books the Pazer *with Galgal* is known as פ׳ גדול or פזר פרה קרני (the form of which is likened to טית), and that *without*, as פ׳ קטן (like final צדי). But for the three Books no such distinction is observed in Codd., the sign of פ׳ קטן being that almost always employed, whether Galgal precedes or not.
⁸ lxxv. 9. ⁹ xliv. 4.
¹⁰ v. 12. Ben-Asher and Ben-Naphtali differ in the way mentioned, the former pointing וישמחו, the latter וישמחו.
¹¹ xxvii. 6. ¹² xxxii. 7. ¹³ i. 1.

אַל־תִּֽהְיוּ ׀ כְּסוּס בְּפֶרֶד ׀ בְּקֶרֶב בֵּיתִי ². ואן כאן תחת אלחרף אלאול מלך כאן
אלכאדם שופר רפע מתל וַאֲנִי ׀ אָשִׁיר עֻזֶּךָ ³ אָהַבְתָּ צֶדֶק ⁴. ואן צאר אלכאדם
עלי אלחרף אלתאלת ואלראבע ומא זאד כאן אלכאדם שופר רפע מתל
בְּשָׁלוֹם יַחְדָּו ⁵ אֱלֹהִים צְבָאוֹת ⁶ אלא מוצע ואחד והו חֶלְקָם בַּחַיִּים ⁷ פאנה מע
אלתאלת והו במארכה. ואדא כאן אלכאדם מע חרף ודלך אלחרף דנש פהו
אבדא מארכה שא ⁷ᵃ אן יכון מע אלתאני או מע אלתאלת או מא זאד ען דלך
מתל מְשֹׁרֵר עֲנִיִּים ⁸ רַבִּים אֹמְרִים ⁹ מא סוי לַמְנַצֵּחַ אַל־תַּשְׁחֵת בשלח שאול ¹⁰
אָנָּה יְהֹוָה כִּי אֲנִי ¹¹ לֹא־תִשָּׂא פְשָׁעוֹ ¹². וקאלו אן אדא כאנת אלזרקה פי כלמתין
לא תכון אלאולה במקף בל בכאדם אלא כִּי־יְהֹוָה הוּא אֱלֹהִים ¹³ יְקַלְלוּ־הֵמָּה ¹⁴.
ואן כאן קד קאלו אן יְקַלְלוּ כלף יְקַלְלוּ הֵמָּה. וקד וגדת גיר הדין אלמוצעין ¹⁵:

אלסלסלה. משהור אלסלסלה פי אלתלתה אספאר כונהא קאימה בנפסהא
ולא יבדמהא אבדא כאדם ואחד בל קד יבדמהא כאדמין פי מוצעין והמא
עַל־כֵּן זָחַלְתִּי וָאִירָא ׀ ¹⁶ כֹּל אֲשֶׁר יִוָּעֵד ו ¹⁷. ומתי כאן קבל אלסלסלה אתנחה
כאנת קאימה בנפסהא אעני תכון לחן מתל וַיִּרְמֹס לָאָרֶץ חַיָּי וּכְבוֹדִי ו ¹⁸
תִּשְׂבְּחַנִי נֶצַח עַד־אָנָה ו ¹⁹. ואדא לם יכן קבלהא אתנחה כאנת כאדם מתל
אֵין ׀ יְשׁוּעָתָה לּוֹ בֵאלֹהִים סֶלָה ²⁰ והי תמאניה כדאם פי אלתלתה אספאר
יְשׁוּעָתָה ²⁰ דֻּמִיָּה [תְּהִלָּה] ²¹ מַלְאַךְ־יְהֹוָה ²² בְּפָרֵשׁ שַׁדַּי ²³ יִשְׂאוּ [הָרִים] ²⁴ שִׂיאָתֶן ²⁵
לְוִית חֵן ²⁶ הֱיַחְתְּךָ [אִישׁ] ²⁷. ויגעלו מתל אלפסק עלאמה ללחן מנהא:

אלרביע ²⁸ אדא כדמה כאדם ואחד קד יכון שופר מקלוב וקד יכון מארכה
וקד יכון שופר תכסירי. אלשרט פי הדא אלאכתלאפאת הו אן תנטר אן
כאן בעד אלרביע תאבעתה פאלכאדם מארכה מתל אֲנִי שָׁכַבְתִּי וָאִישָׁנָה ²⁹
בָּלָה שְׁאֵרִי וּלְבָבִי ³⁰. וכדלך אן כאן בעדה סוף פסוק כאן איצא אלכאדם
מארכה מתל מִצִּיּוֹן מִכְלַל־יֹפִי אֱלֹהִים הוֹפִיעַ ³¹. וכדלך אן כאן קבלה לגרמיה

---

¹ Ps. xxxii. 9.   ² ci. 7.   ³ lix. 17.   ⁴ xlv. 8.   ⁵ iv. 9.
⁶ lxxx. 15.   ⁷ xvii. 14.   ⁷ᵃ Query סוא 'equally.'   ⁸ xii. 6.   ⁹ iv. 7.
¹⁰ lix. 1.   ¹¹ cxvi. 16.   ¹² Job vii. 21. In B and C this ex. is wanting.
¹³ Ps. c. 3.   ¹⁴ cix. 28.   ¹⁵ A. adds זיאדה ללמעלם סייד עלי צאחב אלכתאב.
¹⁶ Job xxxii. 6.   ¹⁷ xxxvii. 12.   ¹⁸ Ps. vii. 6.   ¹⁹ xiii. 2.
²⁰ iii. 3.   ²¹ lxv. 2.   ²² xxxiv. 8.   ²³ lxviii. 15.   ²⁴ lxxii. 3.
²⁵ cxxxvii. 9.   ²⁶ Prov. i. 9.   ²⁷ vi. 27.
²⁸ The rules that follow are very defective. Those given in הראיה אלקאר are fuller
and more complete, but so far from correct, that I have not thought it worth while
to copy them. The Heb. (3. 12 ff.) supplies one omission.
²⁹ Ps. iii. 6.   ³⁰ lxxiii. 26.   ³¹ l. 2. For the R'bîia here, see p. 75, note 3.

APPENDIX. 109

כאן אלכאדם איצׄא מארכה ולאנה יכון בעדה תאבעתה מתל אַזְכִּיר ¹ רַהַב
וּבָבֶל לְיֹדְעָי ¹. ואלשרט פי וגוב אלשופר אלמקלוב הו אן אלרביע אדא כאן
הו אול אלפסוק וליס בעדה תאבעתה כאן אלכאדם שופר מקלוב מתל
שָׁאַל² רֶכֶב אֱלֹהִים ³. אלרביע אדא כדמה כאדמין וכאן בעדה אכר
אפסוק⁴ כאן אלכאדם אלאול רחויה ואלתאני מארכה מתל בְּדַרְךָ עֵדְוֹתֶיךָ
שָׂשְׂתִּי⁵ גַּמֹל עַל־עַבְדְּךָ אֶחְיֶה וְאֶשְׁמְרָה דְבָרֶךָ ⁶. והדא אלגנס לא יכתלף אדא
צער לה תלתה כדאם ואנמא יכתלף אלאול מן אלתלתה כדאם יכון שופר
מקלוב מתל כִּי מֶלֶךְ כָּל־הָאָרֶץ אֱלֹהִים ⁷. וכדא אן כדמה ארבעה כדאם מא
אכתלף אלדרחויה ואלמארכה ואנמא יכתלפאן אלאולין אלאול יכון צנורית
ואלתאני שופר [מקלוב] מתל זָבַרְתִּי מִשְׁפָּטֶיךָ מֵעוֹלָם יְהֹוָה ⁸ מא סוי ואחד
תכתלף פיה אלדרחויה ואלמארכה והו בְּפֶרֶשׁ שַׁדַּי מְלָכִים בָּהּ ⁹:

אללגרמיה. אללגרמיה הו מן אלאלחאן אלדי יתניר כדאמה פי אלואחד
ועשרין ספרא פקד יכדמה שופר מקלוב מתל אֲשֶׁר פָּרִיוֹ ¹⁰ ומארכה יַתְיַצְבוּ ¹¹
ושופר תכסיר וַתִּגְעַשׁ וַתִּרְעַשׁ ¹² וצנורית הַדְרִיכֵנִי בַאֲמִתֶּךָ ¹³. ומא צח ענדי
פיה עלה אדכרהא. וכתיר ממא יגעל אלנאס אללגרמיה פסק ואלדי יפצל בין
אללגרמיה ואלפסק ונהין׳ אלואחד הו אן בעץׄ אלמצאחף אלגיאד תרי מן
ברא ¹⁴ מכתוב קדאם אללגרמיה לגרמיה וקדאם אלפסק פסק וקד יכון דלך
רמז וגיד רמז גיר אן ליס גמיע אלמצאחף תפעל דלד׳ ואלונה אלאכר אן
אלפאסקאת פי כל ספר מעדודה פלו כאן כל מא כאן פי אלתלתה אספאר
הו פסק למא אחתאגו אן יעדוהא קט ואנמא יעדוהא פי כל ספר לתתמיז
מן אללגרמיה לאן שכל אלפסק ואללגרמיה ואחד והו אלעצאה אלתי בין
אלכלמתין:

אליתיב הו מן אלאלחאן אלדי יתניר אלדי שכלה מן שכל אליתיב אלדי פי
אלואחד ועשרין ספרא. אליתיב יכון בגיר כאדם ויכון לה כאדם פכאדמה
אלשופר אדא כאן בין אלחרף אלדי עליה אליתיב ובין אלחרף אלמתהדם
עליה שופר מלכין ומא זאד והו אלחרף אלאול מן אלכלמה ינב לה אלשופר

---

¹ Ps. lxxxvii. 4. ² ii. 8. ³ lxviii. 18. ⁴ I. e. סוף פסוק. ⁵ cxix. 14.
⁶ cxix. 17. Samuel (p. 125) rightly adds here: ואם אין אחריו סלוק ויש רודפין
אחריו הראשון מהפך והשני מרכא בְּוֹ בָּכֹחַ לְבִּי וְנָצַרְתִּי (xxviii. 7).
⁷ xlvii. 8. ⁸ cxix. 52. ⁹ lxviii. 15. ¹⁰ i. 3.
¹¹ ii. 2. The Gaya here is made Mer'kha! ¹² xviii. 8. ¹³ xxv. 5.
¹⁴ ترى من بَرّا, 'thou wilt see on the outside (the margin),' see p. 92, note 1.

בכו' מִי הִקְדִּימַנִי וַאֲשַׁלֵּם[1] כִּי מְבָרְכָיו[2] כִּי עֲוֺנֹתַי[3] כִּי לַחֲמוּ[4] עֵין שְׁזָפַתּוּ[5] הִוָּה
רָאוּ[6] שֶׁקֶר הַסּוּס[7] ואמתאלה. וארא כאן כאדמה מעה פי אלכלמה פינטר אן
כאן וסטהא פיה אחד מלכין אלואחד חלֶם ואלאחר קָמֵן ובין אלחלם או
אלקמץ ובין חרף אליתיב שוא פאן אחד אלמלכין ירפע בשופר כקו' יִלְפְּתוּ[8]
הֵמִירְאָתִי[9] בְּהִשָּׁפְטוֹ[10] ואמתאל דלך' וממא פי וסט אלכלמה אלחלם קולה
וַיֹּאמְרוּ לֹא יִרְאֶה יָהּ[11] וִירוֹמְמֵךְ לָרֶשֶׁת[12] ואמתאלהמא' פאן כאן פי וסט
אלכלמה גיר הדין אלמלכין לם תרפע בשופר כקו' לְתַאֲוָה[13] בְּמַקְהֵלוֹת[14] וכדלך
אן תניר שרט אלשוא ועלי אחד אלמלכין חאצר לם תרפע בשופר כקו'
מֵהֵיכָלֶךָ[15] ואמתאלה[16]:

אלאתנחה. אלאתנחה ארא כדמהא כאדם ואחד קד יכון מדה שופר
ויכון מדה מארכה' פאלדי יונב אלמארכה אשיא ח' [אלואחד] אן תכון
אלאתנחה הי אול לחן פי אלאפסוק[17] כקו' נָבוֹאָה לְמִשְׁכְּנוֹתָיו[18] שָׁקַדְתִּי וָאֶהְיֶה[19]
ואמתאלהמא' ואלתאני אן תכון אלאתנחה בעד רביע מתל הַשָּׁמַיִם מְסַפְּרִים
כְּבוֹד־אֵל[20] וַאֶשְׁחָקֵם כְּעָפָר עַל־פְּנֵי־רוּחַ[21] אֲדֹנָי נֶגְדְּךָ כָל־תַּאֲוָתִי[22] ואמתאל
דלך' ואלתאלת תכון אלאתנחה [בעד] תאבעה אלרביע מתל שִׁיר הַמַּעֲלוֹת
זְכוֹר־יְהוָה לְדָוִד[23] יָבֹא אֱלֹהֵינוּ וְאַל־יֶחֱרַשׁ אֵשׁ־לְפָנָיו תֹּאכֵל[24] ואמתאלהמא'
ואלראבע תכון אלאתנחה בעד תאבעה אלזרקה מתל וּצְפוּנְךָ תְּמַלֵּא בִטְנָם
יִשְׂבְּעוּ בָנִים[25] ואמתאלה' ואלכאמס אן יכון מוצע אלכאדם עלי אול חרף מן
כלמתה מתל זֶה שַׁדַּוּנִי[26] לֹא עָמָד[27] ואנת תציב פי הדאיה אלקאר[28] ונהא
סאדס[29] גיר אן אלכארג ענה כתיר. וממא לם תתבת לה הדה אלשרוט כאן
אלכאדם שופר מתל וַצֵּאן יָדוֹ[30] מוּסַר אָבִיךָ[31] הֵקִים כָּל־אַפְסֵי־אָרֶץ[32] ואמתאל
דלך. אלאתנחה ארא כדמהא כאדמין יכונא אלכאדמין תארה שופרין ותארה
דחויה ומארכה' אלשרט' פי דלך אן כאן בין כלמה אלאתנחה ובין כלמה

---

[1] Job xli. 3.   [2] Ps. xxxvii. 22.   [3] xxxviii. 5.   [4] Prov. iv. 17.
[5] Job xx. 9.   [6] Ps. cvii. 24.   [7] xxxiii. 17.   [8] Job vi. 18.   [9] xxii. 4.
[10] Ps. cix. 7.   [11] xciv. 7.   [12] xxxvii. 34.   [13] Prov. xviii. 1.
[14] Ps. lxviii. 27.   [15] ib. 30.
[16] הדאיה אלקאר gives the rules for D'chî with two and three servi, but incorrectly.
[17] אפסוק occurs elsewhere in the text for פסוק.
[18] Ps. cxxxii. 7.   [19] cii. 8.   [20] xix. 2.   [21] xviii. 43.   [22] xxxviii. 10.
[23] cxxxii. 1.   [24] l. 3.   [25] xvii. 14.   [26] ib. 9.   [27] i. 1.
[28] See p. 103.   [29] MS. has כאדם!! Of course, the Heb. has ששי.
[30] xcv. 7. I substitute this for the false cx. וְצֵאן מַרְעִיתוֹ (c. 3), which is given in both the Arab. and Heb. texts.   [31] Prov. i. 8.   [32] xxx. 4.

APPENDIX. 111

אלכאדם אלקריב אליה פאסקה כאן אלכאדם אבדא דחויה ואלתאני מארכה
מתל בָּרְכוּ עַמִּים ׀ אֱלֹהֵינוּ ׀ הֲלוֹא־מְשַׂנְאֶיךָ יְהוָה ׀ אֶשְׂנָא [2] מא סוי מוצעין בדחויה
ומארכה וליס בינהמא פסק והמא הִנֵּה־זֹאת חֲקַרְנוּהָ כֶּן־הִיא [3] הַקְשֵׁב אִיּוֹב
שְׁמַע־לִי [4] פאן לם תכן פאסקה צאר אלכאדמין שופרין מתל שָׂמוֹ אָדוֹן
לְבֵיתוֹ [5] בְּרֹב שַׂרְעַפַּי בְּקִרְבִּי [6]. ואעלם אן אלדחויה לא תכדם אלא אלרביע
ואלאתנחה ואלשוכב פי אלטפחה מתל נִצְּבָה שֵׁגַל לִימִינְךָ [7]. ומעני קולי
שוכב הו אן תחטֹה בגיר חרכה [8] מתל נִצְּבָה ומעני דחויה הו אנך תרפעהא
אלי ורא נחו אלכמס נגמאת [9] נחו קולך אָמְרֵי הַאֲזִינָה ׀ יְהוָה [10]. פאלשוכב
אבדא לאלטפחה ואלדחויה אבדא לאלרביע ואלאתנחה פאחפטה לאנה משכל [11]:

אלטפחה מן אלאלחאן אלתי יתגיר שכלהא. פאדא כאן קבלהא לא ולא
וכאנת אלטפחה עלי אלחרף אלאול או אלתאני או אלתאלת כאנת לא במקף
מתל וְלֹא־בָטַחְתִּי [12] ואמתאלהא. ואדא כאנת עלי אלחרף אלראבע ומא זאד
כאן לא במארכה מתל וְלֹא נֶאֱמָנוּ [13]. ואדא ראית לָא שָׁמֵעוּ [14] וְלֹא בְחַדוּ [15]
פלים הו עלי אלחרף אלתאלת בל עלי אלראבע לאן שָׁמְעוּ אלקאמצה פי
צמנהא אלף וכדלך בְּחַדוּ פי צמן אלנקטה יוד. אלטפחה אדא כדמתהא
אלמארכה וכאן קבל חרף אלמארכה נקטה אָ או אֶי או אוֹ כאן דלך אלחרף
ירפע רפעא יסירא כפיפא לתעתדל אלנגמה [16]. לאן אלאן כתיר ממן ינגם
עלי חרף ליס עליה תנגים ויחרך אמא אלי אספל ואמא אלי פוק או תרניח [17]
לא יכון דלך אלחרף יסתחק מנה שי בתה. ואלקאר יגב אן יסוק חרוף
אלכלמה מן גיר חרכה בתה חרף אלי חרף אלתנגים והו אלחרף אלדי
עליה אלטעם אמא כאדם ואמא לחן פיננמה וסואה לא ידכלה תנגים בתה.

---

[1] Ps. lxvi. 8.   [2] cxxxix. 21.   [3] Job v. 27.   [4] xxxiii. 31.
[5] Ps. cv. 21.   [6] xciv. 19.   [7] xlv. 10.
[8] 'That thou bring it down, without a movement, or impulse,' הנעה Heb.
[9] 'That thou bring it up behind, like the five tones,' perhaps referring to some ascending scale in use.   [10] v. 2.
[11] The omission here of the rules for three or more משרתים is partially supplied in the Heb., and more fully in הדאיה אלקאר, but in neither case correctly.
[12] Again a false ex. Perhaps the author was thinking of כִּי־בָטַחְתִּי (cxix. 42), which would have been quite right, for the rule applies to all small words resembling לא.   [13] Ps. lxxviii. 37.   [14] Job iii. 18.   [15] xv. 18.
[16] It may be noticed that the melody of Mer'kha was *below*. There was a rising and falling inflection, producing the equilibrium spoken of.
[17] A word seems left out here, Heb. יכריע הכרעה, 'he makes a preponderance, lays a stress.' This passage is wanting in הדאיה אלקאר.

APPENDIX.

ויקול לי אן הדה אלהמזה¹ אלתי נעלוהא פי מוצע לא יתם ללקאר² פיה
פסאד אלנגמה בתחריכה חרף לא ינב אן יחרך לאן אדא רפע אלחרף בהא
אלי פוק קלילא תעדלת אלנגמה³. והדה אלהמזה יחלו אלשיל בהא פי לחנין
פי אלטפחה ואלסלוק מתל קֹרֶץ שְׂפָתָיו· שָׂמֵחַ לְאֵיד⁵ וּבְרָקִים רָב⁶ ופי
אלסלוק חָכְמָה תּוֹדִיעֵנִי⁷· וקד יעמלהא בעץ אלסופרים פי גיר הדין אללחנין
ומע ניר אלתלתה מלוך אלמדבורה. ויקול לי אלאן אנהם נעלוהא לאסקאט
אלשופר מן כלמתהא ולוגוב אלמארכה לאן כל כלמה יכון עליהא הדה
אלהמזה לא יכון פיהא שופר ולא בד להא מן מארכה. ואעלם אן
אלטפחה הי אלנקטה מן פוק אלכלמה ויקול לי אנהם געלו אלעצאה עלי
אלחרף אלאול ליא יטן אן אלנקטה רביע פאלקאר מא יגעל באלה אלא
אלי אלעצאה אלתי מע אול חרף מתל וְחַטָּאִים בעדה⁸· גיר אן מתי אשבל
עליה אימא הו חרף אלתנגים רנע אלי אלנקטה נגם⁹ חרפהא. אליתיב
איצא לא יכתב אלא מע אול חרף וקד יכון חרף אלתנגים וקד לא יכון
חרף אלתנגים. וכתיר ממא ישבל עלי אלקאר דלך פינגם אלחרף אלאול אלדי
עליה אליתיב ולא יכון הו אלחרף אלדי יסתחק אלתנגים פמא ירגע פיה אלא
אלי¹⁰ אלתלקין· גיר אן בעץ אלסופרים יגעל תחת חרף אלתנגים פי אלמואצע
אלמשכלה עצאה שבל אלמארכה וליסת הי מארכה בל ליעלם אנה אלחרף

¹ On this המזה, or מתינה, see p. 70, note 10. One is surprised to find הֶמְזֶה employed to designate what must have been a kind of *secondary tone*. I am glad therefore to be able to give an explanation of the term from the point of view of Jewish grammarians. The following passage occurs in a MS. recently acquired by the Bodleian Library, very similar, in its contents, to the 'Manuel du Lecteur' (Opp. Add. Quo. 158, p. 12): ואיצא שכל אבר יסמי המוזה ויסמי דרבן מענאה מהמאו והו לא לחן ולא כאדם ואנמא יעמל ליהו אלחרף אלדי הו עליה זר אלגעיה לאן אלגעיה תמד אלחרף ואלהמזה תהמו (? תהמזה) ותכון מן פוק אלחרף וצורתה מתל אלאוזלה. We are here told that, whilst Gaya *prolongs* the letter, Hamza *gives a movement*, or *impulse*, to it. (Rt. هَمَزَ, *impulit, trusit*.) This agrees with what is said in the text above, l. 2, where we also learn that the movement, or impulse, was *upwards*. It was, however, clearly a mistake to borrow a *terminus technicus* from Arabic grammarians, and employ it in a sense so different from that which properly belongs to it. ² Heb. לא יחכן לקרוא בה.

³ تَعَجَّلَتِ النَّغْمَةُ. So Par. נשתווחה הנעימה. But this could not have been the author's meaning. Read rather עדלת عَدَلَتِ, 'deviates,' 'goes wrong;' similarly Ox. and Vat. נשחתה, 'is spoilt.'

⁴ Prov. xvi. 30.   ⁵ xvii. 5.   ⁶ Ps. xviii. 15.
⁷ li. 8. Hardly a correct ex., for we require Qámeṣ, not Qámeṣ-chatûph.
⁸ i. 5.   ⁹ Query ונגם.
¹⁰ Query עלי, 'he does not retract it, except on instruction.' Heb. על דרך הלימוד.

APPENDIX. 113

אלמנגם מתל עוּרָה הנבל וכנור¹ בְּיוֹם צָרָתִי² לאן לא יצח אן יקרא אליתיב
עלי אלריש ואלתו נגמיע פנעלו אלעצאבה תפצל.   אלטפחה אדא כדמהא
באדמין קד יכונאן מארכתין וקד יכון אלאול שוכב ואלתאני מארכה.
פאלשרט פי וגוב אלמארכה פי אלאול קיל אן תכון מע אול חרף או מע
אלתאני ויכון אלאול תחתה שוא מתל כִּי אֵלֶיךָ³ זְכֹר חֶרְפָּתְךָ מִנִּי־נָבָל כל
היום⁴ ואמתאלהמא. פאן זאל אלבאדם ען אול חרף וכאן תחת אלאול מלך
צאר אלבאדם אלאול באדם מתל שוכב עֵדוּת יְהוָה נֶאֱמָנָה⁵ מִצְוַת יְהוָה בָּרָה⁶ והדא
ילוח לי אנה כלף בינהם⁷ :

אלסלוק.   אלסלוק אדא לם יבן לה באדם פלא בלאם עליה מתל
כְּמִצְוֹתֶיךָ⁸. פאדא כדמה באדם ואחד קד יכון שופר רפע וקד יכון מארכה
וקד יכון שופר תכסיר. אלשרט פי וגוב אלשופר אלרפע כונה מע אול חרף
מתל שִׁפְטֵי־אָרֶץ⁹ בִּינָה הַגִיגִי¹⁰ ואמתאלהמא. ואן צאר מע אלחרף אלתאני
וכאן תחת אלאול שוא וגב אלשופר איצא מתל וְרֹמּוּ סֶלָה¹¹ בְּצֹאן מַרְעִיתֶךָ¹²
ואמתאל דלך. ואלשרט פי וגוב אלמארכה כונהא מע אלחרף אלתאני אדא
כאן תחת אלאול מלך מתל וְאַחַר כָּבוֹד תִּקָּחֵנִי¹³ תָּרוּם יְמִינֶךָ¹⁴ ואמתאלהמא.
ואדא צאר מע אלתאלת ומא זאד לא תתגיר אלמארכה מתל אֲשֶׁר־תִּדְפֶּנּוּ
רוּחַ¹⁵ בַּעֲדַת צַדִּיקִים¹⁶ ואמתאלהמא וקד יכרג ען הדא שואד.   ואלשרט פי וגוב
אלשופר אלתכסיר הו אן יכון קבלה לגרמיה מתל מִפְּנֵי אַבְשָׁלוֹם בְּנוֹ¹⁷
שָׁם אֱלֹהֵי יַעֲקֹב¹⁸ ואמתאלהמא. וקד אכתלף פי אלכלמה אלתי פיהא אחד
חרוף אהח״ע ויכון פי אלכלמה חרף רגש פאן אלבעץ יבאלף אלשרט ויקראה
אלי פוק¹⁹ מתל כָּל־פֹּעֲלֵי אָוֶן²⁰ אַתָּה תְשַׁבְּחֵם²¹ ואמתאלהמא ואדא כאן
כלמה צגירה מתל בָּל וְעַל וְאֵת וכאנת במוקף פהם יגרוהא בע״ן אלכלמה
מתל כָּל־פֹּעֲלֵי אָוֶן²⁰.   וקד יכדם אלסלוק שוכב פי תלתה מואצע והי יַעַמְדוּ
מָיִם²² וּמִמַּעֲמַקֵּי מָיִם²³ וַיַּהַפְכוּ אָרֶץ²⁴.   אלסלוק אדא כדמה באדמין פאלאול
אבדא במאילה ואלתאני שופר רפע מתל וְכֹל אֲשֶׁר־יַעֲשֶׂה יַצְלִיחַ²⁵ אֲשֶׁר
הִתְעַתְּדוּ לְגַלִּים²⁶ וקד כרג ען דלך שואד מתל וְנִכְאֵה לֵבָב לְמוֹתֵת²⁷ . וקד

---

¹ Ps. lvii. 9.   ² lxxxvi. 7.   ³ ib. 4.   ⁴ lxxiv. 22.   ⁵ xix. 8.   ⁶ ib. 9.
⁷ So for the last three cxx., Ben-Asher and Ben-Naphtali differ. See p. 76, note 7.
⁸ cxix. 10.   ⁹ ii. 10.   ¹⁰ v. 2.   ¹¹ iv. 5.   ¹² lxxiv. 1.   ¹³ lxxiii. 24.
¹⁴ lxxxix. 14.   ¹⁵ i. 4.   ¹⁶ ib. 5.   ¹⁷ iii. 1.   ¹⁸ xx. 2.
¹⁹ I. e. with שׁוֹפָר רְסַע.   ²⁰ Ps. v. 6.   ²¹ lxxxix. 10.   ²² civ. 6.
²³ lxix. 15.   ²⁴ Job xii. 15.   ²⁵ Ps. i. 3.   ²⁶ Job xv. 28.   ²⁷ Ps. cix. 16.

Q

אכתלף פי אלכאדם אלתאני וחו אן בעצהם אדֹא לם יכן בין חרף אלמאילה
וביו חרף אלשופר מלך אצלא נעל אלשופר מארכה מתל מִדַּבֵּר צֶדֶק סֶלָה[1]
וְעָפָי הוּא אֱלֵי־חָרֶב[2]. אלסלוק אדֹא כדמה תלתה כדאם מא תתגיר
אלכאדמין ואנמא יתגיר אלכאדם אלאול וחו אן כאן מע אול חרף כאן
שופר מקלוב מתל כִּי לֹא־עָזַבְתָּ דֹרְשֶׁיךָ יְהוָֹה[3] ואן צאר מע אלחרף אלתאני
צאר שופר תכסיר מן פוק מתל מָגֵן וְחֶרֶב וּמִלְחָמָה סֶלָה[4] ואן צאר מע
אלתאלת ומא זאד צאר מקל מתל אֶבְחָנְךָ֫ עַל־מֵי מְרִיבָה סֶלָה[5] והדֹא עלי
אלאשהר. ואלשופר אדֹא כאן קבל אלסלוק אן כאן אלסלוק מע אכר מלך
כאן רפעה אלשופר חפיפה מתל לֹא יָשָׁב[6] וארא כאן אלסלוק בעדה מלך
כאן רפעה אלשופר בהמזה[7] אלי פוק ליואזי תקל אלסלוק פיגו כפיף מע
כפיף ותקיל מע תקיל פיעתדל אלתנגים:

תאבעה אלאזרקה. תאבעה אלזורקה מא חסבוהא לא מע אלאלחאן ולא
מע אלכדאם. והי תגי עלי תלתה צֹרוב אלואחד מתל מֶרְכְּבֹי אִישׁ[8] ואלתאני
מתל בַּעֲצַת רְשָׁעִים[9] ואלתאלת אדֹא כאן מע אול חרף כאן שופר מקלוב
מתל יִמְחַץ רֹאשׁ אֹיְבָיו[10] מִי זֶה מֶלֶךְ הַכָּבוֹד[11]. וליס הדה אלעצֹאצה אלתי
תחת אֹיְבָיו וְהַכָּבוֹד מארכה לאנהא ליס מתצל במא בערהא[12] ואנמא הי
עלאמה ללחרף אלדֹי יננם לאנה ישכל מתל זִבְחֵי אֱלֹהִים רוּחַ נִשְׁבָּרָה[13] לולם
יגעל מע אלרֵישׁ עלאמה אנה חרף אלתנגים לקרית עלי אלבא[14]:

פצל פי חצץ אלכדאם[15]. חצה אלגלגל פי אלפזר. חצה אלמקל פי
אלסלוק. חצה אלשופר אלטקלוב פי סבעה מואצֹע פי אלפזר ואלזורקה
ואללגרמיה ואלרביע ואליתיב ואלאתנחה ואלסלוק. חצה אלצנארה[16] פי

---

[1] Ps. lii. 5.   [2] Job xv. 22.   [3] Ps. ix. 11.   [4] lxxvi. 4.   [5] lxxxi. 8.   [6] i. 1.

[7] I question whether המזה is right here, although Par. has also מתיבה. There is nothing corresponding in הראיה אלקאר.

[8] xxxi. 21.   [9] i. 1.   [10] lxviii. 22.   [11] xxiv. 8.

[12] Simson (p. 75[b]) adds: כי הורדף מעמיד התיבה כמו אתנחתא ומקמיץ התיבה הפתוחה כאתנחתא גם לפעמים מתש כה האתנחתא.

[13] li. 19.   [14] 'Then it would have been read on the ב,' נִשְׁבָּרָה (as in Ps. xxxiv. 21). Samuel (p. 126) concludes this section with רודפי רביע הם שנים האחרונים של ורקא כנון הוֹרֵנוּ יהוה דרכך (xxvii. 11).

[15] This list is so full of mistakes that I do not think it worth while to particularize them.

[16] צנארה is another name for צנורית, regularly used in הראיה אלקאר.

APPENDIX.

כמסה מואצׄע מכצוצה פי אללגרמיה פי מכאן מכצוץ ואלרביע ואליתיב
ואלאתנחה ואלסלוק פי אמכנה מכצוצה והי תכון מעינה ללשופר אלמקלוב·
ומא צח לי פי אלתצניר שרט פאדכרה ¹. חצׄה אלשופר אלרפע
פי אלזרקה ואלאתנחה פי מואצׄע מכצוצה. חצׄה שופר אלתכסיר פי
אלרביע ואללגרמיה ואליתיב ואלאתנחה ואכר אלפסוק פי מואצׄע מכצוצה.
חצׄה אלמארכה פי אלאלחאן כלהא פי מואצׄע מכצוצה. חצׄה אלדחויה פי
אלרביע ואלאתנחה פי מואצׄע מכצוצה. חצׄה אלמאילה פי אכר אלפסוק
פי מואצׄע מכצוצה. חצׄה אלשוכב פי אלטפחה ופי אלסלוק פי תלתה
מואצׄע יַעֲמְדוּ מָיִם וְאכְוַיה. אלסלסלה אדא באנת כאדם כדמת אתנחה
ורביע וסלוק:

פצל פי מנאורה אלאלחאן. הדׄה אלתמאניה אלחאן ליס פיהא ואגב אלואחד
בעד אלאכׄר אלא אלסלסלה פאנהא אדא כאנת לחן לא בד מן אן יכון
קבלהא אתנחה. אלפזור ימכן בעדה זרקה כִּי כָלוּ בְיָגוֹן חַיָּ² וּרבִיעַ פַּח לִי ³
ולגרמיה וַיֵּרֶד מֵי אָסַף־רוּחַ · בְּחָפְנָיו · ויתיב יִגְאָלֵהוּ חֹשֶׁךְ וְצַלְמָוֶת⁵ וטפחה לְדָוִד
אֵלֶיךָ יְהֹוָה⁶ וסלוק וַיֹּאמַר אֶרְחָמְךָ יְהֹוָה חִזְקִי ⁷. אלזרקה אדא תבעתהא
תבעתהא ארבעה אלחאן · אלפזור חָכְמָה כִּי־כְפֻלַיִם לְתוּשִׁיָּה וְדַע ⁸ ואלרביע
בָּרוּךְ אֲדֹנָי יוֹם יוֹם יַעֲמָס־לָנוּ⁹ ואמתאל דלך ואליתיב אָבְחַר דַּרְכָּם וְאֵשֵׁב
רֹאשׁ וְאֶשְׁכּוֹן¹⁰ ואמתאל דלך ואלאתנחה נַּס־אֲנִי · אוֹדְךָ בִכְלִי־נֶבֶל אֲמִתְּךָ אֱלֹהָי
אֲזַמְּרָה לְךָ בְכִנּוֹר¹¹ ואמתאלה · ואן לם יכן בעדהא תאבעתהא לם ימכן
בעדהא אלא אלרביע פקט כקו׳ הַאֲזִינָה אֶל־דִּמְעָתִי¹² בַּשָּׁמַיִם הֶרֶךְ נָחָשׁ¹³.
אלרביע ימכן בעדה כמסה· אלזרקה מְמָתִים מֵחֶלֶד חֶלְקָם בַּחַיִּים¹⁴ ואמתאלה
ואליתיב חַסְדּוֹ וּבַלַּיְלָה¹⁵ ואמתאלה ואלאתנחה כְּמוֹכֶם לֹא־נֹפֵל אָנֹכִי מִכֶּם¹⁶
ואמתאלה ואללגרמיה אַשְׁרֵי הָאִישׁ אֲשֶׁר לֹא הָלַךְ¹⁷ ואמתאלה ואלסלוק פֶּתַח
דְּבָרֶיךָ יָאִיר [מֵבִין פְּתָיִים]¹⁸ ואמתאלה. אללגרמיה ימכן בעדה אלפזור טָמְנוּ

---

¹ The word תצניר is a denominative from צנארה and *Nom. Verbi* of the second Form, the sense apparently being: 'And what is clear to me, there is a condition in regard to the making (placing) of Ṣinnorīth, and so I mention it.' The condition has been named in the words immediately preceding.

² Ps. xxxi. 11.   ³ cxl. 6.   ⁴ Prov. xxx. 4.   ⁵ Job iii. 5.
⁶ Ps. xxv. 1.   ⁷ xviii. 2.   ⁸ Job xi. 6.   ⁹ Ps. lxviii. 20.
¹⁰ Job xxix. 25.   ¹¹ Ps. lxxi. 22.   ¹² xxxix. 13.   ¹³ Prov. xxx. 19.
¹⁴ Ps. xvii. 14.   ¹⁵ xlii. 9.   ¹⁶ Job xii. 3.   ¹⁷ Ps. i. 1.
¹⁸ cxix. 130.

APPENDIX.

גְּאִים ׀ פַּח לִי¹ וזרקה וְיַגֶּד־לְךָ² תַּעֲלֻמוֹת חָכְמָה² ואלרביע אָכְלוּ וַיִּשְׁתַּחֲווּ ׀ כָּל־
דִּשְׁנֵי־אֶרֶץ³ ואליתיב על־כן ׀ לֹא־יָקֻמוּ רְשָׁעִים⁴ ואתנחה כִּי שָׁמָּה ׀ יָשְׁבוּ כִסְאוֹת
לְמִשְׁפָּט⁵ ואלסלוק שֵׁם ׀ אֱלֹהֵי יַעֲקֹב⁵. ואליתיב יכמן בעדה תלתה אלחאן
אתנחה יְהוָה עֹז לְעַמּוֹ יִתֵּן⁷ ואמתאלה ואלרביע בְּפִי שְׁלֹשֶׁת הָאֲנָשִׁים⁸
ואלסלוק מוצעין וְדֶרֶךְ רַע וּפִי תַהְפֻּכוֹת [שָׂנֵאתִי]⁹ אִישׁ־עָנִי וְאֶבְיוֹן וְנִכְאֵה לֵבָב
לְמוֹתֵת¹⁰. אלאתנחה יכמן בעדהא לחנין טפחה וְעַתָּה מְלָכִים הַשְׂכִּילוּ
[הִוָּסְרוּ]¹¹ וסלוק לְמֹצְאֵיהֶם וּלְכָל־בְּשָׂרוֹ מַרְפֵּא¹². אלטפחה יכמן בעדהא
לנרמיה יְשַׁנְּתִּי אָז ׀ יָנוּחַ לִי¹³ וסלוק מְאֹד עָמְקוּ מַחְשְׁבֹתֶיךָ¹⁴. כל טפחה יכון
בעדהא לנרמיה לא בד ממא אן יכון בעד אללגרמיה סלוק ויכון קבל
אלטפחה אתנחה:

פצל פי אחצה¹⁵ כדאם הדה כם יכון לכל לחן מן כאדם. כדאם אלפזר
תלתה מארכה ושופר מקלוב וגלגל. כדאם אלזרקה תלתה שופר מקלוב
ומארכה ושופר רפע. כדאם אלרביע [סתה] מארכה ושופר מקלוב וצנארה
ושופר תכסיר ודחויה וסלסלה. כדאם אללגרמיה ארבעה מארכה ושופר
תכסיר ושופר מקלוב וצנארה. כדאם אליתיב במסה אלשופר תכסיר
ושופר מקלוב וצנארה ומארכה. כדאם אלאתנחה סבעה שופר ודחויה
מארכה ושופר תכסיר ושופר מקלוב וצנארה וסלסלה. כדאם אלטפחה
אתנאן שובב ומארכה. כדאם אלסלוק תמאניה שופר ומארכה ומאילה
ושופר תכסיר ומקל ושופר מקלוב וצנורית וסלסלה:

ואליק מא תתבת הדה אלחאן אלכדא¹⁶. בעד אלפזר [לנרמיה בעד]
אללגרמיה זרקה בעד. אלזרקה רביע בעד אלרביע יתיב ואתנחה בעד אליתיב
אתנחה בעד אלאתנחה טפחה בעד אלטפחה סלוק:

והדה אלתמאניה אלחאן אלחאן אן תכון כלהא רום פואסיק עלי אלאשהר
אלא אליתיב¹⁷ ואלסלוק פאנהמא שואר׳ ודאך אן אלטפחה לא תכון פי

---

¹ Ps. cxl. 6. ² Job xi. 6. ³ Ps. xxii. 30. ⁴ i. 5. ⁵ cxxii. 5.
⁶ xx. 2. ⁷ xxix. 11. ⁸ Job xxxii. 5. ⁹ Prov. viii. 13.
¹⁰ Ps. cix. 16. ¹¹ ii. 10. ¹² Prov. iv. 22. ¹³ Job iii. 13.
¹⁴ Ps. xcii. 6. ¹⁵ I.e. אחצא, احصاء, 'the numbering.'
¹⁶ 'And these accents are most suitably fixed as follows.' We should have expected תרתיב, 'are most frequently arranged,' אכתר מא תרתבת is the technical term for this sequence. The list here given corresponds to the Zarqa-table in the prose accentuation. ¹⁷ It is clear that for יתיב we must read מפחה.

APPENDIX. 117

אלתלתה אספאר אלא פי נצף אלפסוק אלתאני ולא תכון פי נצפה אלאול
כמא תכון אלטפחה פי אול אלפסוק פי אלואחד ועשרין ספר מתל בְּרֵאשִׁית[1]
פלדלך ביֵנת אן אלטפחה לא תוגד האהנא פי אלנצף אלאול אלא שאד פי
תלתה מואצע פאתנין מנהם בגיר כאדם והמא לַמְנַצֵּחַ לְדָוִד מִזְמוֹר: קוה קויתי
יהוה[2] לַמְנַצֵּחַ לְדָוִד לְהַזְכִּיר: אלהים להצילני[3] ואלדי בכאדם שִׁיר מִזְמוֹר
לִבְנֵי־קֹרַח: גדול יהוה ומהלל מאד[4]. ואמא אלסלוק פלא יוגד פי אלואחד
ועשרין ספרא פי אול פסוק[5] לאן לא יבדמה אלא כאדם ואחד ופסוק מן
בלמתין לא יוגד ופי הדה אלתלתה אספאר יכדמה אויד מן כאדם פלדלך נא
האהנא אול פסוק וביאן דלך אן ליס פי אלפסוק לחן סואהי ודאך אנך תגדה
פי עשרה[6] מואצע תלתה מנהא להא כאדמין והי [שִׁיר מִזְמוֹר לְדָוִד[7]] שִׁיר
מִזְמוֹר לְאָסָף[8] מִזְמוֹר לְדָוִד לְהַזְכִּיר: יהוה אל בקצפך[9] ומנהא סבעה בשופרות
תכסיר והי למנצח לבני־קרח משכיל: אלהים באזנינו שמענו[10] למנצח לבני־
קרח מזמור: רצית יהוה ארצך[11] למנצח על־נגינת לדוד[12]: למנצח על־שושנים
לדוד[13]: הושיעני אלהים[14] למנצח על־הגתית לאסף[14]: למנצח לבני־קרח מזמור:
כל העמים תקעו כף[15] למנצח לעבד־יהוה לדוד: נאם פשע[16]:

ואגתמאע הדה אלתמאניה אלחאן וגד פי פסוק על זאת יתפלל כל חסיד
אליך[17]. ומא יגמע סבעה אלחאן פהו פסוק אשרי האיש[18] לדוד אליך יהוה
אקרא[19] ראיתה כי אתה עמל וכעס תביט[20]:

תם אלמכתצר בחמד אללה ⸪

---

[1] Gen. i. 1.   [2] Ps. xl. 1.   [3] lxx. 1.   [4] xlviii. 1.
[5] Here and in the lines following there is in the text אפסוק for פסוק.
[6] סבעה for תמאניה, and in the next line עשרה for אחד עשר has הראיה אלקאר, adding xlix. 1.
[7] cviii. 1. This ex. fails in the text, but is in the Heb.   [8] lxxxiii. 1.
[9] xxxviii. 1.   [10] xliv. 1.   [11] lxxxv. 1.   [12] lxi. 1.   [13] lxix. 1.   [14] lxxxi. 1.
[15] xlvii. 1.   [16] xxxvi. 1.   [17] xxxii. 6.   [18] i. 1.   [19] xxviii. 1.   [20] x. 14.

INDEX

OF THE PRINCIPAL PASSAGES, CORRECTED OR EXPLAINED.

In the right-hand column, the first figure indicates the *page*, the second the *line*, n. stands for *note*.

PSALMS.

1. 3	....	7. 16
4. 8	....	42. n.
4. 9	....	52. 11
5. 3	....	52. 27
5. 5	....	85. n. 8
5. 12	....	89. 6
7. 10	....	43. 28
9. 14	....	64. 2
11. 1	.....	6. n.; 52. 29
11. 6	....	36. 2
13. 3	....	89. 7
17. 14	....	56. n. 6
18. 1	....	76. n. 8
18. 7	....	73. 2
19. 14	....	36. 5
22. 25	....	89. 8
23. 4	....	89. 9
27. 6	....	89. 10
29. 7	....	51. 20
31. 12	....	89. 11
32. 5	....	53. 1; 89. 12
34. 8	....	95. 2
35. 7	....	52. 15
42. 5	....	36. 8
42. 9	....	36. 17
44. 25	....	52. 16
45. 13	....	84. n.
48. 15	....	44. 9
49. 15	....	73. 6
55. 13	....	90. n. 2
59. 6	....	89. 22
62. 12	....	64. 4
66. 12	....	36. 21
68. 20	....	69. n. 8
71. 3	....	36. 25
73. 8	....	64. 5
75. 7	....	26. n. 2
76. 8	....	36. 28
80. 6	....	46. n. 20
89. 6	....	53. 3
89. 48	....	43. 31
90. 1	....	53. 20
90. 10	....	89. 25
92. 9	....	29. 29
93. 5	....	36. 31
94. 12	....	64. 7
95. 7	....	51. 22
102. 8	....	29. 23
106. 37	....	26. n. 3
106. 38	....	89. 13
109. 16	....	69. n. 8
110. 4	....	30. 11
115. 1	....	90. 12
116. 1	....	29. 24
119. 20	....	29. 27
119. 138	....	53. 5
120. 1	....	29. 28
122. 4	....	89. 14
123. 2	....	89. 15
125. 3	....	73. 8
133. 2	....	56. n. 8
137. 9	....	95. 2
138. 2	....	89. 16
144. 14	....	55. n. 2
145. 5	....	25. 36

PROVERBS.

1. 10	....	34. 20
4. 6	....	101. 2

6. 3	.... 88.	21
7. 15	.... 26.	3
8. 13	.... 69.	n. 8
14. 6	.... 51.	24
14. 13	.... 51.	26
14. 14	.... 52.	18
15. 31	.... 51.	28
17. 12	.... 61.	15
21. 4	.... 29.	30
21. 8	.... 85.	n. 6
21. 29	.... 61.	16
21. 30	.... 26.	5
22. 3	.... 52.	1
27. 10	.... 89.	17
27. 22	.... 100.	2
28. 23	.... 64.	9

JOB.

4. 8	.... 26.	1
6. 14	.... 52.	20
9. 30	.... 53.	6
10. 8	.... 30.	1
10. 15	.... 37.	1
11. 6	.... 73.	18

15. 22	.... 53.	8
17. 15	.... 52.	21
17. 16	.... 52.	23
18. 2	.... 85.	n. 5
19. 21	.... 53.	9
20. 25	.... 37.	4
22. 18	.... 52.	3
24. 9	.... 53.	11
28. 3	.... 37.	9
29. 15	.... 53.	26
29. 25	.... 52.	25
31. 15	.... 53.	13
31. 16	.... 53.	15
32. 6	.... 91.	n. 4
33. 27	.... 30.	13
34. 20	.... 37.	12
37. 12	.... 37.	15
37. 23	.... 52.	5
38. 2	.... 60.	n. 8
38. 32	.... 52.	9
39. 10	.... 53.	17
39. 12	.... 101.	3
39. 13	.... 52.	7
39. 25	.... 37.	18
40. 2	.... 53.	19

ERRATA.

Page 20, note 53, *for* נוֹחַת *read* נָחַת
,, 31, note 18, *for* 'four' *read* 'three,' *and delete* 'Ps. xviii. 31'
,, 33, l. 17 from bottom, *for* 'lx' *read* 'lxi'
,, 33, note 25, *for* 'at end' *read* 'p. 75'
,, 40, l. 14 from bottom, *point* אָחֲוֶה
,, 82, note 6, *for* 'B. M. 16' *read* 'B. M. 17'

SELECT LIST OF STANDARD WORKS

PRINTED AT

The Clarendon Press, Oxford.

DICTIONARIES	. . Page 1.
ENGLISH AND ROMAN LAW	. . . ,, 2.
HISTORY, BIOGRAPHY, ETC.	. . . ,, 3.
PHILOSOPHY, LOGIC, ETC. .	. . . ,, 6.
PHYSICAL SCIENCE . . .	. . . ,, 7.

1. DICTIONARIES.

A New English Dictionary on Historical Principles, founded mainly on the materials collected by the Philological Society. Imperial 4to. In Parts, price 12s. 6d. each.

Vol. I (**A** and **B**), half morocco, 2l. 12s. 6d.
Part IV, Section 2, **C—CASS**, beginning Vol. II, price 5s.
Part V, **CASS—COL.** *In the Press.*
Edited by James A. H. Murray, LL.D.
Vol. III (**E, F,** and **G**), Part I, edited by Henry Bradley. *In the Press.*

An Etymological Dictionary of the English Language, arranged on an Historical Basis. By W. W. Skeat, Litt.D. *Second Edition.* 4to. 2l. 4s.

An Anglo-Saxon Dictionary, based on the MS. collections of the late Joseph Bosworth, D.D. Edited and enlarged by Prof. T. N. Toller, M.A., Owens College, Manchester. Parts I-III. A-SAR. 4to. stiff covers. 15s. each. Part IV (completing the Work) *in the Press.*

An Icelandic-English Dictionary, based on the MS. collections of the late Richard Cleasby. Enlarged and completed by G. Vigfússon, M.A. With an Introduction, and Life of Richard Cleasby, by G. Webbe Dasent, D.C.L. 4to. 3l. 7s.

A Greek-English Lexicon, by H. G. Liddell, D.D., and Robert Scott, D.D. *Seventh Edition, Revised and Augmented throughout.* 4to. 1l. 16s.

An Intermediate Greek-English Lexicon, abridged from the above. Small 4to. 12s. 6d.

Oxford: Clarendon Press. London: HENRY FROWDE, Amen Corner, E.C.

A Latin Dictionary, founded on Andrews' edition of Freund's Latin Dictionary, revised, enlarged, and in great part rewritten by Charlton T. Lewis, Ph.D., and Charles Short, LL.D. 4to. 1*l.* 5*s.*

A School Latin Dictionary. By Charlton T. Lewis, Ph.D. Small 4to. 18*s.*

A Sanskrit-English Dictionary. Etymologically and Philologically arranged, with special reference to Greek, Latin, German, Anglo-Saxon, English, and other cognate Indo-European Languages. By Sir M. Monier-Williams, D.C.L. 4to. 4*l.* 14*s.* 6*d.*

Thesaurus Syriacus: collegerunt Quatremère, Bernstein, Lorsbach, Arnoldi, Agrell, Field, Roediger: edidit R. Payne Smith, S.T.P. Vol. I, containing Fasc. I-V, sm. fol. 5*l.* 5*s.*
Fasc. VI. 1*l.* 1*s.* Fasc. VII. 1*l.* 11*s.* 6*d.*

2. ENGLISH AND ROMAN LAW.

Anson. *Principles of the English Law of Contract, and of Agency in its Relation to Contract.* By Sir W. R. Anson, D.C.L. *Fifth Edition.* 8vo. 10*s.* 6*d.*

—— *Law and Custom of the Constitution.* Part I. Parliament. 8vo. 10*s.* 6*d.*

Bentham. *An Introduction to the Principles of Morals and Legislation.* By Jeremy Bentham. Crown 8vo. 6*s.* 6*d.*

Digby. *An Introduction to the History of the Law of Real Property.* By Kenelm E. Digby, M.A. *Third Edition.* 8vo. 10*s.* 6*d.*

Gaii *Institutionum Juris Civilis Commentarii Quattuor;* or, Elements of Roman Law by Gaius. With a Translation and Commentary by Edward Poste, M.A. *Second Edition.* 8vo. 18*s.*

Gentilis, Alberici, I.C.D., I.C., *De Iure Belli Libri Tres.* Edidit T. E. Holland, I.C.D. Small 4to. half morocco, 21*s.*

Hall. *International Law.* By W. E. Hall, M.A. *Second Edition.* 8vo. 21*s.*

Holland. *Elements of Jurisprudence.* By T. E. Holland, D.C.L. *Fourth Edition.* 8vo. 10*s.* 6*d.*

—— *The European Concert in the Eastern Question;* a Collection of Treaties and other Public Acts. Edited, with Introductions and Notes, by T. E. Holland, D.C.L. 8vo. 12*s.* 6*d.*

Justinian. *Imperatoris Iustiniani Institutionum Libri Quattuor;* with Introductions, Commentary, Excursus and Translation. By J. B. Moyle, B.C.L., M.A. 2 vols. 8vo. 21*s.*

Oxford: Clarendon Press.

Justinian. *The Institutes of Justinian,* edited as a recension of the Institutes of Gaius, by T. E. Holland, D.C.L. *Second Edition.* Extra fcap. 8vo. 5s.

—— *Select Titles from the Digest of Justinian.* By T. E. Holland, D.C.L., and C. L. Shadwell, B.C.L. 8vo. 14s.

Also sold in Parts, in paper covers, as follows :—

Part I. Introductory Titles. 2s. 6d.
Part II. Family Law. 1s.
Part III. Property Law. 2s. 6d.
Part IV. Law of Obligations (No. 1). 3s. 6d.
Part IV. Law of Obligations (No. 2). 4s. 6d.

—— *Lex Aquilia.* The Roman Law of Damage to Property: being a Commentary on the Title of the Digest 'Ad Legem Aquiliam' (ix. 2). With an Introduction to the Study of the Corpus Iuris Civilis. By Erwin Grueber, Dr. Jur., M.A. 8vo. 10s. 6d.

Markby. *Elements of Law* considered with reference to Principles of General Jurisprudence. By Sir William Markby, D.C.L. *Third Edition.* 8vo. 12s. 6d.

Pollock and Wright. *An Essay on Possession in the Common Law.* By Sir F. Pollock, M.A., and R. S. Wright, B.C.L. 8vo. 8s. 6d.

Raleigh. *The English Law of Property.* By Thos. Raleigh, M.A. *In the Press.*

Stokes. *The Anglo-Indian Codes.* By Whitley Stokes, LL.D.
Vol. I. Substantive Law. 8vo. 30s.
Vol. II. Adjective Law. 8vo. 35s.

Twiss. *The Law of Nations* considered as Independent Political Communities. By Sir Travers Twiss, D.C.L.
Part I. On the Rights and Duties of Nations in time of Peace. New Edition. 8vo. 15s.
Part II. On the Rights and Duties of Nations in time of War. Second Edition. 8vo. 21s.

3. HISTORY, BIOGRAPHY, ETC.

Bluntschli. *The Theory of the State.* By J. K. Bluntschli. Translated from the Sixth German Edition. 8vo. half bound, 12s. 6d.

Boswell's *Life of Samuel Johnson, LL.D.*; including Boswell's Journal of a Tour to the Hebrides, and Johnson's Diary of a Journey into North Wales. Edited by G. Birkbeck Hill, D.C.L. In six volumes, medium 8vo. With Portraits and Facsimiles. Half bound, 3l. 3s.

Burnet's *History of His Own Time,* with the Suppressed Passages and Notes. 6 vols. 8vo. 2l. 10s.

—— *History of James II,* with Additional Notes. 8vo. 9s. 6d.

Calendar *of the Clarendon State Papers,* preserved in the Bodleian Library. In three volumes. 1869-76.
Vol. I. From 1523 to January 1649. 8vo. 18s.
Vol. II. From 1649 to 1654. 16s.
Vol. III. From 1655 to 1657. 14s.

HISTORY, BIOGRAPHY, ETC.

Calendar *of Charters and Rolls* preserved in the Bodleian Library. 8vo. 1*l*. 11*s*. 6*d*.

Carte's *Life of James Duke of Ormond.* 6 vols. 8vo. 1*l*. 5*s*.

Clarendon's *History of the Rebellion and Civil Wars in England.* Re-edited from a fresh collation of the original MS. in the Bodleian Library, with marginal dates and occasional notes, by W. Dunn Macray, M.A., F.S.A. 6 vols. Crown 8vo. 2*l*. 5*s*.

—— *History of the Rebellion and Civil Wars in England.* To which are subjoined the Notes of Bishop Warburton. 7 vols. medium 8vo. 2*l*. 10*s*.

—— *History of the Rebellion and Civil Wars in England.* Also his Life, written by himself, in which is included a Continuation of his History of the Grand Rebellion. Royal 8vo. 1*l*. 2*s*.

—— *Life, including a Continuation of his History.* 2 vols. medium 8vo. 1*l*. 2*s*.

Clinton's *Fasti Hellenici.* The Civil and Literary Chronology of Greece, from the LVIth to the CXXIIIrd Olympiad. *Third Edition.* 4to. 1*l*. 14*s*. 6*d*.

—— *Fasti Hellenici.* The Civil and Literary Chronology of Greece, from the CXXIVth Olympiad to the Death of Augustus. *Second Edition.* 4to. 1*l*. 12*s*.

—— *Epitome of the Fasti Hellenici.* 8vo. 6*s*. 6*d*.

—— *Fasti Romani.* The Civil and Literary Chronology of Rome and Constantinople, from the Death of Augustus to the Death of Heraclius. 2 vols. 4to. 2*l*. 2*s*.

Clinton's *Epitome of the Fasti Romani.* 8vo. 7*s*.

Earle. *Handbook to the Land-Charters, and other Saxonic Documents.* By John Earle, M.A., Professor of Anglo-Saxon in the University of Oxford. Crown 8vo. 16*s*.

Finlay. *A History of Greece from its Conquest by the Romans to the present time,* B.C. 146 to A.D. 1864. By George Finlay, LL.D. A new Edition, revised throughout, and in part re-written, with considerable additions, by the Author, and edited by H. F. Tozer, M.A. 7 vols. 8vo. 3*l*. 10*s*.

Fortescue. *The Governance of England:* otherwise called The Difference between an Absolute and a Limited Monarchy. By Sir John Fortescue, Kt. A Revised Text. Edited, with Introduction, Notes, etc., by Charles Plummer, M.A. 8vo. half bound, 12*s*. 6*d*.

Freeman. *History of the Norman Conquest of England; its Causes and Results.* By E. A. Freeman, D.C.L. In Six Volumes. 8vo. 5*l*. 9*s*. 6*d*.

—— *The Reign of William Rufus and the Accession of Henry the First.* 2 vols. 8vo. 1*l*. 16*s*.

—— *A Short History of the Norman Conquest of England.* Second Edition. Extra fcap. 8vo. 2*s*. 6*d*.

Gascoigne's *Theological Dictionary* ('*Liber Veritatum*'): Selected Passages, illustrating the Condition of Church and State, 1403–1458. With an Introduction by James E. Thorold Rogers, M.A. Small 4to. 10*s*. 6*d*.

Oxford: Clarendon Press.

HISTORY, BIOGRAPHY, ETC. 5

George. *Genealogical Tables illustrative of Modern History.* By H. B. George, M.A. Third Edition. Small 4to. 12s.

Gross. *The Gild Merchant:* a Contribution to English Municipal History. By Charles Gross, Ph.D. 2 vols. 8vo. *Nearly ready.*

Hodgkin. *Italy and her Invaders.* With Plates and Maps. By T. Hodgkin, D.C.L. Vols. I–IV, A.D. 376–553. 8vo. 3*l.* 8*s.*

—— *The Dynasty of Theodosius;* or, Seventy Years' Struggle with the Barbarians. By the same Author. Crown 8vo. 6s.

Hume. *Letters of David Hume to William Strahan.* Edited with Notes, Index, etc., by G. Birkbeck Hill, D.C.L. 8vo. 12s. 6d.

Kitchin. *A History of France.* With Numerous Maps, Plans, and Tables. By G. W. Kitchin, D.D. In three Volumes. *Second Edition.* Crown 8vo. each 10s. 6d.

Vol. I. to 1453. Vol. II. 1453–1624. Vol. III. 1624–1793.

Lucas. *Introduction to a Historical Geography of the British Colonies.* By C. P. Lucas, B.A. With Eight Maps. Crown 8vo. 4s. 6d.

—— *Historical Geography of the Colonies.* Vol. I. By the same Author. With Eleven Maps. Crown 8vo. 5s.

Luttrell's *(Narcissus) Diary.* A Brief Historical Relation of State Affairs, 1678–1714. 6 vols. 8vo. 1*l.* 4*s.*

Magna Carta, *a careful Reprint.* Edited by W. Stubbs, D.D., Bishop of Oxford. 4to. stiched, 1s.

Metcalfe. *Passio et Miracula Beati Olaui.* Edited from a Twelfth-Century MS. by F. Metcalfe, M.A. Small 4to. 6s.

Oxford. *Manuscript Materials relating to the History of Oxford;* contained in the Printed Catalogues of the Bodleian and College Libraries. By F. Madan, M.A. 8vo. 7s. 6d.

Ranke. *A History of England, principally in the Seventeenth Century.* By L. von Ranke. Translated under the superintendence of G. W. Kitchin, D.D., and C. W. Boase, M.A. 6 vols. 8vo. 3*l.* 3*s.*

Rawlinson. *A Manual of Ancient History.* By George Rawlinson, M.A. Second Edition. Demy 8vo. 14s.

Ricardo. *Letters of David Ricardo to T. R. Malthus* (1810–1823). Edited by James Bonar, M.A. 8vo. 10s. 6d.

Rogers. *History of Agriculture and Prices in England,* A.D. 1259–1793. By James E. Thorold Rogers, M.A.

Vols. I and II (1259–1400). 8vo. 2*l.* 2*s.*

Vols. III and IV (1401–1582). 8vo. 2*l.* 10*s.*

Vols. V and VI. (1583–1702). 8vo. 2*l.* 10*s.*

—— *First Nine Years of the Bank of England.* 8vo. 8s. 6d.

—— *Protests of the Lords, including those which have been expunged, from 1624 to 1874;* with Historical Introductions. In three volumes. 8vo. 2*l.* 2*s.*

Smith's *Wealth of Nations.* A New Edition, with Notes, by J. E. Thorold Rogers, M.A. 2 vols. 8vo. 21s.

London: HENRY FROWDE, Amen Corner, E.C.

Sprigg's *England's Recovery ;* being the History of the Army under Sir Thomas Fairfax. 8vo. 6s.

Stubbs. *Select Charters and other Illustrations of English Constitutional History, from the Earliest Times to the Reign of Edward I.* Arranged and edited by W. Stubbs, D.D., Lord Bishop of Oxford. *Fifth Edition.* Crown 8vo. 8s. 6d.

—— *The Constitutional History of England, in its Origin and Development.* Library Edition. 3 vols. Demy 8vo. 2l. 8s.

Also in 3 vols. crown 8vo. price 12s. each.

—— *Seventeen Lectures on the Study of Medieval and Modern History, delivered at Oxford* 1867–1884. Crown 8vo. 8s. 6d.

Stubbs. *Registrum Sacrum Anglicanum.* An attempt to exhibit the course of Episcopal Succession in England. By W. Stubbs, D.D. Small 4to. 8s. 6d.

Wellesley. *A Selection from the Despatches, Treaties, and other Papers of the Marquess Wellesley, K.G., during his Government of India.* Edited by S. J. Owen, M.A. 8vo. 1l. 4s.

Wellington. *A Selection from the Despatches, Treaties, and other Papers relating to India of Field-Marshal the Duke of Wellington, K.G.* Edited by S. J. Owen, M.A. 8vo. 1l. 4s.

Whitelock's *Memorials of English Affairs from* 1625 *to* 1660. 4 vols. 8vo. 1l. 10s.

4. PHILOSOPHY, LOGIC, ETC.

Bacon. *Novum Organum.* Edited, with Introduction, Notes, &c., by T. Fowler, D.D. 8vo. 14s.

—— *Novum Organum.* Edited, with English Notes, by G. W. Kitchin, D.D. 8vo. 9s. 6d.

—— *Novum Organum.* Translated by G. W. Kitchin, D.D. 8vo. 9s. 6d.

Berkeley. *The Works of George Berkeley, D.D., formerly Bishop of Cloyne; including many of his writings hitherto unpublished.* With Prefaces, Annotations, and an Account of his Life and Philosophy, by Alexander Campbell Fraser, LL.D. 4 vols. 8vo. 2l. 18s.

The Life, Letters, &c., separately, 16s.

Bosanquet. *Logic; or, the Morphology of Knowledge.* By B. Bosanquet, M.A. 8vo. 21s.

Butler's *Works, with Index to the Analogy.* 2 vols. 8vo. 11s.

Fowler. *The Elements of Deductive Logic, designed mainly for the use of Junior Students in the Universities.* By T. Fowler, D.D. *Ninth Edition,* with a Collection of Examples. Extra fcap. 8vo. 3s. 6d.

—— *The Elements of Inductive Logic, designed mainly for the use of Students in the Universities.* By the same Author. *Fourth Edition.* Extra fcap. 8vo. 6s.

—— *The Principles of Morals* (Introductory Chapters). By T. Fowler, D.D., and J. M. Wilson, B.D. 8vo. boards, 3s. 6d.

Oxford: Clarendon Press.

Fowler. *The Principles of Morals.* Part II. By T. Fowler, D.D. 8vo. 10s. 6d.

Green. *Prolegomena to Ethics.* By T. H. Green, M.A. Edited by A. C. Bradley, M.A. 8vo. 12s. 6d.

Hegel. *The Logic of Hegel;* translated from the Encyclopaedia of the Philosophical Sciences. With Prolegomena by William Wallace, M.A. 8vo. 14s.

Hume's *Treatise of Human Nature.* Reprinted from the Original Edition in Three Volumes, and edited, with Analytical Index, by L. A. Selby-Bigge, M.A. Crown 8vo. 9s.

Locke's *Conduct of the Understanding.* Edited by T. Fowler, D.D. Second Edition. Extra fcap. 8vo. 2s.

Lotze's *Logic,* in Three Books; of Thought, of Investigation, and of Knowledge. English Translation; Edited by B. Bosanquet, M.A. Second Edition. 2 vols. Crown 8vo. 12s.

—— *Metaphysic,* in Three Books; Ontology, Cosmology, and Psychology. English Translation; Edited by B. Bosanquet, M.A. Second Edition. 2 vols. Crown 8vo. 12s.

Martineau. *Types of Ethical Theory.* By James Martineau, D.D. Third Edition. 2 vols. Crown 8vo. 15s.

—— *A Study of Religion:* its Sources and Contents. Second Edition. 2 vols. Crown 8vo. *Immediately.*

5. PHYSICAL SCIENCE.

De Bary. *Comparative Anatomy of the Vegetative Organs of the Phanerogams and Ferns.* By Dr. A. De Bary. Translated and Annotated by F. O. Bower, M.A., F.L.S., and D. H. Scott, M.A., Ph.D., F.L.S. Royal 8vo., half morocco, 1l. 2s. 6d.

—— *Comparative Morphology and Biology of Fungi, Mycetozoa and Bacteria.* By Dr. A. De Bary. Translated by H. E. F. Garnsey, M.A. Revised by Isaac Bayley Balfour, M.A., M.D., F.R.S. Royal 8vo., half morocco, 1l. 2s. 6d.

—— *Lectures on Bacteria.* By Dr. A. De Bary. Second Improved Edition. Translated by H. E. F. Garnsey, M.A. Revised by Isaac Bayley Balfour, M.A., M.D., F.R.S. Crown 8vo. 6s.

Goebel. *Outlines of Classification and Special Morphology of Plants.* A new Edition of Sachs' Text-Book of Botany, Book II. By Dr. K. Goebel. Translated by H. E. F. Garnsey, M.A. Revised by Isaac Bayley Balfour, M.A., M.D., F.R.S. Royal 8vo., half morocco, 1l. 1s.

Sachs. *Lectures on the Physiology of Plants.* By Julius von Sachs. Translated by H. Marshall Ward, M.A., F.L.S. Royal 8vo., half morocco, 1l. 11s. 6d.

—— *A History of Botany.* Translated by H. E. F. Garnsey, M.A. Edited by I. Bayley Balfour, M.A., M.D., F.R.S. Crown 8vo. *In the Press.*

Solms-Laubach. *Introduction to Fossil Botany.* By Count H. von Solms-Laubach. Authorised English Translation, by H. E. F. Garnsey, M.A. Edited by Isaac Bayley Balfour, M.A., M.D., F.R.S. *In the Press.*

Annals of Botany. Edited by Isaac Bayley Balfour, M.A., M.D., F.R.S., Sydney H. Vines, D.Sc., F.R.S., and W. G. Farlow, M.D.
Vol. I. Parts I–IV. Royal 8vo., half morocco, gilt top, 1*l.* 16*s.*

Biological Series. (*Translations of Foreign Biological Memoirs.*)
I. *The Pysiology of Nerve, of Muscle, and of the Electrical Organ.* Edited by J. Burdon-Sanderson, M.D., F.R.SS. L. & E. Medium 8vo. 1*l.* 1*s.*
II. *The Anatomy of the Frog.* By Dr. Alexander Ecker, Professor in the University of Freiburg. Translated, with numerous Annotations and Additions, by G. Haslam, M.D., Scientific Assistant in the Medical Department in the University of Zürich. Demy 8vo. *Nearly ready.*
III. *Contributions to the History of the Physiology of the Nervous System.* By Professor Conrad Eckhard. Translated by Miss Edith Prance. *In Preparation.*
IV. *Essays upon Heredity and Kindred Biological Problems.* By Dr. August Weismann, Translated and Edited by E. B. Poulton, M.A., Selmar Schönland, Ph.D., and Arthur E. Shipley, M.A. Medium 8vo. 16*s.*

Prestwich. *Geology, Chemical, Physical, and Stratigraphical.* By Joseph Prestwich, M.A., F.R.S. In two Volumes.
Vol. I. Chemical and Physical. Royal 8vo. 1*l.* 5*s.*
Vol. II. Stratigraphical and Physical. With a new Geological Map of Europe. Royal 8vo. 1*l.* 16*s.*
New Geological Map of Europe. In case or on roller. 5*s.*

Rolleston and Jackson. *Forms of Animal Life.* A Manual of Comparative Anatomy, with descriptions of selected types. By George Rolleston, M.D., F.R.S. *Second Edition.* Revised and Enlarged by W. Hatchett Jackson, M.A. Medium 8vo. 1*l.* 16*s.*

Oxford
AT THE CLARENDON PRESS
LONDON: HENRY FROWDE
OXFORD UNIVERSITY PRESS WAREHOUSE, AMEN CORNER, E.C.

www.ingramcontent.com/pod-product-compliance
Lightning Source LLC
Chambersburg PA
CBHW022131160426
43197CB00009B/1237